TRANSATLANTIC MIRRORS

TRANSATLANTIC MIRRORS

Essays in Franco-American Literary Relations

Edited by
SIDNEY D. BRAUN *and*
SEYMOUR LAINOFF

TWAYNE PUBLISHERS

Boston   1978

TRANSATLANTIC MIRRORS
Copyright © 1978 by Sidney D. Braun and Seymour Lainoff
Please see Acknowledgments page for information
on selections that are protected by separate copyrights

Printed on permanent/durable acid-free paper and bound
in the United States of America

Published in 1978 by Twayne Publishers
A Division of G. K. Hall & Co.
70 Lincoln Street, Boston, Massachusetts 02111

First Printing, September 1978

Library of Congress Cataloging in Publication Data
Main entry under title:

Transatlantic mirrors.

1. Literature, Comparative—American and French—
Addresses, essays, lectures. 2. Literature, Comparative
—French and American—Addresses, essays, lectures.
I. Braun, Sidney David, 1912-   II. Lainoff,
Seymour.
PS159.F5T7   809   78-18344
ISBN 0-8057-9008-X

203057

Preface

THE AIM OF THIS VOLUME is to present, in an intelligible if not always chronological order, a collection of literary essays by French and American writers—novelists, poets, essayists—which reflect not only the views these two countries have held of each other, but also, and more particularly, their seminal literary influences on each other. Such a collection, to our knowledge at least, has never before been presented; the ideas expressed in these essays should contribute to a better understanding of the spiritual and literary relationships of these two countries, however different at times their outlook may have been.

We were inspired in the preparation of this volume by Edmund Wilson's *The Shock of Recognition* (1943), which assembled records, largely among American writers, of the fresh thrill of discovery felt by these writers when they encountered some of their contemporaries or predecessors. Our hope is that this volume records the thrill of discovery and the enhancement of knowledge—and sometimes the disillusionment—felt by French and American writers as they confronted their transatlantic counterparts.

These essays span the history of these mutual influences from the end of the eighteenth century to almost the present day. The reader will note that often the romance, primitivism, fantasy, youthful vigor, and individualism of certain American writers appealed to French writers who typified a more stratified civilization, while the French classical spirit—disciplined, critical, and sophisticated—affected many American writers.

This collection does not intend to be definitive or exhaustive, but rather to serve as a useful introduction, both as anthology and as critical comment. Though some of these essays have been reprinted more than once and are easily available, they have never before been assembled in one volume. Other essays in this anthology can be presently obtained only by digging, such as Whitman's essay on Taine and Motley's on Balzac. The selections by Sainte-Beuve, Larbaud, and Edith Wharton (writing in French), translated by the editors, have not ever before, to our knowledge, been translated. The general introduction and the separate introductions to the selections are intended to synthesize facts and impressions hitherto scattered. These introductions, therefore, should convey a brief history of the more important aspects of Franco-American literary relationships. A selective bibliography of secondary sources follows at the end of the volume.

S. D. B.
S. L.

About the Editors

SIDNEY D. BRAUN is Professor of French at Lehman College, where he has served as Chairman of the Department of Romance Languages, and at the Graduate Center, The City University of New York. He has also taught at the University of Washington (Seattle), University of Illinois, Wayne State University, and Yeshiva University, and lectured at the École Libre des Hautes Études (New York). Professor Braun received the degrees of A.B., A.M., and Ph.D. from New York University, and studied at the Sorbonne in Paris. He has been a Fulbright Research Professor attached to the Sorbonne, and in 1960 was awarded the Palmes Académiques by the French government and the Grande Médaille d'Argent de la Ville de Paris. His published works include *Dictionary of French Literature, Correspondance André Gide-André Suarès, The "Courtisane" in the French Theatre from Hugo to Becque, André Suarès: Hero Among Heroes,* and numerous articles and reviews in *PMLA, Romanic Review, Symposium, Criticism, Walt Whitman Review, Europe, The French Review, Modern Language Notes,* and *Modern Language Quarterly.* He has also been Assistant Literary Editor of *The French Review,* and is currently a member of the Advisory Board to *Nineteenth Century French Studies.*

SEYMOUR LAINOFF is Professor of English Literature at Yeshiva University. He has also taught at The City College of New York and Hofstra University. He received his B.A. degree at Brooklyn College, his M.A. at Columbia University, and his Ph.D. at New York University. Professor Lainoff has participated in panel discussion on American literature on television, both on WNBC and WNYC, and has been awarded a National Foundation of Jewish Culture grant and a New York State War Veterans Regents Fellowship. He has published numerous articles and reviews, including studies on Henry

7

James, Stephen Crane, Shirley Jackson, and American fiction, in *Modern Fiction Studies, College English, Nineteenth Century Fiction, Studies in English Literature, Criticism, Symposium, Explicator,* and other journals.

Contents

Acknowledgments

THE EDITORS thank all the copyright owners who granted permission to reprint the texts and translations in this collection.

We hereby acknowledge our appreciation and gratitude to: The Atlantic Monthly Company and to Jean-Paul Sartre for permission to include "American Novelists in French Eyes" by Jean-Paul Sartre, copyright © 1946. To Farrar, Straus Giroux, Inc., for permission to include "Hawthorne's 'The Scarlet Letter' " and "Henry James' 'The Bostonians' " by François Mauriac, translated from the French by Gerard Hopkins, copyright © 1960 by Eyre & Spottiswoode. To Mr. Charles E. Feinberg, Detroit, for permission to include the Walt Whitman article on Hippolyte Taine, edited by Roger Asselineau, which appeared in *Etudes Anglaises* (1957). To Harcourt Brace Jovanovich, Inc., for permission to include "Baudelaire" by T. S. Eliot, copyright 1932, 1936, 1950, 1960, 1964. To *Yale French Studies* and to André Malraux for permission to include "Preface to Faulkner's *Santuary*," which had been published in French in the *Nouvelle Revue Française* in 1933. To New Directions for permission to include part of "Blaise Cendrars" from the *Henry Miller Reader*, edited by Lawrence Durrell, copyright © 1959, and for "Irony, Laforgue, and Some Satire" by Ezra Pound, copyright 1918, 1920, 1935. To the *New England Quarterly* for permission to include the essay on Emerson by the Comtesse d'Agoult [Daniel Stern], translated from the French by Bessie Howard, 1937. To the Pennsylvania State University Press for permission to include "New Notes on Edgar Poe," from *Baudelaire as a Literary Critic*, selected essays introduced and translated by Lois Boe Hyslop and Francis E. Hyslop, Jr., copyright © 1964. To Random House, Inc., Alfred A. Knopf, Inc., for permission to include "Herman Melville," from *Lyrical and Critical Essays* by Albert Camus, translated by Ellen Conroy Kennedy, edited by Philip Thody, copyright © 1968 by

Alfred A. Knopf, Inc. To Alfred A. Knopf, Inc., for permission to reprint "The New American Novelists" from *Imaginary Interviews* by André Gide, translated by Malcolm Cowley, copyright 1944 by Jacques Schiffrin. To Mr. Armitage Watkins, New York, for permission to translate an article by Edith Wharton in French, which appeared in the *Revue Hebdomadaire* on June 21, 1936.

Introduction

FRENCH AND AMERICAN WRITERS have exerted upon one another a considerable literary influence. French authors have found in their American counterparts invigorating outlooks not present in their own literature; witness Baudelaire's response to Poe as poet-outlaw outside society or the response of modern French novelists to the virile pessimism of the American novel in the 1930s and 1940s. Similarly, American writers have found in the French equally exciting pathbreakers; in such manner did Henry James read Balzac, and Frank Norris, Zola. French and American literatures have vivified one another intermittently, if not continuously. One might venture the cautious generalization, set forth by Harry Levin, among others, in his *Refractions* (New York, 1966), that the French have sought in American literature an untutored vigor, a syncopation, or romance not easily discovered in the French tradition (though the French have no great affection for Mark Twain, a quintessential American) and that American authors have sought in the French an intellectual discipline, a critical curiosity, and a civilized demeanor not easily discovered in American writers (though nineteenth-century Realism and Naturalism in French fiction seemed shocking at first, in a sense, too "primitive," for many Americans). If the generalization holds true, one must, of course, be alert to exceptions.

I

French exploration of the New World dates back to the sixteenth century; but this was in the natural course of historical and geographic development, inspired by the broader intellectual horizons of the Renaissance. With the eighteenth century, however, France, through several of its voyagers seeking, in America, spiritual and emotional solace, received encouragement to spread its ideas of freedom and enlightenment. Americans, by living example, and French authors, by precept, abetted one another toward freedom and revolution. Montesquieu's *Spirit of Laws* (1748) already anticipated the political privileges and advantages of a democratic form of government, with its separation of powers, urging on those who, for reasons of religious or political freedom, had left England and other European states to settle across the Atlantic. At a time, too, when Rousseau was questioning in several of his works the values of progress and civilization as opposed to Nature, embodied in the Noble Savage, America served up its own form of republicanism, which helped produce the French Revolution. (Even Voltaire, though he rejected the myth of the Noble Savage and deplored French excursions into America, had great praise for William Penn and his Quakers, extolling their noble simplicity of religion and manner of living.)

As early as 1731 the exotic appeal of America in France is evident in many of the vivid descriptions of American scenery in *Manon Lescaut;* later, of course, Chateaubriand let his imagination run free in the lush scenery portrayed by his *René* (1802) and *Atala* (1801). But even before Chateaubriand was to feed his imagination with his visit, in 1791, to parts of the United States, Crèvecoeur, a Frenchman who had served with Montcalm in the war against the English, settled, after marrying a New England girl, on the frontier. His *Letters from an American Farmer* (1782), written in English, presented America as the "golden mean" between the primitive and the excessively civilized. Crèvecoeur's praise of America was symptomatic of the high regard with which the French viewed America during the American Revolution and the first stages of the French Revolution. Both as a source of romantic exoticism and of republican sentiment, America inspired French writers during the second half of the eighteenth century.

Just as French travelers, like Chateaubriand and Crèvecoeur, found an elemental greatness in the New World, so, too, American visitors to France, notably Benjamin Franklin and Thomas Jefferson, impressed French leaders with the freshness of their personalities and their sturdy republicanism. In the realm of literature, James Fenimore Cooper, the most highly regarded of American writers in France as late as the 1830s and 1840s, was to leave an indelible impression on both Balzac and Sainte-Beuve. Through his descriptions of virgin forests, early frontiers, and Indian wars, Cooper attracted the interest of Honoré de Balzac, the father of the *Human Comedy*, who found, in an analysis of *The Pathfinder*, much originality. Such descriptions, Balzac was convinced, were unlike those found in English or European literature. Sainte-Beuve, on the other hand, saw in Cooper's *Red Rover* a mirror and testament of the American democratic way of life. Sainte-Beuve also wrote admiring essays on Jefferson and Franklin, and, in reviewing Tocqueville on America, emphasized Tocqueville's positive assessments of the American scene.

But, it should be noted that, toward the end of the 1790s a countercurrent of French opinion, as Durand Echeverria indicates, began to assert itself, occasioned both by the growth of anti-revolutionary sentiment among French writers in exile and by the reports of French travelers that the young American republic, after all, was not another Eden but a real country with real problems, such as the blight of slavery, political factions, and an expanding commercialism of spirit. Le Comte Constantin de Volney's strictures in *View of the Climate and Soil of the United States* (Eng. trans., 1804) led to Stendhal's adverse comments in *Of Love* (1822); Chateaubriand's later conservatism gave rise to his observation of emergent disunity in the American scene, as recorded in his *Memoirs from beyond the Grave* (1849). Tocqueville, writing in the Age of Jackson, attempted a balanced picture of American democracy, presenting flaws as well as virtues. His *Democracy in America* (1835-1840), although acclaiming democratic institutions and foreseeing the various literary possibilities that were to ensue therefrom, also forecast the inevitable commercialism and debasement of literature that would follow in such a climate; one of the reasons of this debasement, he felt, was the unavoidable lowering of standards in a democracy. Tocqueville's criticisms were amplified and rendered more bitter, in the 1850s, by Baudelaire in his essays on Poe. The euphoria with which Frenchmen greeted the new republic in the 1770s and 1780s was to be dissipated in the next fifty years, to be replaced by more complex and contradictory assessments.

II

The American authors who made up what F. O. Matthiessen referred to as the American Renaissance in his volume of that name (1941)—especially Emerson, Hawthorne, Melville, Whitman, and

Thoreau—won recognition in France slowly. This lateness of acceptance was abetted, in some instances, by the fact that America itself
was slow to recognize the value of these writers.

It was a truism among French critics and authors in the first part of
the nineteenth century that American literature was reluctant to free
itself from its chains to Britain; Philarète Chasles, *Anglo-American
Literature and Manners* (Eng. trans. 1852), elaborated this thesis.
The French saw a paradox in the emergence of a new nation amid
challenging natural surroundings and the derivativeness of its literature. Cooper, in the 1830s and 1840s, despite his debt to Sir Walter
Scott, seemed the one exception, with his description of the frontier
and prairie and native figures like Leatherstocking.

In the 1840s a less patronizing note was heard from the Comtesse
d'Agoult, who saw in Emerson the personification of American
genius disdainful of authority and tradition. Consequently, during
the 1850s, Émile Montégut and E. D. Forgues commenced to write
intelligent articles on Emerson, Hawthorne, and Poe in the *Revue
des Deux Mondes.* Least sympathetic to American culture was
Baudelaire, who, for reasons not exclusively esthetic, wished to make
Edgar Allan Poe known in France; the latter personified, in his mind,
the saintly victim of American materialism and mediocrity. This
American "outcast," however, it should be quickly stated, was to be
later deified by such great French poets as Mallarmé and Valéry for
more purely literary reasons.

After Poe, the American poet who perhaps had the most impact in
France was Walt Whitman, who, until about 1888, was seen by
certain hostile French writers and critics as the epitome of American
physical and naturalistic values; but later, he was extolled for his
individualism and as a prophet of democracy; and still later, he was to
be admired for his poetic originality, for his rhythm and freedom
from conventional verse forms, which linked him with several of the
French Symbolist poets. (It should be noted, perhaps, that Longfellow's poems had great popularity in France, among general French
readers, constituting what is called today "middle-brow" culture;
later Bret Harte, Jack London and Upton Sinclair enjoyed the same
popularity.) Nineteenth-century French writers regarded Hawthorne as adversely affected by Puritanism and pointed to his seeming
melancholy and introspection. Thoreau was strangely neglected until
the 1920s and Melville was ignored into the 1930s.

III

How did the American writers and public view, during this same period, their counterparts across the sea? From Emerson, who wrote on Montaigne, through Henry James, Irving Babbitt, and Paul Elmer More, who wrote on Sainte-Beuve, and James Gibbons Huneker and Ezra Pound, who wrote on Rémy de Gourmont, American writers paid tribute to French critical acumen and the French intellectual tradition. However, during much of the nineteenth century, largely because of the American legacy of Puritanism, Americans regarded French fiction as immoral. Through the 1850's, except for John Lothrop Motley, the historian, who commended Balzac for his realism and social perception, American reviewers, by and large, expressed their unhappiness with writers who seemed to glory in the indecent. Dismay was sometimes compounded with a certain respect. As Harry Levin writes: "It was as the habitat of natural man that our continent had originally appealed to the French. Yet our own men of letters, inhibited by nineteenth-century notions of gentility, sometimes envied the freedom of their Gallic confrères to explore all manner of subjects. James wrote a letter to Howells . . . wistfully confiding that Edmond de Goncourt's latest yellowback would set out to investigate—if I may quote James verbatim— a 'whorehouse de province' " (*Refractions*, p. 218). Slowly but surely, Realism, and Balzac in particular, were accepted on the American scene during the 1870s. Edward Eggleston began his Hoosier novels under the inspiration of the French critic and historian Hippolyte Taine. Resistance to French Realism gave way to acceptance; Realism in American fiction was stimulated and developed. In 1912, at his seventy-fifth birthday gathering William Dean Howells said: "I would fain help to have it remembered that we studied from the French masters . . . to imitate nature, and gave American fiction the bent which it still keeps wherever it is vital."

For similar reasons, Zola's novels met with much resistance in the United States in the 1870s and 1880s. The seamy and vulgar, apparently the subject-matter of Zola's novels, were not palatable to American literary taste. Interestingly enough, however, several American writers, most prominent among them Frank Norris, gave proof of their inherent debt to Zola. Other writers, furthermore, took Zola into their favor for ingenious reasons: Howells, for

example, the chief American advocate of Realism, was touched by
Zola's humanitarianism, by his social and moral conscience. Norris,
on the other hand, was grateful to Zola for having added a new
dimension—one which he found lacking in American literature,
which he characterized as "romantic" and which he identified with
sensationalism. Henry James, of course, while admiring the French
novelists and learning from them, gave only grudging acceptance to
Flaubert, praising the latter's having raised Art to its greatest dignity;
Zola, he charged, unlike what had so often been said of him, was
sometimes guilty of violating the rule of observation and specific
knowledge, while Maupassant, he added, neglected the reflective side
of human nature. Among French novelists James found Balzac most
rewarding—Balzac, "the father of us all," whose grasp of both the
conflicting economic and moral sides of man's nature and of the
formulating yet repressing role of society in the life of the individual
James tried to imitate.

If Poe and Whitman influenced French poetry and the French
Symbolists in particular, French poetry during the nineteenth and
into the twentieth century exercised a similar function for American
poets. Lafcadio Hearn, who aspired to poetic prose, aimed to
promote French romanticism and its Bohemian outlook. The French
Symbolists, who received their first American critical appreciation in
articles by Aline Gorren (*Scribner's*, 1893), the most informed of
these critics, Theodore Child (*Harper's*, 1896), and Thomas Sergeant
Perry (*Cosmopolitan*, 1892), were known to and studied by Richard
Hovey, Trumbull Stickney, and Amy Lowell, whose volume *Six
French Poets* (1915) included studies of those within and outside the
Symbolist inheritance. Hearn, Hovey, Amy Lowell, Stickney, and
others influenced by French poetry searched for a more artistic
consciousness, a less didactic view in poetry, a "purer" poetry than
they cound find in the Anglo-American late-Victorian tradition. But
French poetic influence manifested itself most profoundly in the
poetry of Ezra Pound and T. S. Eliot. Ezra Pound was drawn to
Théophile Gautier's precise imagery and to Jules Laforgue's
irony—aspects which reflect some of his own characteristics. T. S.
Eliot, whose interest in French poetry perhaps transcended that of
any other major American poet, was drawn to Baudelaire, Mallarmé,
and Valéry, as well as to Laforgue; his knowledge of Baudelaire
reveals itself in "The Wasteland" (1922), and his essay on Baudelaire
discusses Baudelaire's Satanism, from which Eliot educes certain

theological conclusions. We may generalize, therefore, that just as American novelists found in French Realism and Naturalism a more liberated subject matter and a higher standard of artistic integrity, so American poets found in their French counterparts a more challenging and a more complex poetic statement.

IV

In the course of the twentieth century, in the realm of fiction at least, the pendulum of influence has swung the other way. Several modern French writers have apotheosized a few American writers. Melville, for example, has been placed by both Gide and Camus among the greatest geniuses of the West, mainly because of his search for meaning in existence. Gide and Camus have been obsessed with the same search. François Mauriac, on the other hand, seemed more interested in Hawthorne, because, like himself, the latter was attracted to the problems of religion as against physical desire. Interestingly enough, Mauriac, the ardent Catholic, saw hypocrisy and pharisaism in the American Puritan mentality, as set forth in both Hawthorne and James. But, again, Valery Larbaud, who wrote on Poe, Whitman, and Thoreau, among others, was attracted to Thoreau's *Walden,* which exemplifies the attempt to discover the realities of the self.

Following the Second World War unrivalled supremacy was granted the "cinq grands"—William Faulkner, Ernest Hemingway, John Dos Passos, Erskine Caldwell, and John Steinbeck—by such writers as Jean-Paul Sartre and André Malraux. In modern American fiction the French found both the violence and the virile pessimistic ambiance that animated their own writings and reflected the spirit of the age. In addition, they found it necessary to borrow much of American narrative technique for the expression of their own art.

The influence of twentieth-century American poetry in France seems less pervasive. Attempts to bring this poetry to the attention of the French public commenced with Eugene Jolas, in his *Anthologie de la nouvelle poésie américaine* (1928). And the 380-page summer issue of *Mesures* (1939) was devoted to American literature, beginning with Cotton Mather and Benjamin Franklin, and notably to translations of American poets from Emily Dickinson through Allen Tate. Jean Prévost, novelist and essayist killed while fighting with the *maquis* in 1944, further demonstrated his interest in the United States (he had written a critical study of Hemingway and a volume on American civilization called *Usonie*, 1939) by publishing his study *Robert Frost, le Poète et le Sage* (May, 1939). Despite this efflorescence of interest in modern American poetry in the 1930s, this body of poetry did not have the vitalizing influence in France that American fiction had.

It is clear from our rapid survey that much of the fascination France and America have held for each other lies in the fact that, whatever they found wanting in themselves, they searched for in their cultural counterpart; and when this was found, they eventually appropriated it to themselves. This mutual attempt to learn from each other has enriched the literary record of both countries.

PART I

French Images of America

MICHEL-GUILLAUME ST. JEAN DE CRÈVECOEUR

(1735–1813)

What Is an American?

St. Jean de Crèvecoeur, born in France of an aristocratic lineage, came to the New World at the age of nineteen and joined the army of Montcalm against the English. He later settled in the United States. After residing more than twenty years in the New World, he spent the last twenty-three years of his life in his ancestral Normandy. The work with which he is always identified, *Letters from an American Farmer,* written in English, was published in London in 1782; an enlarged French version was published in Paris, where he was then living, a year later. A part of his Third Letter, "What Is an American?," is reproduced here. In this letter, Crèvecoeur, in the manner of Rousseau, idealizes the American scene as a golden mean between the primitive and the excessively civilized. The American, Crèvecoeur writes, has shed his European past and has assumed a new and better identity. For Crèvecoeur, America embodied a dream of a fresh and bountiful existence. He expresses the euphoric attitudes toward America held by many Frenchmen just after the American Revolution.

Bibliography: A good sketch of Crèvecoeur's life by Stanley T. Williams appears in the *Dictionary of American Biography* (1930).

The text is reprinted from *Letters from an American Farmer* (London, 1782), pp. 45–53.

WHAT IS AN AMERICAN?

(1782)

I wish I could be acquainted with the feelings and thoughts which must agitate the heart and present themselves to the mind of an enlightened Englishman, when he first lands on this continent. He must greatly rejoice, that he lived at a time to see this fair country discovered and settled; he must necessarily feel a share of national pride, when he views the chain of settlements which embellishes these extended shores. When he says to himself, this is the work of my countrymen, who, when convulsed by factions, afflicted by a variety of miseries and wants, restless and impatient, took refuge here. They brought along with them their national genius, to which they principally owe what liberty they enjoy, and what substance they possess. Here he sees the industry of his native country, displayed in a new manner, and traces in their works the embryos of all the arts, sciences, and ingenuity which flourish in Europe. Here he beholds fair cities, substantial villages, extensive fields, an immense country filled with decent houses, good roads, orchards, meadows, and bridges, where an hundred years ago all was wild, woody, and uncultivated!

What a train of pleasing ideas this fair spectacle must suggest! It is a prospect which must inspire a good citizen with the most heartfelt pleasure. The difficulty consists in the manner of viewing so extensive a scene. He is arrived on a new continent; a modern society offers itself to his contemplation, different from what he had hitherto seen. It is not composed, as in Europe, of great lords who possess everything, and of a herd of people who have nothing. Here are no aristocratical families, no courts, no kings, no bishops, no ecclesiastical dominion, no invisible power giving to a few a very visible one; no great manufacturers employing thousands, no great refinements of luxury. The rich and the poor are not so far removed from each other as they are in Europe. Some few towns excepted, we are all tillers of the earth, from Nova Scotia to West Florida. We are a people of cultivators, scattered over an immense territory, communicating with each other by means of good roads and navigable rivers, united by the silken bands of mild government, all respecting the laws, without dreading their power, because they are equitable. We are all animated with the spirit of an industry which is unfettered and unrestrained, because each person works for himself. If he travels through our rural districts he views not the hostile castle, and the haughty mansion, contrasted with the clay-built hut and miserable cabin, where cattle and men help to keep each other warm, and dwell in meanness, smoke, and indigence.

A pleasing uniformity of decent competence appears throughout our habitations. The meanest of our log-houses is a dry and comfortable habitation. Lawyer or merchant are the fairest titles our towns afford; that of a farmer is the only appellation of the rural inhabitants of our country. It must take some time ere he can reconcile himself to our dictionary, which is but short in words of dignity, and names of honor. There, on a Sunday, he sees a congregation of respectable farmers and their wives, all clad in neat homespun, well mounted, or riding in their own humble wagons. There is not among them an esquire, saving the unlettered magistrate. There he sees a parson as simple as his flock, a farmer who does not riot on the labor of others. We have no princes, for whom we toil, starve, and bleed: we are the most perfect society now existing in the world. Here man is free as he ought to be; nor is this pleasing equality so transitory as many others are. Many ages will not see the shores of our great lakes replenished with inland nations, nor the unknown bounds of North America entirely peopled. Who can tell how far it extends? Who can tell the millions of men whom it will feed and contain? for no European foot has as yet travelled half the extent of this mighty continent!

The next wish of this traveller will be to know whence came all these people? they are a mixture of English, Scotch, Irish, French, Dutch, Germans, and Swedes. From this promiscuous breed, that race now called Americans have arisen. The eastern provinces must indeed be excepted, as being the unmixed descendants of Englishmen. I have heard many wish that they had been more intermixed also: for my part, I am no wisher, and think it much better as it has happened. They exhibit a most conspicuous figure in this great and variegated picture; they too enter for a great share in the pleasing perspective displayed in these thirteen provinces. I know it is fashionable to reflect on them, but I respect them for what they have done; for the accuracy and wisdom with which they have settled their territory, for the decency of their manners; for their early love of letters; their ancient college, the first in this hemisphere; for their industry; which to me who am but a farmer, is the criterion of everything. There never was a people, situated as they are, who with so ungrateful a soil have done more in so short a time. Do you think that the monarchical ingredients which are more prevalent in other governments, have purged them from all foul stains? Their histories assert the contrary.

In this great American asylum, the poor of Europe have by some means met together, and in consequence of various causes; to what purpose should they ask one another what countrymen they are? Alas, two thirds of them had no country. Can a wretch who wanders about, who works and starves, whose life is a continual scene of sore affliction or pinching penury; can that man call England or any other kingdom his country? A country that had no bread for him, whose fields procured him no harvest, who met with nothing but the frowns of the rich, the severity of the laws, with jails and punishments; who owned not a single foot of the extensive surface of this planet? No! urged by a variety of motives, here they came. Every thing has tended to regenerate them; new laws, a new mode of living, a new social system; here they are become men: in Europe they were as so many useless plants, wanting vegetative mould, and refreshing showers; they withered, and were mowed down by want, hunger, and war; but now by the power of transplantation, like all other plants they have taken root and flourished! Formerly they were not numbered in any civil list of their country, except in those of the poor; here they rank as citizens.

By what invisible power has this surprizing metamorphosis been performed? By that of the laws and that of their industry. The laws, the indulgent laws, protect them as they arrive, stamping on them the symbol of adoption; they receive ample rewards for their labors; these accumulated rewards procure them lands; those lands confer on them the title of freemen; and to that title every benefit is affixed which men can possibly require. This is the great operation daily performed by our laws. From whence proceed these laws? From our government. Whence that government? It is derived from the original genius and strong desire of the people, ratified and confirmed by government. This is the great chain which links us all, this is the picture which every province exhibits, Nova Scotia excepted. There the crown has done all; either there were no people who had genius, or it was not much attended to: the consequence is, that the province is very thinly inhabited indeed; the power of the crown, in conjunction with the mosquitoes, has prevented men from settling there. Yet some part of it flourished once, and it contained a mild harmless set of people. But for the fault of a few leaders the whole were banished. The greatest political error the crown ever committed in America, was to cut off men from a country which wanted nothing but men! What attachment can a poor European emigrant have for a country where he had nothing? The knowledge of the language, the love of a few kindred as poor as himself, were the only cords that tied him: his country is now that which gives him land, bread, protection, and consequence: *Ubi panis ibi patri,* is the motto of all emigrants.

What then is the American, this new man? He is either an European, or the descendant of an European; hence that strange mixture of blood, which you will find in no other country. I could point out to you a man, whose grandfather was an Englishman, whose wife was Dutch, whose son married a French woman, and whose present four sons have now four wives of different nations. *He* is an American, who, leaving behind him all his ancient prejudices and manners, receives new ones from the new mode of life he has embraced, the new government he obeys, and the new rank he holds. He becomes an American by being received in the broad lap of our great *Alma Mater.*

Here individuals of all nations are melted into a new race of men, whose labors and posterity will one day cause great change in the world. Americans are the western pilgrims, who are carrying along with them that great mass of arts, sciences, vigor, and industry, which began long since in the east; they will finish the great circle. The Americans were once scattered all over Europe; here they are incorporated into one of the finest systems of population which has ever appeared, and which will hereafter become distinct by the power of the different climates they inhabit. The American ought, therefore, to love his country much better than that wherein either he or his forefathers were born. Here the rewards of his industry follow with equal steps the progress of his labor; his labor is founded on the basis of nature, *self-interest;* can it want a stronger allurement? Wives and children, who before in vain demanded of him a morsel of bread, now, fat and frolicsome, gladly help their father to clear those fields whence exuberant crops are to arise to feed and clothe them all; without any part being claimed, either by a despotic prince, a rich abbot, or a mighty lord. Here religion demands but little of him; a small voluntary salary to the minister, and gratitude to God; can he refuse these?

The American is a new man, who acts upon new principles; he must therefore entertain new ideas, and form new opinions. From voluntary idleness, servile dependence, penury, and useless labor, he has passed to toils of a very different nature.

This is an American.

CHARLES-AUGUSTIN SAINTE-BEUVE
(1804–1869)

Cooper's *The Red Rover*

SAINTE-BEUVE, among the foremost of French literary critics, revealed in his *Causeries du lundi* (1851-62) and *Nouveaux lundis*
(1863-70), collections of articles printed earlier in periodicals, a
strong interest in American political life and culture. His discerning
articles on Jefferson and Franklin praise the republican spirit, the
practicality mixed with idealism, and the moderation in religious
matters of these Americans, and his exposition of Alexis de Tocqueville's *Democracy in America* stresses the virtues Tocqueville
observed in American democratic life rather than the dangers Tocqueville also detected. Sainte-Beuve pointed to the fact that the
American Revolution had been followed by decades of peaceful
progress and democratic change.

In his essay on James Fenimore Cooper's *The Red Rover*, Sainte-
Beuve comments favorably not only on Cooper's stalwart republicanism, but also on his characterization and imaginative grasp of the
novel's ocean setting. He is more critical of Cooper's plotting.
Cooper had written *The Red Rover* in 1827 in France, and the novel
enjoyed an immediate success both in that country and in America.
Sainte-Beuve, at the beginning of his review, assumes the novel has
secured a wide audience.

Bibliography: Lander MacClintock, "Sainte-Beuve and America,"
PMLA, 60 (1945), 422–36.

The essay, first published on April 16, 1828, in *Le Globe,* is found
in *Oeuvres,* I., ed. Maxime Leroy (Paris: Gallimard, 1956),
pp. 283–87. It is here translated for the first time by the editors.

COOPER'S *THE RED ROVER*
(1828)

AN ADMIRABLE SCENE from the *Red Rover,* at the time of its publication, has been cited in *Le Globe.* Although somewhat late, we are today returning to this fine work that everyone has read; and without seeking to give it a dry and useless analysis, we shall talk about it for a while with our readers like two people who enjoy recalling an old acquaintance.

Since his first writings, which placed him at the head of those imitating Walter Scott, M. Cooper continued to perfect himself as he went along; he secured a better knowledge of his talent by bringing it into play; his style, at first timid and uncertain, became firmer, broader, more original; he dared have his own qualities and faults; in a word, without ever ceasing to belong to the tradition of the Scottish novelist, he followed his separate path, and the Colonist emancipated himself. To begin with his faults, he doubtlessly has rather serious ones. Ordinarily, his novels suffer from the *fable.* At times the *fable* is weak and poorly knit, at other times tortured and obscure, and almost always improbable; one would think, upon seeing it unfold painfully, turn and revolve, that it was conceived after its completion, and that the accidents of its progress were foreseen and ordered in a strange design. The river, so to speak, is there only to flow and follow its slope; its owner wishes to make something of it, and uses it as a means to an end. M. Cooper does not, in fact, recount for the sake of relating a story, but rather to describe. This observation, once it is well understood, will give us the key to his talent.

Gifted with a controlled and profound sensitivity, a vast and untroubled imagination, he early saw the most magnificent spectacles of nature; he saw or dreamed, in the midst of these sublime spectacles, of some human beings in harmony with the virgin forests, the limitless prairies, and the sky, higher there than elsewhere. The struggles of civilization with nature, especially those of right and liberty against oppression and force, came to cast upon these youthful portraits shades no less varied than vivid. As a descriptive poet, a reflective poet, and a sincere patriot, he sought above all, within the framework of the historical novel, an opportunity to pour out his soul, to release his imagination, to sing the praises of a country and a cause that he loved. He also portrayed, in faithful and indelible strokes, mores that are unknown to Europe and that America itself sees each day receding and disappearing. But less versatile, less accomplished than [Sir Walter] Scott, he could not, like him, in the midst of so many preoccupations, control, almost as if it were a game, a plot both complicated and facile, or tangle and disentangle the threads, put them aside and go back to them in turn, and set skillfully in their tight fabric his brilliant adornments. Moreover, it is not that M. Cooper is at all lacking in this creative faculty that engenders and gives birth to new characters, by virtue of which [Francois] Rabelais produced *Panurge;* [Alain René] Le Sage, *Gil Blas;* and [Samuel] Richardson, *Clarissa.* One cannot forget, once they have been known, Hawk Eye and Tom Coffin. Therefore, in spite of their faults, the novels of the American author are those that elicit the greatest pleasure and emotion; and enough superior things of beauty redeem the obscurities and improbabilities.

Nowhere do these beautiful qualities reveal themselves more numerous and striking than in the *Red Rover.* After having been a seaman like [Tobias] Smollett, M. Cooper wanted, like the author of *Roderick Random,* to describe mores and scenes of the sea; but it is with more poetry and, so to speak, more love, that he did it. No one better than he understood the ocean, its murmurs and hues, its calm and tempests; no one had such a keen and true feeling for a boat and for its sympathetic relationships with the crew. He is unfailing in rendering these vague and profound impressions. The *Dauphin* of the *Rover,* having come out of the same stock as the *Ariel* of the *Pilot,* seems to have been given life the moment it felt the waves under its pins and the seamen aboard. At times it is a seabird that skims over the foam with its wings, and gracefully follows the contours of the waves; at other times, it is a warhorse that crashes down, rights itself and quivers with terror. Good Richard Fid cannot prevent himself from comparing the elegant slenderness of its shrouds and stays to the figure of Nelle Dalle, *when the ropes of the corset have been tightened,* and, according to him, all these pulleys, placed just at the proper distance from each other, are like the eye of a dear child, whose face is a pleasure to see. When the *Caroline* plunges and goes to the bottom, Wilder hears the hollow and menacing sounds that come out of the depths of the hold, similar to the roarings of some dying monster, and good Richard also teaches us that a ship about to sink makes lamentations like any other living thing. I would say, if I dared, that in this novel the two ships are the two principal characters, and that the *Dauphin* is of more interest than the rover himself.

The latter recalls Byron's Conrad and Walter Scott's *Cleveland*. Roderic is nothing but the tender and discreet page-boy of *Lara*. But the author found a way of rejuvenating and nationalizing, in some sort, his hero through feelings that he gives him in anticipation of later events. The bloody Jolly Roger already presages American independence; the pirate himself hopes and foresees this independence in the near future; he proclaims it in advance as if to absolve himself. When he is insulted one day by the proud Islanders, his wounded heart beats only for revenge. A Spanish galleon laden with gold, or a rich Dutch cargo, is not worth in his eyes the honor of humiliating the German who sits on the throne of England, or the pleasure of sinking *Saint-George*. A few more years, and the sea-rover will be a Paul Jones, just as the Greek pirate will be a Canaris; only, I would not prefer that the hero, on his death-bed, should have in his hand this roller *which had served him as a pillow,* and that, through a sudden effort, at the moment of expiring, he should unfurl the national flag, while exclaiming: "We triumph." That resembles too much the theatrical deaths of our Olympic Circus. It appears to us, moreover, that the novel would have gained more probability, without losing interest, if the rover had been less skillful in disguises; if he had had diversions, and, as we say, less long and frequent *absences;* as if he had not been precisely Mistress Wallis's brother, Henry's uncle, Gertrude's relative; if Mistress Willys had waited not so long to recognize him, etc. We would also like, even if we were to seem very hard to please, that the tailor Homespun would speak a bit less of his *five long and bloody wars,* and that the excellent Richard Fid would fill his conversation a little less with nautical expressions. In wishing to be true, the author has outdone nature: the sea-men, tailors and craftsmen also speak like other men. As for the black loyal Guinea, otherwise called the *African Scipio,* he lacks nothing in order to interest and move to pity. His cordial nature, artlessness, naive distrust of himself, sublime devotion to Henry, and especially the friendship, more familiar but yet respectful, which unites him to Richard, everything in him attracts and pleases; among the Negroes he is almost what Rebecca of *Ivanhoe* is among Jewish women. One can only render praise to the character of Henry Wilder; in him the author has realized the American type in all his purity. What dominates Henry is something honest, orderly, and serious; ideas of order and duty are uppermost in his mind; his lively sensibility is hidden beneath solemn and cold outward appearances; in the delicate and even equivocal situation in which he finds himself, he does not, for one single moment, depart from discretion, candor, or courage; in a word, if there is something of Paul Jones in the rover, there is something of Washington in this young man. From the moment that he enters as captain aboard the *Caroline* to that of his return aboard the *Dauphin,* the whole action turns on him, and he sustains it admirably; it is the most beautiful part of the book. His conduct during the tempest, amidst the complaints of the crew, his determination to climb the mast after the lieutenant's refusal to do so, his firm will to remain aboard the abandoned ship as long as one plank remains afloat—all these strong and true feelings spread in the midst of so many heart-rending scenes a strong touch of moral sublimity that accentuates and completes their effect; and when, after the tempest, at night, under the moonbeams, one sees Wilder, at the helm of the longboat, bending forward, as if to hear the gentle breathing of the sleeping Gertrude, the reader, who has passed through all the stages of anguish, delightfully enjoys this moment of pure intoxication, and succumbing to the sensations that inundate him, would gladly say, together with the poet: *It is enough for one who must die.*

HONORÉ DE BALZAC

(1799–1850)

Cooper's *The Pathfinder*

Balzac, author of *La Comédie Humaine*, the huge collective work
depicting contemporary French society, was attracted to the American romancer James Fenimore Cooper (1789–1851), whose settings,
in the Leatherstocking series, were very different—the more primitive milieu of the early American frontier. Balzac, like other French
readers, was entranced by Cooper's descriptions of virgin forests and
his narrations of daring incident. In the most striking phrase in his
review of *The Pathfinder* (1840), Balzac recognizes what we today
call the mythic qualities of Natty Bumpo; Balzac calls the Pathfinder
a "moral hermaphrodite," a "statue," sexless and passionless, who
combines in perfection the best moral qualities of savage and civilized
man. Unlike Sainte-Beuve, Balzac subordinates Cooper's powers of
characterization to his ability to create an atmosphere and, in
Bumpo, an ideal conception.

Cooper was the most highly regarded of American writers in
France well into the 1840s. French critics found in Cooper what
they sought in American literature generally: an "original" view of
the American scene, not oriented toward England or Europe.
Cooper exerted a considerable influence on French fiction. Balzac's
fiery peasants in *Les Chouans* (1829) and Dumas's underworld
characters in *Les Mohicans de Paris* (1854) are indebted to Cooper's
fighting Indians, and lesser figures, like Gabriel Ferry and Eugène
Sue, imitated Cooper in numerous novels. Victor Hugo was lavish in
his praise of Cooper.

Balzac's review was originally published in *La Revue Parisienne*
(July 25, 1840); the translation used here is by Auguste D'Avezac,
brother-in-law of Edward Livingston, and was printed in *The Evening Post* (March 26, 1841). D'Avezac sent his translation to Cooper.

Bibliography: Fernand Baldensperger, "James Fenimore Cooper in France," *Franco-American Pamphlets,* Second Series, No. 12 (New York: 1940).

Balzac's review can be found in "Lettres sur la littérature," *Oeuvres Complètes,* XXIII, Paris: Calmann-Levy, 1879, 262–85. D'Avezac's excerpted translation appeared on page 1 of the New York *Evening Post* on the date indicated.

COOPER'S *THE PATHFINDER*

(1840)

AFTER TWO FEEBLE WORKS Cooper has redeemed himself by his "Lake Ontario". It is a beautiful book, worthy of "The Last of the Mohicans," "The Pioneers," and "The Prairie," which it serves to complete. At this moment, Cooper is the sole author worthy of being placed beside Sir Walter Scott. He is not equal to him, but he possesses the same order of genius; and he owes the high place which he occupies in modern literature to two faculties: that of painting the ocean and its mariners, and of idealizing the magnificent scenery of America. I am unable to comprehend how the author of "The Pilot" and "The Red Rover," and the four romances just cited, should have been the author of his other works, with the single exception of "The Spy." These seven works constitute the only and real titles of his fame. I do not pronounce this opinion lightly. I have read again and again the productions of the Romancer, or to say the truth, the historian of America, and I feel, in common with Sir Walter Scott, the same admiration for his two faculties, to which I may add the grand original conception of Leatherstocking, that sublime personage, who connects "The Pioneers," "The Mohicans," "The Prairie," and "Lake Ontario." Leatherstocking is a statue, a magnificent moral hermaphrodite, born between the savage and the civilized states of man, who will live as long as literature endures. I question whether the extraordinary works of Sir Walter Scott furnish a creation so grandiose as that of the hero of the Savannahs and the forests of America. Gurth, in "Invahoe," approximates to him: and we feel that if the great Scotchman had seen America, he would have been able to create Leatherstocking. The conception, above all, of this man, half Indian and half civilized, elevates Cooper to the rank of Sir Walter Scott.

I love these simple stories; they discover great power of conception, and always abound in fertility. The early part of the work embraces a description of the Oswego, one of the tributary rivers of Lake Ontario, along the shores of which lurk the Iroquois, for the purpose of making the party captive. Here Cooper is himself again. His description of the forest, the running stream, with its rapids and waterfalls, the artifices of the savages, who endeavor to outwit the Great Serpent, Jasper, and the Pathfinder, furnishes a succession of admirable pictures, which in this work, as well as its antecedents, are inimitable. Here is sufficient to dishearten all the romancers who have the ambition to follow in the footsteps of the American author. Never did the art of writing tread closer upon the art of the pencil. This is the school for the study of literary landscape-painters. All the secrets of the art are revealed. The magical prose of Cooper not only embodies the spirit of the river, its shores, the forests and its trees; but it exhibits the minutest details, combined with the grandest outline. . . . When the spirit of solitude communes with us, when the first calm of these eternal shades pervades us, when we hover over this virgin vegetation, our hearts are filled with emotion. Page after page is filled with naturally presented dangers, without any effort at stage effect. It seems as though we were seeking under these magnificent trees for the print of a moccasin. . . . We know not how this metamorphosis of genius is accomplished, but it is impossible to separate the soil, the vegetation, the waters, their extent, and their configuration, from the interests that agitate us. In short, the personages become what they really are, of little importance among the sublime scenery which surrounds them.

The skirmishes with the Indians, and their devices, are never monotonous, and bear no resemblance to those which we find in the previous works of Cooper. The description of the fort, the encampment and repose of the party, and the target-shooting are *chefs d'oeuvre.* We owe to the author our warmest gratitude for his choice of these humble personages. With the exception of the young woman, who is not true to nature, and whose qualities are painfully and uselessly dwelt upon, his other figures are drawn from nature, if we may use a term borrowed from the *ateliers.* It is unfortunate that the English sailor and Lieutenant Muir, the pivots of a drama so simple and so naif, should be failures. More reflection, and a little more breadth, would have rendered this work faultless. The voyage across Lake Ontario is a delicious miniature, rivalling the finest ocean-scenes of Cooper. In short, the expedition to the Thousand Islands, the fights with the Iroquois, commanded by a French captain, possess an interest equal to that master-piece of genius, "The Last of the Mohicans." The Pathfinder predominates here as well as elsewhere; and this profoundly melancholy personage is in some degree explained.

A serious charge remains to be stated against our author. Undoubtedly, Cooper's renown is not due to his countrymen, nor to the English: he owes it mainly to the ardent admiration of France; of our noble and beautiful country, which pays more attention to foreign men of genius than to our own poets. Cooper has been perfectly understood and appreciated in France. The universality of our language has made his works known among nations who are acquainted with that of England [sic]. I am therefore the more astonished to see France, and the French officers who were in Canada in 1750, ridiculed, in the person of Captain Sanglier. They were gentlemen, and history attests the glory of their conduct. Is it for an American, whose position entitles him to a high sense of honor, to invest a French officer with a gratuitously odious character, when the only succor which America received during her struggle for independence came from France? The noble or ignoble character of Captain Sanglier is not material to the plan of the drama, and nobleness of character would have furnished the author with an additional scene of beauty. It is pitiful to see enlightened men adopting the vulgar prejudices of the multitude. But Cooper shares this fault in common with Scott, who repaid the sincere admiration of France by writing "Paul's Letters to his Kinsfolk." My censure is however the more just in the instance of Cooper, whose works contain not a single trace of kindness toward France.

The difference between these authors arise [sic] mainly from the nature of the subjects to which their talents have been directed. From those chosen by Cooper, nothing could be drawn from philosophy, nor from the deep workings of the human mind. When his work is once read, the mind looks back to it, to embrace it as a whole. Both are certainly great historians, but both have cold hearts.

ALEXIS DE TOCQUEVILLE

(1805–1863)

American Literature

FEW VOYAGES to the United States have proven so intellectually profitable as that made by the young Alexis de Tocqueville and his companion, Gustave-Auguste de Beaumont de la Bonninière (1802–66), over a nine-month period in 1831 and 1832. Their reason for visiting America was to study penal conditions in this country; and their joint report (1838) proved a major source of French prison-reform endeavors for many years. In addition, young Beaumont wrote a novel, influential in France, called *Marie: A Slave in America* (1835; not translated into English until 1958), which, in its fictional framework, wove in many sociological comments on American institutions, particularly slavery. Tocqueville's separate accomplishment was the classic study of the United States during the era of Jackson:*Democracy in America,* the first two volumes of which appeared in a French edition in 1835, with the next two volumes following in 1840.

Tocqueville, recognizing and even welcoming the ascent of democratic institutions in America, nevertheless pointed to the dilemmas as well as the strengths of American democracy. The dangers confronting the democratic state include the possible tyranny of the majority, the mobility and restlessness of constantly changing patterns, and the lowering and leveling out of intellectual standards.

In the selections chosen here, from Chapters XIII and XIV of Part II, Book I, Tocqueville embraces some stereotypes of French literary opinion in his times, soon to be set aside by critics like Montégut, Forgues, and the Countess d'Agoult. He repeats the familiar charge that America had no original literature, that American writers were enchained to their British counterparts. In his presentation of this charge, however, he nowhere mentions specifically the name of any American writer. Evidencing no particular knowledge of Cooper,

37

Washington Irving, or earlier writers, he fell prey to the then current grand generalization.

Like other French critics, Tocqueville anticipated that American literature, when it would emerge, would "bear marks of an untutored and rude vigour of thought—frequently of great variety and singular fecundity." Earlier French writers had believed that American originality would arise from conditions of a more primitive splendor. But Tocqueville, thinking more in terms of the evolving democratic society he had witnessed, thought that America—lacking an aristocratic or classical literary tradition, yet opening up the possibilities of a literary career to all talents—would necessarily give birth to powerful but eccentric productions. Tocqueville laid to rest the idyllis visions of the New World held by Crèvecoeur and Chateaubriand, and replaced the image of the noble farmer or woodsman with that of the rising bourgeois who supported Jackson. Except for this significant change, Tocqueville was conventional in his literary judgments. In his brief chapter, "Trade and Literature," also reprinted below, Tocqueville forsaw, accurately enough, the growing commercialism and debasement of literature in a modern democracy.

Bibliography: The standard study is G. W. Pearson, *Tocqueville and Beaumont in America* (New York: 1938). For French opinions in the age of Tocqueville, see Harold E. Mantz, *French Criticism of American Literature Before 1850* (New York: 1917).

The translation here is by Tocqueville's English contemporary, Henry Reeve, from *Democracy in America*, Part the Second (London: Saunder and Otley, 1840), III, pp. 109–23.

AMERICAN LITERATURE

(1840)

WHEN A TRAVELLER goes into a bookseller's shop in the United States, and examines the American books upon the shelves, the number of works appears extremely great; whilst that of known authors appears, on the contrary, to be extremely small. He will first meet with a number of elementary treatises, destined to teach the rudiments of human knowledge. Most of these books are written in Europe; the Americans reprint them, adapting them to their own country. Next comes an enormous quantity of religious works, Bibles, sermons, edifying anecdotes, controversial divinity, and reports of charitable societies; lastly, appears the long catalogue of political pamphlets. In America, parties do not write books to combat each others' opinions, but pamphlets which are circulated for a day with incredible rapidity, and then expire.

In the midst of all these obscure productions of the human brain, are to be found the more remarkable works of that small number of authors, whose names are, or ought to be, known to Europeans.

Although America is perhaps in our days the civilized country in which literature is least attended to, a large number of persons are nevertheless to be found there who take an interest in the productions of the mind, and who make them, if not the study of their lives, at least the charm of their leisure hours. But England supplies these readers with the larger portion of the books which they require. Almost all important English books are republished in the United States. The literary genius of Great Britain still darts its rays into the recesses of the forests of the New World. There is hardly a pioneer's hut which does not contain a few odd volumes of Shakespere. I remember that I read the feudal play of Henry V. for the first time in a log-house.

Not only do the Americans constantly draw upon the treasures of English literature, but it may be said with truth that they find the literature of England growing on their own soil. The larger part of that small number of men in the United States who are engaged in the composition of literary works are English in substance, and still more so in form. Thus they transport into the midst of democracy the ideas and literary fashions which are current amongst the aristocratic nation they have taken for their model. They paint with colours borrowed from foreign manners; and as they hardly ever represent the country they were born in as it really is they are seldom popular there.

The citizens of the United States are themselves so convinced that it is not for them that books are published, that before they can make up their minds upon the merit of one of their authors, they generally wait till his fame has been ratified in England, just as in pictures the author of an original is held to be entitled to judge of the merit of a copy.

The inhabitants of the United States have then at present, properly speaking, no literature. The only authors whom I acknowledge as American are the journalists. They indeed are not great writers, but they speak the language of their countrymen, and make themselves heard by them. Other authors are aliens; they are to the Americans what the imitators of the Greeks and Romans were to us at the revival of learning, an object of curiosity, not of general sympathy. They amuse the mind, but they do not act upon the manners of the people.

I have already said that this state of things is very far from originating in democracy alone, and that the causes of it must be sought for in several peculiar circumstances independent of the democratic principle. If the Americans, retaining the same laws and social condition, had had a different origin, and had been transported into another country, I do not question that they would have had a literature. Even as they now are, I am convinced that they will ultimately have one; but its character will be different from that which marks the American literary productions of our time, and that character will be peculiarly its own. Nor is it impossible to trace this character beforehand.

I suppose an aristocratic people amongst whom letters are culti- vated; the labours of the mind, as well as the affairs of state, are conducted by a ruling class in society. The literary as well as the political career is almost entirely confined to this class, or to those nearest to it in rank. These premises suffice to give me a key to all the rest.

When a small number of the same men are engaged at the same time upon the same objects, they easily concert with one another, and agree upon certain leading rules which are to govern them each and all. If the object which attracts the attention of these men is literature, the productions of the mind will soon be subjected by them to precise canons, from which it will no longer be allowable to depart. If these men occupy an hereditary position in the country, they will be naturally inclined, not only to adopt a certain number of fixed rules for themselves, but to follow those which their forefathers laid down for their own guidance; their code will be at once strict and tradi- tional. As they are not necessarily engrossed by the cares of daily life,—as they have never been so, any more than their fathers were before them—they have learned to take an interest, for several generations back, in the labours of the mind. They have learned to understand literature as an art, to love it in the end for its own sake, and to feel a scholar-like satisfaction in seeing men conform to its rules. Nor is this all: the men of whom I speak began and will end their lives in easy or in affluent circumstances; hence they have naturally conceived a taste for choice gratifications, and a love of refined and delicate pleasures. Nay more, a kind of indolence of mind and heart, which they frequently contract in the midst of this long and peaceful enjoyment of so much welfare, leads them to put aside, even from their pleasures, whatever might be too startling or too acute. They had rather be amused, than intensely excited; they wish to be interested, but not to be carried away.

Now let us fancy a great number of literary performances executed by the men, or for the men, whom I have just described, and we shall readily conceive a style of literature in which everything will be regular and pre-arranged. The slightest work will be carefully touched in its least details; art and labour will be conspicuous in everything; each kind of writing will have rules of its own, from which it will not be allowed to swerve, and which distinguish it from all others. Style will be thought of almost as much importance as thought; and the form will be no less considered than the matter: the diction will be polished, measured, and uniform. The tone of the mind will be always dignified, seldom very animated; and writers will care more to perfect what they produce, than to multiply their productions. It will sometimes happen, that the members of the literary class, always living amongst themselves and writing for themselves alone, will lose sight of the rest of the world, which will infect them with a false and laboured style; they will lay down minute literary rules for their exclusive use, which will insensibly lead them to deviate from common sense, and finally to transgress the bounds of nature. By dint of striving after a mode of parlance different from the vulgar, they will arrive at a sort of aristocratic jargon, which is hardly less remote from pure language than is the coarse dialect of the people. Such are the natural perils of literature amongst aristocracies. Every aristocracy which keeps itself entirely aloof from the people becomes impotent—a fact which is as true in literature as it is in politics.[1]

Let us now turn the picture and consider the other side of it: let us transport ourselves into the midst of a democracy, not unprepared by

[1]All this is especially true of the aristocratic countries which have been long and peacefully subject to a monarchical government. When liberty prevails in an aristocracy, the higher ranks are constantly obliged to make use of the lower classes; and when they use, they approach them. This frequently introduces something of a democratic spirit into an aristocratic community. There springs up, moreover, in a privileged body, governing with energy and an habitually bold policy, a taste for stir and excitement, which must infallibly affect all literary performances.

ancient traditions and present culture to partake in the pleasures of the mind. Ranks are there intermingled and confounded; knowledge and power are both infinitely subdivided, and, if I may use the expression, scattered on every side. Here then is a motley mutlitude, whose intellectual wants are to be supplied. These new votaries of the pleasures of the mind have not all received the same education; they do not possess the same degree of culture as their fathers, nor any resemblance to them—nay, they perpetually differ from themselves, for they live in a state of incessant change of place, feelings, and fortunes. The mind of each member of the community is therefore unattached to that of his fellow-citizens by tradition or by common habits; and they have never had the power, the inclination, nor the time to concert together. It is however from the bosom of this heterogeneous and agitated mass that authors spring; and from the same source their profits and their fame are distributed.

I can without difficulty understand that, under these circumstances, I must expect to meet in the literature of such a people with but few of those strict conventional rules which are admitted by readers and by writers in aristocratic ages. If it should happen that the men of some one period were agreed upon any such rules, that would prove nothing for the following period; for, amongst democratic nations, each new generation is a new people. Amongst such nations, then, literature will not easily be subjected to strict rules, and it is impossible that any such rules should ever be permanent.

In democracies it is by no means the case that all the men who cultivate literature have received a literary education; and most of those who have some tinge of belles-lettres, are either engaged in politics, or in a profession which only allows them to taste occasionally and by stealth the pleasures of the mind. These pleasures, therefore, do not constitute the principal charm of their lives; but they are considered as a transient and necessary recreation amidst the serious labours of life. Such men can never acquire a sufficiently intimate knowledge of the art of literature to appreciate its more delicate beauties; and the minor shades of expression must escape them. As the time they can devote to letters is very short, they seek to make the best use of the whole of it. They prefer books which may be easily procured, quickly read, and which require no learned researches to be understood. They ask for beauties, self-proffered, and easily enjoyed; above all, they must have what is unexpected and new. Accustomed to the struggle, the crosses, and the monotony of

practical life, they require rapid emotions, startling passages,—truths
or errors brilliant enough to rouse them up, and to plunge them at
once, as if by violence, into the midst of a subject.

Why should I say more? or who does not understand what is about
to follow, before I have expressed it? Taken as a whole, literature in
democratic ages can never present, as it does in the periods of
aristocracy, an aspect of order, regularity, science, and art; its form
will, on the contrary, ordinarily be slighted, sometimes despised.
Style will frequently be fantastic, incorrect, overburdened, and
loose,—almost always vehement and bold. Authors will aim at
rapidity of execution, more than at perfection of detail. Small
productions will be more common than bulky books: there will be
more wit than erudition, more imagination than profundity; and
literary performances will bear marks of an untutored and rude
vigour of thought,—frequently of great variety and singular fecundity. The object of authors will be to astonish rather than to please,
and to stir the passions more than to charm the taste.

Here and there, indeed, writers will doubtless occur who will
choose a different track, and who will, if they are gifted with superior
abilities, succeed in finding readers, in spite of their defects or their
better qualities; but these exceptions will be rare, and even the
authors who shall so depart from the received practice in the main
subject of their works, will always relapse into it in some lesser
details.

I have just depicted two extreme conditions: the transition by
which a nation passes from the former to the latter is not sudden but
gradual, and marked with shades of very various intensity. In the
passage which conducts a lettered people from the one to the other,
there is almost always a moment at which the literary genius of
democratic nations has its confluence with that of aristocracies, and
both seek to establish their joint sway over the human mind. Such
epochs are transient, but very brilliant: they are fertile without
exuberance, and animated without confusion. The French literature
of the eighteenth century may serve as an example.

I should say more than I mean, if I were to assert that the literature
of a nation is always subordinate to its social condition and its
political constitution. I am aware that, independently of these causes,
there are several others which confer certain characteristics on literary productions; but these appear to me to be the chief. The relations
which exist between the social and political condition of a people and

the genius of its authors are always very numerous: whoever knows the one, is never completely ignorant of the other.

THE TRADE OF LITERATURE

DEMOCRACY not only infuses a taste for letters among the trading classes, but introduces a trading spirit into literature.

In aristocracies, readers are fastidious and few in number; in democracies, they are far more numerous and far less difficult to please. The consequence is, that among aristocratic nations no one can hope to succeed without immense exertions, and that these exertions may bestow a great deal of fame, but can never earn much money; whilst among democratic nations, a writer may flatter himself that he will obtain at a cheap rate a meagre reputation and a large fortune. For this purpose he need not be admired, it is enough that he is liked.

The ever-increasing crowd of readers, and their continual craving for something new, insures the sale of books which nobody much esteems.

In democratic periods the public frequently treat authors as kings do their courtiers; they enrich, and they despise them. What more is needed by the venal souls which are born in courts, or which are worthy to live there?

Democratic literature is always infested with a tribe of writers who look upon letters as a mere trade; and for some few great authors who adorn it, you may reckon thousands of idea-mongers.

FRANÇOIS RENÉ DE CHATEAUBRIAND
(1768–1848)

On America and American Literature

IN HIS WRITINGS ON AMERICA, there are at least two Chateaubriands. First, there is the young Frenchman who, in *Atala* (1801), a prose romance—soon translated into Italian, German, Spanish, and English, both in England and in the United States—spread through Europe the appeal of an exotic and mysterious America and of a noble Indian savage with a viable civilization of his own. In *Atala* the myth of an uncultivated semi-paradise across the sea, mingled with the allure of a romantic Christianity, reached its apex. Chateaubriand explored this theme further in *René* (first separate publication, 1805) and *Voyage en Amérique* (1827), in which he was to compare Washington favorably with Napoleon. He had traveled to America in 1791 and had spent about five months there. He later pretended that his writings on America derived principally from his American experience, though it has been long evident that they are strongly indebted to his imagination, later recastings, and his readings, including William Bartram's *Travels* (1792), descriptions of the Floridas, Georgia, and the Carolinas which rapidly gained popularity.

So powerful was the effect of *Atala* that the American writer, Timothy Flint, who traveled from Massachusetts to the Mississippi Valley in 1816, incorporated into his *Recollections of the Last Ten Years* (1826) nature descriptions imitative of Chateaubriand. Robert Dale Owen's *Pocahontas* (1837), modeled after *Atala*, was only one of many American plays inspired by Chateaubriand. On the other hand, Caroline Kirkland, author of *A New Home—Who'll Follow?* (1839), consisting of sharp sketches of Midwestern life, found *Atala* no accurate guide. Moving with her husband from the East to the

45

Michigan Territory in 1835, she expected to live in an atmosphere redolent of *Atala* and found the real West very different. "I had . . . dwelt with delight in Chateaubriand's Atala, where no such vulgar inconvenience is once hinted at, and my floating vision of a home in the woods was full of important omissions, and always in a Floridian clime. . . ." Her books were born of disillusionment with the French romancer.

The second and later Chateaubriand, conservative in political and cultural matters, expresses himself in the excerpt below, from Part I, Book VI, of his *Memoirs from Beyond the Grave (Mémoires d'outre-tombe*, 1849–50). In this later period Chateaubriand shared the misgivings about contemporary America revealed in travel literature by emigrés who had lived in America in the late 1790s and in the first decade of the nineteenth century, notably Le Comte Constantin de Volney's *Tableau du Climat et du Sol des États-Unis* (1803) and La Rochefoucauld-Liancourt's *Voyages dans les États-Unis d'Amérique* (1799). These aristocratic observers, less sympathetic to the French and American revolutions than a Lafayette or a Crèvecoeur, pointed particularly to the forces working for disunity in the American scene and to the effects of materialism and rawness on the intellectual life of the nation. They constitute a reaction to the almost universally sympathetic and even idealizing picture of American life current among the French just before and during the American Revolution. Chateaubriand reiterates these arguments, with considerable sagacity and insight. In addition, Chateaubriand shows small regard for early nineteenth-century American literature, an attitude, incidentally, expressed more flatly and without qualifications by Stendhal. (In Chapter 50, "Love in the United States," in *Of Love* [1822], the famous novelist—citing Volney—describes Americans as too pragmatic and nonpassionate to produce a worthwhile literature.)

Bibliography: Indispensable for an understanding of French attitudes toward America until Tocqueville is Gilbert Chinard, "The American Dream," in *Literary History of the United States*, ed. Robert E. Spiller et al., Chapter 15 (3rd edition, New York: 1963). A good longer study is Durand Echeverria, *Mirage in the West: A History of the French Image of American Society to 1815* (Princeton: 1957). An interesting sidelight is revealed in Richmond L. Hawken, *Madame de Staël and the United States* (Cambridge: 1931). Mme. de Staël, instrumental in introducing Romanticism into French literature and hostile to Napoleon, was an admirer of the United States, made financial investments in this country, and contemplated emigration. A correspondent of Jefferson, Gouverneur Morris, and John Quincy Adams, she made no extended comments on American literature. In studies on Chateaubriand, Emma K. Armstrong, "Chateaubriand's America," *PMLA*, 22 (1907), 345–70, still has value. A more recent examination, "Chateaubriand and Early America," by the French "New Novelist" Michel Butor, translated by Derek Coleman, can be found in Butor, *Inventory* (New York: 1968).

These excerpts from *Memoirs from Beyond the Grave* were translated by Alexander Teixeira de Mattos (New York: G. P. Putnam's Sons, 1902), pp. 250–58. Footnotes in the text are the translator's.

ON AMERICA AND AMERICAN LITERATURE

(1850)

. . .THE UNITED STATES must not be searched for that which distinguishes man above the other beings of creation, for that which constitutes his certificate of immortality and the ornament of his days: literature is unknown in the new republic, although called for by a multitude of institutions. The American has replaced intellectual by positive operations. Do not impute to him as an inferiority his mediocrity in the arts, for it is not in that direction that he has turned his attention. Cast through various causes upon a desert soil, he made agriculture and commerce the first objects of his cares: before thinking, one must live; before planting trees, one must fell them, in order to till the ground.

The primitive colonists, it is true, their minds steeped in religious controversy, carried the passion for disputation into the very heart of the forests; but it was necessary for them first to shoulder their axes and march to the conquest of the desert: their sole pulpit, in the intervals between their labours, was the elm they were engaged in squaring. The Americans have not passed through the ages of other nations: they left their childhood and their youth in Europe; the artless words of the cradle were unknown to them; they enjoyed the delights of home only through the medium of their regrets for a native land which they had never seen, and of which they mourned the eternal absence and the charm they had heard of from others.

The new continent had no classical literature, nor romantic literature, nor Indian literature: for the classical, the Americans have no models; for the romantic, no middle-ages; for the Indian, the Americans despise the savages and loathe the sight of the woods as of a prison to which they were once condemned.

And thus it comes that literature as a thing apart, literature properly so-called, does not exist in America; what one finds is applied literature, answering to the different needs of society: the literature of workmen, merchants, sailors, farmers. Americans succeed in mechanics and science, because science has its material side. Franklin and Fulton took possession of lightning and steam for the benefit of mankind. It fell to America to endow the world with the discovery, thanks to which no continent can henceforward escape the mariner's search.

Poetry and imagination, the portion of a very small number of idlers, are regarded in the United States as puerilities appertaining to the first and to the last age of life. The Americans have had no childhood and have as yet had no old age.

Hence it follows that men engaged upon serious studies have necessarily been obliged to take part in the affairs of their country in order to become acquainted with them, and in the same way they inevitably found themselves actors in their revolution. But one melancholy fact must be observed, which is the prompt degeneration of talent, from the first men, who figured in the American troubles, down to the men of these latter days; and yet those men all touch. The old presidents of ths Republic have a religious, simple, lofty, calm character, of which we find no trace in the blood-stained tumults of our own Republic and Empire. The solitude with which the Americans were surrounded reacted upon their nature; they achieved their liberty in silence.

General Washington's farewell address to the people of the United States might have been uttered by the gravest characters of antiquity. . . .

Without loving nature, the Americans have applied themselves to the study of natural history. Townsend set out from Philadelphia and traversed on foot the regions separating the Atlantic from the Pacific Ocean, jotting down numerous observations in his journal. Thomas Say, who travelled in Florida and in the Rocky Mountains, has published a work on American entomology. Wilson, a weaver who became an author, has left some rather finished pictures.

To turn to literature proper, although it does not amount to much, there are, nevertheless, a few writers to be mentioned among the novelists and poets. Brown, the son of a Quaker, is the author of *Wieland*, which is the source and model of the novels of the new school. Unlike his fellow-countrymen:

"I prefer," said Brown, "roaming in the forests to thrashing corn."
Wieland, the hero of the novel, is a Puritan whom Heaven has commanded to kill his wife:

" 'I have brought thee hither,' says he to her, 'to fulfil a divine command. I am appointed thy destroyer, and destroy thee I must.'
"Saying this, I seized her wrists. She shrieked aloud, and endeavoured to free herself from my grasp. . . .
" 'Wieland. . . . Am I not thy wife? And wouldst thou kill me? Thou wilt not; oh! . . .Spare me—spare—help, help—'
"Till her breath was stopped she shrieked for help—for mercy."

Wieland strangles his wife, and experiences unspeakable delights by the side of her dead corpse. The horror of our modern inventions is here surpassed. Brown had trained his mind by reading *Caleb Williams*,[1] and in *Wieland* he copied a scene from *Othello*.

At the present day, the American novelists Cooper[2] and Washington Irving[3] are obliged to take refuge in Europe to find chronicles and a public. The language of the great English writers has been "creolized," "provincialized," "barbarized," without gaining anything in energy in the midst of a virgin nature; it has become necessary to draw up catalogues of American expressions.

As to the American poets, their language has charm, but they rarely rise above the common-place. Still, the *Ode to the Evening Breeze*, the *Sunrise on the Mount*, the *Torrent*, and some other poems, deserve a passing glance. Halleck[4] has sung the death of Bozzaris, and George Hill[5] has wandered among the Ruins of Athens:

[1]*Caleb Williams*, by William Godwin (1756–1836), father of Mary Wollstonecraft, Shelley's second wife, appeared in 1794, one year before the publication of *Wieland*.—T.
[2]James Fenimore Cooper (1780–1851), probably the most popular of American novelists.—T.
[3]Washington Irving (1783-1859). He was American Minister in Madrid for a short period (1842).—T.
[4]Fitz-Greene Halleck (1795-1867), author of *Marco Bozzaris*. The curious will find a criticism of his work in Poe's *Literati of New York*.—T.
[5]George Hill (*b.* 1796), author of the *Ruins of Athens*, and a few shorter poems.—T.

> Alas! for her, the beautiful, but lone,
> Dethroned queen![6] . . .

And again:

> There sits the queen of temples[7]—grey and lone.
>   She, like the last of an imperial line,
> Has seen her sister structures, one by one,
>   To time their gods and worshippers resign.[8]

It pleases me, a traveller on the shores of Hellas and Atlantis, to hear the independent voice of a land unknown to antiquity lamenting the lost liberty of the old world.

But will American preserve her form of government? Will the States not become divided? Has not a representative of Virginia already maintained the theory of ancient liberty with slaves, the result of paganism, against a representative of Massachusetts, defending the cause of modern liberty without slaves, as Christianity made it? Are not the Northern and Southern States opposed in mind and interests? Will not the Western States, so far removed from the Atlantic, wish to have a separate government? On the one hand, is the federal bond sufficiently powerful to maintain the union, and to compel each State to draw closer to it? On the other hand, if the presidential power be increased, will not despotism come with the guards and privileges of the dictator?

The isolation of the United States has permitted them to spring into being and to increase: it is doubtful whether they would have been able to exist and grow in Europe. Federal Switzerland subsists in our midst; but why? Because she is small, poor, cantoned in the bosom of the mountains, a nursery of soldiers for kings, a goal for travellers.

Separated from the old world, the population of the United States still inhabits the solitude: its deserts have been its liberty; but already the conditions of its existence are altering . . . .

I have said that the Northern, Southern, and Western States were divided in interests; that is common knowledge: if these States break up the union, will they be reduced by force of arms? In that case,

---

[6]*Ruins of Athens*, II.—T.
[7]The Parthenon.—T.
[8]*Ruins of Athens*, XVII.—T.

what a leaven of hatred will be spread through the social body! Will the dissenting States maintain their independence? In that case, what discords will not break out among those emancipated States! Those republics across the sea, once uncoupled, would no longer form aught save feeble units without weight in the social balance, where they would be successively subjugated by one of their number (I leave on one side the serious question of alliances and foreign intervention). Kentucky, peopled as it is with a race of men bred in the open air, harder and more soldier-like, would seem destined to become the conquering State. In this State devouring the others, the power of one would soon rise upon the ruins of the power of all. . . .

The commerical spirit is beginning to take possession of them; self-interest is becoming their national vice. Already the speculations of the banks of the different States clash with one another, and bankruptcies threaten the fortunes of the community. So long as liberty produces gold, an industrial republic does wonders; but when the gold is acquired or exhausted, it loses it love of independence, which is not based upon a moral sentiment, but arises from the thirst for gain and the passion for trade. . . .

The enormous inequality of fortunes threatens still more seriously to kill the spirit of equality. There are Americans with incomes of one or two millions a year; and already the Yankees of high society are no longer able to live as Franklin did: the true "gentleman," disgusted with his new country, goes to Europe in search of the old; one meets him at the inns, making "tours" in Italy like the English, tours marked by extravagance or spleen. These ramblers from Carolina or Virginia buy ruined abbeys in France, and lay out English gardens with American trees at Melun. Naples sends it singers and perfumers to New York, Paris its fashions and dancers, London its grooms and prize-fighters: exotic delights which do not add to the gaiety of the Union. There they amuse themselves by jumping into the Falls of Niagara, amid the applause of fifty thousand planters, semi-savages whose merriment is with difficulty aroused by the sight of death. . . .

A cold and hard egotism reigns in the towns; piastres and dollars, bank-notes and silver, the rise and fall of stocks, these form the sole subject of conversation: one imagines one's self on 'Change or in the counting-house of a large shop. The newspapers, huge in dimensions, are filled with business articles or scurrilous gossip. Could the Americans be unconsciously submitting to the law of a climate in which vegetable nature seems to have benefited at the expense of living nature, a law combated by some distinguished minds, and yet not put entirely out of court by its refutation? It might be worth while to inquire whether the American has not been too soon used up in philosphic liberty, as the Russian has been in civilized despotism.

To sum up, the United States give the idea of a colony, not of a parent country; they have no past, their manners owe their existence to the laws. These citizens of the New World took rank among the nations at the moment when political ideas were entering upon an upward phase: this explains why they change with such extraordinary rapidity. A permanent form of society seems to become impracticable in their case, thanks, on the one hand, to the extreme weariness of individuals; on the other, to the impossibility of remaining in one spot, the necessity for movement, by which they are dominated: for one is never very firmly fixed where the household gods are wandering gods. Placed on the ocean road, at the head of progressive opinions as new as his country, the American seems to have received from Columbus a mission to discover fresh worlds rather than to create them.

PART II

American Classics Through French Eyes

Comtesse d'Agoult: Emerson (1846)
Stuart Merrill: Whitman (1912)
Valery Larbaud: Thoreau (1922)
Albert Camus: Melville (1953)
François Mauriac: Hawthorne's *The Scarlet Letter* and
James's *The Bostonians* (1959)

Emerson

THE EARLY FRENCH ESTIMATE of Ralph Waldo Emerson (1803–1882) reprinted below remains one of the best. Written by "Daniel Stern," a penname for the Comtesse d'Agoult, it first appeared in the *Revue Indépendante* on July 25, 1846. The Comtesse d'Agoult had been the mistress of Franz Liszt, the mother of Cosima Wagner, and Richard Wagner's mother-in-law. After her liaison with Liszt was terminated in 1844, she undertook a career in letters, in which she was to establish a reputation that was to stamp her as a remarkable woman.

She thought of Emerson as an American original, with the novelty French readers expected to find in American literature: "In a word, Emerson seems to me the personification of the American genius, genius impatient of all authority and disdainful of all tradition, because it acknowledges no ancestors and desires no debt to a past which was servitude." Émile Montégut (1825–1895), writing on Emerson a year later in the *Revue des Deux Mondes*, likewise saw him as a representative American, rendering original and fruitful ideas. It was Montégut, too, who, in 1851, first translated The First Series of Emerson's *Essays* (1841).

Despite these early appraisals, Emerson remained comparatively little known during the next few decades. However, Baudelaire referred to him in the 1860s. Next to Poe, Emerson was the American author Charles Baudelaire read most carefully. The latter was particularly affected by Emerson's *Conduct of Life* (1860), which offered practical advice and encouragement. (See Margaret Gilman, "Baudelaire and Emerson," *Romantic Review*, 1943, pp. 211–22.)

From 1890, Emerson has had a considerable following in France, especially among moralists and philosophers. The Belgian poet, Maurice Maeterlinck, in a long essay on Emerson (Brussels: 1894), found grounds in Emerson for philosophic optimism. A French philosopher of the twentieth century, Henri Bergson, acknowledged his debt to Emerson. Other French writers who have praised Emerson or have shown an influence were Henri-Frédéric Amiel and Marcel Proust.

Bibliography: A considerable body of scholarship on Emerson exists in French, beginning with Marie Dugard's critical biography in 1907, continuing with several volumes by Régis Michaud in the 1920s, and up through Maurice Gonnard's *Individuel et Société dans l'Oeuvre de Ralph Waldo Emerson* (1963). A brief but helpful sketch of Emerson in France is found in *The Emerson Handbook* by Frederick Ives Carpenter (New York: 1953), pp. 241–43.

The translation here is by Bessie D. Howard, reproduced from *New England Quarterly*, 10 (1937), 447–63. The footnotes are the translator's.

EMERSON

(1846)

MEN OF TALENT AND GENIUS, artists, writers, philosophers, and poets reach renown in two altogether different ways. Some find the approach easy, the doorway open. They are familiar only with the smiles of the gods hence find no sanctuary forbidding; they enter as a matter of course, often without realizing it, their minds on other things. These are destiny's favorite children who, born of a propitious union and baptized by the fairies, receive what might be called the gift of fame.

The others, on the contrary, find all the approaches blocked from the very beginning. They are lost in the crowd where no one senses their presence nor gives them place. If, finally, modest and persevering, they succeed in slipping into the inner court, it is at evening, in the shadows, where they wait a long time for the revealing light of day.

Emerson seems to me to belong somewhat to these latter.

For some years this rare spirit has been appreciated in his own country by a young and studious élite, yet there is no glamour of celebrity about him. I do not believe I am mistaken in stating that his name is still almost unknown in Europe. It was mentioned for the first time by M. Philarète Chasles in an article on American literary tendencies and more recently during some remarkable lectures given by a distinguished foreign poet[1] who quoted him on different occasions à *propos* of certain enigmatic opinions on the language of animals and the transmigration of souls. But, referred to in that way, without any special significance attached to it, Emerson's name awoke no curiosity in an audience taken up with more vital questions. No one, I feel sure, in that whole assembly, no one, except myself, thought of keeping it in mind.

When I made enquiry about the works mentioned by the illustrious professor, I learned they were not to be found at any of our bookshops. It was necessary to write to London, where I was finally able to procure a volume of the Essays with a preface by T. Carlyle, from which I drew the meagre information I am going to set down here. It will be neither long nor detailed nor even unusual, for charmed as he shows himself to be, Carlyle himself has only very incomplete data, namely: that the author's name is Ralph Waldo Emerson; that he was born in Massachusetts; that his first studies were in theology; that he was, but no longer is, a Unitarian minister and that, in spite of outstanding intellectual qualities which seemed to destine him for public life, he has preferred to live quietly, "sit still" and remain in solitude. It is easy to be seen that there is nothing particularly revealing in that! It is only a meagre sketch without which it would be impossible to draw such a vague figure in the imagination. Indeed if we knew anything less, we should know nothing at all. The Essays once read, it becomes difficult to explain such ignorance of so luminous a spirit, so compelling a moralist as Emerson. It is understandable, perhaps, when one considers that he lives without concern for reputation, far from the world, on the other side of the ocean; especially it is understandable when one considers that he is thinking and writing among a people whose spiritual life, still scarcely manifest, is, in a sense, stifled by the great hub-bub of its three-fold industrial, political and commercial activity.

Who among us, in fact, imagines that in the United States of America there are thinkers, artists or philosophers worthy of the name? Who concerns himself with American letters or thought? And shall we not admit, in our own defense, that we are excusable for not paying scrupulous attention to the part of that vast organism which

[1]Mickiewicz, in his course on Slavic literature, published under the title *Messianism and the Official Church*. Adam Mickiewicz (1798–1855), a Polish poet born in Lithuania, was professor of Slavic literature at the College de France.

still lies dormant, while the other is growing visibly, unfolding its strength and multiplying under our astounded eyes, the wonders of its powerful vitality?

Nothing resembles our old states of Europe less than the new continent of America. Another origin stamped it with another character; other influences are leading it on to other destinies. This young giant, born in the bright sunlight of liberty, has not been much concerned with learning to read nor given to the contemplative life. What would he seek in the class-room—this young giant whose quick-surging blood calls into the wide outdoors and whose robust nature sweeps on to bold adventures? The time has not come for him to read and write and meditate. He must live, live with exuberance and tumult, like a violent, headstrong child. He must swim in his tempestuous seas, stride over his mountains, set fire to his forests, torment his slaves. He needs noise and confusion more than rhythm and harmony! Wait until he is tired. Wait until the flood waters of his life are calm and can catch the reflection of the light from above.

Already certain signs indicate that the moment is near. The demands of the spirit are beginning to awake in the vigorous body dominated a short while ago by the excess of its physical energy. A visible transformation is taking place. I know that that is not the common opinion; I know that it is the accepted thing to say that the United States will never possess art nor literature of its own because its origin, devoid of the marvelous, was not consecrated by mysterious theogonies, because its recently established traditions have not been gathered together by rhapsodists and because its history, born yesterday, has not had and could not have its Iliad or its Niebelungen. The soundness of that argument is, however, more apparent than real. It would be difficult to show that the civilization of peoples in the course of the centuries will always have to follow identical processes. The daily and complaisant error of man is to measure infinite motives by his own limited perception and to persist in limiting the possible.

If Orpheus's lyre did not calm the roarings in the wilderness of the new world, if no Amphyon built magic cities there, if no bard evoked the thunder-god from the top of a sacred rock and if Valleda did not gather with his golden reapinghook the immortal mistletoe hung from the branches of the virgin oak, does that mean that the mysteries of grace and harmony will never be revealed to the children of the great Washington? And that the divine tremor will never stir the hearts of these brave and free men? We must admit that such an induction would be, at the least, bold. No, it will not be that way. Life calls forth life. Some crudeness is inseparable from the first flights of strength, but let us be careful not to base our judgment of the whole future of such a people on the passing conditions of their existence and in ignorance of the secret laws of their development, which resembles no other. Let us have confidence in the creative force of free institutions and let us not close our eyes disdainfully to the first flickerings of the new art of these new people. These flickerings are still weak, uncertain, vacillating, why deny it? Neither W. Irving nor Bryant nor Longfellow nor the famous woman with the charming name of Maria dell Occidente[2] give evidence of relationship to that kind of genius which characterizes the artistic ideal of a nation. Nevertheless, the sum-total of the works of these talented people is already creating an atmosphere more favorable to genius, which is penetrating the soil, making it more fertile for the great sower of the word who is to come.

Among these precursors or rather outside their ranks, alone and rising in strong direct flight toward the high regions of thought, I single out to-day Emerson. Why this choice, why this preference? On what found it or how justify it? It will be neither by the number nor the brilliance of his works. I have already said that one volume of Emerson has come into my hands, and in that volume he shows no special faculty for writing. I do not detect in him a political sense; he could not lay claim to the title of philosopher. So completely does he defy all classification by his independent strides I could scarcely bring myself to call him a moralist. Shall I not say that in my eyes Emerson is more than all that. He is a man of superior nature who, in order to speak the language of the ancients, has the courage and the wisdom *to think and act in conformity with his own nature:* a rarer wisdom and a stauncher courage than one could believe possible in any age, especially in ours.

Born in the midst of a turbulent and adventurous society he prefers to "sit still" and live in silent communion with his own soul because he finds nothing outside himself which corresponds with his exquisite nature. The vain agitation of the cities tires him; in a country retreat he seeks the serenity of meditation. He seeks solitude there

---

[2]Sobriquet given by Southey to Mrs. Maria (Gowen) Brooks (1795–1845), an American poet who was born at Medford, Massachusetts, and died in Cuba. Mrs. Brooks was the author of *Zophiël, or the Bride of Seven* (1825) and other volumes.

but not isolation; for Emerson, it is evident in his writings, has a sensitive intelligence which takes pleasure in a sort of distant enjoyment of things and men of which too close a view wounds him. Like Obermann,[3] his less resigned and less wise brother, he finds no place for himself in any stratum of our social hierarchies; he belongs to no profession. All yokes seem absurd to him, all careers servile, all parties unjust, all flags ridiculous. In a country where everything is conducted by groups and is divided into sects, he belongs to no group, no sect. He can not be tagged with any of the names which give a collective value to the individual; he can not be counted among the Methodists, the Puseyites, the Reformers, the Emancipationists nor especially among the philanthropists. He knows he is a man and wishes to remain a man. But as he is not ignorant of the fact that it is a difficult task in the midst of an ordered society which is divided into classes according to arbitrary conventions, he takes refuge under his rustic roof; rests content in his own strength and communicates with his fellowmen through the intermediary of his writings, which, small in number until now, carry the incontestable stamp of a virile and natural greatness. These are, as Carlyle excellently says, the soliloquies of a true soul, the rich overflowing of a mind which has remained faithful to itself and of which nothing blurs the clear perception.

Emerson, I intimated a while ago, belongs to that aristocratic family of intellectuals whose exquisite and noble instincts make them sensitive to the discord in human affairs, and who refuse to accept the deviations from primitive law, the astounding contradictions between eternal truth and social ethics which make up popular opinion. Deep within him he can hear the sincere muse which dictated the familiar wisdom of Charron; he goes back to the philosophy of Montaigne; he says, with Obermann, that our life could be much easier and simpler than we make it. ("That our life might be much easier and simpler than we make it; that the world might be a happier place than it is; that there is no need of struggle, convulsions and despairs, of the wringing of the hands and the gnashing of the teeth; that we miscreate our own evils.") He adds that there is a "certain fatal dislocation in our relation to nature, distorting all our modes of living." But more consoling than Obermann, he believes that man, obedient to the inner voice, to the divine "afflatus" can set right

[3]Étienne Pivert de Sénancour (1770–1846).

within himself the discord of the world and he cries out with enthusiastic conviction, "to the poet, to the philosopher and to the saint, all things are friendly and sacred, all events profitable, all days holy, all men divine."

The most striking characteristic of Emerson's philosophy, if I may permit myself to call philosophy a capricious collection of meditations which can boast neither well-knit argument nor sustained logic, the root of it and, in my eyes, the very substance of the book, is the religious respect for the human personality and the frankest protest which has ever been made against the oppression of the many in favor of the rights of the individual.

This sentiment persists and is expressed with great force throughout the book. It evidences itself in a strange way, through a mystic naturalism and a perpetual adoration of the "over-soul" which Emerson sees shining through all the phenomena of humanity, giving them new life with its divine breath which he says is called genius when it breathes through the intellect; virtue, when it breathes through the will; love, when it flows through the affections.

In his eyes, the universe is a living symbolism: he divides men into three classes according to the degree to which they understand this symbolism. "One class live to the utility of the symbol, esteeming health and wealth; another class live above this mark, to the beauty of the symbol, as the poet, the artist, the naturalist, and the man of science; a third class live above the beauty of the symbol, to the beauty of the thing signified. The first class have common sense; the second, taste; and the third spiritual perception."

Yet, while exhorting man to lose himself in infinite nature, and renounce self-will, Emerson calls him incessantly back to himself and repeats again and again, in his concise language: "Insist upon thyself." Here is an apparent contradiction; the coexistence of two principles which seem necessarily mutually exclusive and which Emerson reconciles only in the vast unity of God. But this God, what is it? By what name invoke it? By what attributes shall we identify it? The former Unitarian minister does not take the trouble to enlighten us about that; he tells us very plainly, it is true, that it is not the God of tradition, nor of rhetoric. But is it Plato's God, or Spinoza's or Hegel's or Swedenborg's? We do not know; fortunately we do not mind not knowing. The rare charm of the book of Essays is that one asks nothing of it, for it pretends to nothing. Emerson calls himself "an endless seeker" who "unsettles all things" and draws one along after him with his irresistible simplicity. There is no hesitancy about following him, for one breathes in, in his work, a wholesome atmosphere; one smells there, as he naïvely says, the resinous odor of the pine; one thinks he almost hears the buzzing of insects. The straw which the swallow dropped is interwoven into this rustic fabric. "My book should smell of pines and resound with the hum of insects; the swallow over my window should inter-weave that thread or straw he carries in his bill into my web also." Nothing jars in all this, not even the dissonances. The peculiarities are not shocking to us: they are not affected peculiarities but natural and as little studied, as native to Emerson's mentality as the vagaries of certain flowers.

I could sum up all Emerson's contradictions, moreover, in one: the protestant tendency to question in conflict with a vague pantheistic instinct which never completely possesses him. This tendency manifests itself throughout the book by bold negation, the most striking of which is the negation of history. Like Napoleon, Emerson declares that history is only "a fable agreed upon." According to him "Time dissipates to shining ether the solid angularity of facts. No anchor, no cable, no fences avail to keep a fact a fact. Babylon, Troy and Tyre and even early Rome are passing already into fiction. The garden of Eden, the sun standing still in Gibeon is poetry thenceforward to all nations. London and Paris and New York must go the same way." Everything is within us. History if subjective. Man seeks and finds there only the personification of his own feelings: "Civil and natural history, the history of art and literature must be explained from individual history or must remain words."

It is very plain that that is a solitary's conception of things; it is the very natural interpretation of a great soul which feels itself capable of the most heroic acts and the most sublime realizations of human kind. No devotion surprises him; like circumstances would have found in him the same response. No creation of art dazzles him; on contemplating it he identifies himself with it. Neither Plato nor Caesar nor Shakespeare are strangers to him; they show him, as he says so well "his unattained but attainable self." The history of the world lies in germ, in his own heart. He can cry out without exaggeration or hyperbole, with his virile eloquence, "I feel the eternity of man and the identity of his thought."

When Emerson comes to the moral applications of his beliefs, he is, as may well be expected, in radical opposition to popular opinion. The vice he detests most, the only one he attacks with an insistent irony and which he calls the *vice of conformity,* is the greatest force of our modern civilization. It is the cult of convention which impels man to follow the opinions of others, in all things, and subjects him, slavishly, to modes of life contrary to the desires and needs of his own nature. "Our houses," say Emerson, "are built with foreign taste; our shelves are garnished with foreign ornaments; our opinions, our tastes, all our minds follow the past and the distant, as the eyes of a maiden follow the mistress." His power of reason, solid and sure, makes him see in this *conformist* tendency, as he calls it, the source of an evil which, spread to-day into all things, is destroying interest in human life and is depriving personal existence of all greatness. It is the most-to-be-feared evil in democratic society, where people too easily confuse equality with conformity. Emerson understands this only too well; he never tires of insisting what shame and cowardice there is for a reasoning creature in perpetual imitation which he flays as suicide of the will. "Man is timid and apologetic," he says. "We are afraid of truth, afraid of fortune, afraid of death and afraid of each other."

And then, in some pages permeated with a deep feeling for human dignity, he paints, in bold strokes, society which he represents in a state of permanent conspiracy against individual spontaneity, against independence and virility of character, against genius, which, according to his definition, consists in believing that what is true for us in our own soul, is true also for all humanity. "To believe that what is true for you, in your private heart, is true for all men; that is genius." Society does not want creative geniuses: it hounds them with its sarcasm, crushes them with its scorn. If you dare to be a man, if you say to-day what you think to-day, to-morrow what you think to-morrow, you must expect to be misunderstood. "Misunderstood!" cries Emerson. What a stupid word! Is it such a misfortune to be misunderstood? Pythagoras was misunderstood, and Socrates and Jesus, too, and Luther and Copernicus and Galileo and Newton and all the wise and pure spirits which have been made into the flesh. "To be great is to be misunderstood."*

---

*Goethe says almost the same thing in these terms, "I have for many a day been convinced that it is necessary to pass through the world understood or misunderstood." As regards this, I should like to call attention to the ever-increasing influence of Goethe on his contemporaries. There is scarcely a book written to-day where his name is not cited. It is evident that Emerson, too, has known this great modern sage and that he has not touched the hem of his garment in vain. [Daniel Stern]

His protestant turn of mind and his keen antipathy to the sheep-like troop of conformists leads him to a thousand daring assertions. It is evident that he exaggerates his ideas for fear of understating them. He in no way conceals on what deep-rooted prejudice he declares war. Neither does he spare his forces; he renews his attack a hundred times, seizes now one weapon, now another; wrath, sarcasm, everything is fair, everything is put to his purpose. At one time he asserts that no law is sacred except the law of nature; at another he shows that good and evil are empty words, that one passes easily from one to the other; and that the only good is that which suits one's constitution, the only evil that which is contrary to it, "the only right is what is after my constitution, the only wrong what is against it." Furthermore, he would leave, he says, father and mother, wife and brother if his genius bid him; he would like to write over his door "whim."

And when we might think him tired and his arguments exhausted, he suddenly attacks, with a completely renewed fervor, the supreme pretension of the conformists—the virtue of consistency, the exaggerated respect for what we have done and said which rivets us to the past through fear of contradicting ourselves. Emerson sees no more shame in being inconsistent than in being misunderstood. Intellectual consistency or inconsistency, he says, is the obsession of little souls;[4] a great soul is not disturbed by it, it does not drag along after it the "corpse of memory." What does it matter if we are inconsistent? What matters is to act in complete harmony with the impulse of our own heart; what matters is that our actions be honest and sincere. At a distance, the variations of a great soul are effaced. Of what importance are the zigzags of a vessel when it leaves one fixed point and arrives at another fixed point? Of what consequence are the irregularities of the Andes and the Himalayas in relation to the surface of the immense globe?

Here I think I see the reader smile, insinuating that the consistency of the American moralist is not exactly the vice of our modern glory and that philanthropists, poets and especially statesmen, vying with each other, have in our day shown marks of inconsistency sufficient to satisfy the most exacting! He adds that it is probably not the time, in America or elsewhere, to preach the easy ethics of inconsistency. To be frank I must confess that I agree. Variety of opinions, vacillation of thought are not rare and phenomenal things with us:

[4]"A foolish consistency is the hobgoblin of little minds."

but I consider excessively rare, and that after all is the only thing Emerson laments and recommends, the courage of contradiction and the manly sincerity which knows how not to blush at past error.

This virtue, I am bold enough to state, is not one of those which shine in our great men. There is not one whose pride would dare do what Scripture tells us of God himself who, they say, repented. Most of them, whom one could point out, wear themselves out in useless efforts to smooth over, readjust, piece together again as well as possible the scattered fragments of their lives, and to show to the bewildered crowd that, even if they talked white yesterday and they talk black to-day, there results from their words and deeds a grayish shading of the pleasantest sort.* All energy is exhausted in these childish efforts and lofty thoughts are smothered by such petty concerns. "Man is timid and apologetic." How could it be said better in fewer words? In our land, middle-age is spent in explaining youth; old age in excusing and criticizing favorably middle-age; and all ages forget to live in their anxiety to explain how they have lived.

Emerson, therefore, is not wrong in insisting on confidence in oneself (self-reliance), a virtue of the primitive days of society which man neglects to-day because he feels less need of it, protected as he is by strong and free institutions and by the leveling influence of our democratic customs.

But, let us leave the *conformists* and *consistents* and follow Emerson in the minor parts of his Essays. We have just pointed out the two poles of his ethics: adoration of the "over-soul" which reveals to man his affinity with creation and makes him part of universal life; confidence in one's self which delivers one from servitude to the established opinions and conventions of society.

Let us run through with him some intermediary points, touched on less thoroughly, but to which the sincerity of his thought and his picturesque, unexpected expressions lend an incomparable interest and charm.

No thinker, no writer has described better and explained with more shining eloquence the inevitable decline of love in the most noble souls. Or rather, Emerson denies that it is decline; according to

*Peel is perhaps the only person who has given us a great example of self-contradiction; he dared to say to England's face, and Europe's: "I was mistaken." These are words of exalted simplicity which only the consciousness of great strength could dictate. [Daniel Stern]

him it is only a providential transformation. Love, that passion which draws two young and beautiful beings toward one another and absorbs them in mutual ardor, in exclusive, absorbing and wholly personal love, is modified bit by bit. The cult of individual beauty is transformed into adoration of universal beauty; blind passion for a woman or a man lifts itself up to an intellectual idealization which knows neither sex nor individuals nor time. It is progress of the soul which enlarges its sphere more and more, passes from the finite into the infinite and rises by love of the perishable form to the understanding of eternal harmonies.

Emerson recounts, no less happily, the effects of friendship. The only way to have a friend, he says, is to be one: as the only money of God is God himself, who never pays with anything inferior or strange to himself. And further on: "A friend is a person with whom I may be sincere," which leads him to this poetic image about sincerity: "Sincerity is the luxury allowed, like diadems and authority only to the highest rank; *that* being permitted to speak the truth as having none above it to court or conform unto."

These are, to be sure, original and new ways of speaking, a style adapted to the altogether individual thought. When the subject-matter requires it, Emerson's sentence, ordinarily short and somewhat abrupt, takes on long strides, unfolds and rounds itself out. When he speaks of art, for example, he becomes the artist, quite naturally, and without any effort writes like the masters. I know of few things more beautiful than the pages which bring the Essays to a close and which I beg permission to transcribe here in their entirety for fear, in presenting them in part, of altering their somewhat savage charm.[5]

Unthinkingly, and certainly unintentionally, Emerson has sketched, in these two pages, the philosophy of the new art. He completes it moreover by a portrait of the true artist, who, he says, should study with hope and love the work to be done by him, and should consider the climate, the soil, the length of the day, the wants of the people, the habit and form of the government, the social customs: only in this way, and not by copying the Doric and the Gothic styles, will he create works which will satisfy the taste and the spirit of his century and people.

One might well believe, from what precedes, that Emerson would

[5]The original article quotes the final paragraph of Emerson's essay, "Art."

exhort writers and artists to follow their instinct blindly, but in spite of his cult of nature, he does not fall into such exaggeration. Here, as elsewhere, his good sense saves him from overstrained logic. He knows too well by experience that nothing can be lost of one's own strength in companionship with the masters. He has lived too long in the intimacy of Homer and Plato and Phidias and Eschylus; he loves Shakespeare, Ariosto and Schiller too well, not to recognize their ennobling influence. But cleverly discerning the advantages and dangers of such company, he does not confuse blind imitation with intelligent homage. Let us place ourselves, he says with gentle humor, let us place ourselves as well as we can, in Roman and Greek houses, but only to get a better view of our English, French and American constructions. We need a platform, off at a distance, a certain perspective in which to judge the place where we live—and one does not get the Christian idea in the catechism *etc., etc.*

But, enough of quotations! From all that precedes the reader should form a fairly accurate idea of Emerson's book. He will know enough at least to have told himself that he will or will not look further in the clear depths to which I have led him for truths sympathetic to his taste and his temperament. If, perhaps, he asks something more critical, if he wishes to know in a more definite manner what opinion of Emerson one can hold, from the point of view of art, I might add that the Essays are not, as I see them, a planned composition, nor even, properly speaking, a literary work. It is not difficult to see that there is neither plan nor system nor doctrine nor method. A series of isolated chapters without direct connection with each other, as one sees at first glance, will never form what we call a book. The inequality of style and his whims correspond to the arbitrary nature of the divisions; the sentences are short, aphoristic; the ideas go in leaps and bounds and meet at right angles. Emerson seems to disdain, for one can not suppose he is ignorant of it, the art of drawn-out development, of maneuvred transitions and winding sentences. Nevertheless it would be wrong to think that his style is dry and stiff. On the contrary, in his writings, which seem animated by a youthful freshness, Emerson writes as one talks when, wandering in a countryside with one's eyes on the horizon, one gathers a flower, absent-mindedly, along the edge of the path. Again it must be said, the beauty of his work lies in the thought rather than in the form.

Its intrinsic value and what makes me hail its coming as a phenomenon of considerable importance, is, if I may be forgiven for an epithet, its *initial character*. It is not yet art, it is not the majestic oak but the fertile acorn from which we shall see it, in its proper season, start up and grow green. The mingling, heretofore unknown, of the protestant spirit of individualism, or self-reliance, with the pantheistic spirit which inspires this book, the combination and harmonizing of these two antagonisms in a superior intellect forms, incontestably, a new element from whence may be born an original art which might bind itself intimately to the very entrails of American society.

In a word, Emerson seems to me to be the personification of the American genius, genius impatient of all authority and disdainful of all tradition, because it acknowledges no ancestors and desires no debt to a past which was servitude. One feels that the life-giving breath which circulates through the work of the Massachusetts moralist has risen from the depths of the virgin forest and soared over the great waters of the wilderness. It is the natural poetry, the very breath of those hardy regions which man has not yet conquered. Even when Emerson moves away from his native soil, when he searches types of superior beauty in Greece and in Italy, and when he seems to borrow from Plato his sublime idealism, it is not in order to wander after him to far-off, unknown and unseen regions but rather to learn of him how to interpret and glorify the visible and palpable results of the nation's labors, and so reveal to his compatriots the mysterious poetry of science and the divine meaning hidden in the most material operations in industry.

Surely for all of us who believe in the destiny of the West, here is a prophetic signal. When the spirit of a people is concentrated and expressed thus in an individual genius, that people is very near, I believe, a complete consciousness of itself and consequently of a national art. The United States owe their origin to revolt, their greatness to industry; after having been the soldiers of independence it will be given them to become the poets of it; after having constructed marvelous machines it will be given them, Prometheuses triumphant, to animate them with the immortal breath.

STUART MERRILL

(1863–1915)

Whitman

WALT WHITMAN'S INFLUENCE on French literature has been considerable, both as regards subject matter and form. As in the United
States, his poetry initially met with controversy in France. From the
first French reference in 1861—six years after the appearance of the
first edition of *Leaves of Grass*—to 1888, his detractors charged him
with rowdyism, materialism, and elevation of the physical, whereas
his defenders praised his individualism, his championing of the
physical, and his advocacy of democracy. In May, 1888, Gabriel
Sarrazin, in a long article in *La Nouvelle Revue,* turned the tide of
critical opinion in Whitman's favor, stressing his mysticism and
pantheism. Léon Bazalgette, who wrote the first important French
biography of Whitman (1908; revised edition 1909; translated and
bowdlerized into English by Ellen Fitzgerald, 1920), credits Sarrazin
with rendering the first significant salute in French to Whitman. With
Bazalgette, the French view of Whitman as an American prophet, a
heroic personality, a champion of democracy and the common man,
commenced, and this view, held in varying ways by the Unanimists,
particularly Jules Romains, and the socialists, including Daniel
Halévy, prevailed into the 1920s.

The tone of Whitman adulation detected in many of these French
authors can be exemplified in one paragraph from Bazalgette's
introduction to his biography:

> Poet, seer, one hesitates to define terms. He is both and much more
> besides. Through him a whole continent is an exultant voice. In listening to
> him, one seems to hear some huge rough rhapsodist from the antique world
> who had passed over America to confess the desires, the marvels, and the
> faith of the Modern Man.—the Vedic hymns of our ages, fresh, rich,
> multiple. They thrill with the birth of an era. (trans. Ellen Fitzgerald, New
> York: 1920, p. xv)

Today Whitman scholars think of this view as simplistic, for it ignores the art and artifice of the poetry and the complexity of the man. Two French scholars have contributed to a more subtle understanding of Whitman. Jean Catel's studies, *Walt Whitman: La Naissance du Poète* (1929) and *Rhythme et langage dans la première édition des "Leaves of Grass"* (1930), have been termed by Gay Wilson Allen the first attempt in any country at "a combined psychological and esthetic interpretation of Whitman's life and art through his imagery, symbolism, vocabulary, and rhythm." Roger Asselineau's *L'Evolution de Walt Whitman après la première édition des Feuilles d'Herbe* (1954)—translated into English by Asselineau in two volumes as *The Evolution of Walt Whitman* (1962)—stresses Whitman's endeavor to create a personality through the successive stages of his poetry.

It must be noted, too, that Whitman as poet, not as the Gabriel of a new democracy, left his mark among French poets much before the 1920s. The Symbolists saw in Whitman's work the attractive qualities of freedom from conventional verse forms and a fluid use of image and symbol. Arthur Rimbaud read him; the American-born Vielé-Griffin and Jules Laforgue translated him (1886). Later, André Gide, in correspondence with Paul Claudel (1913), objected to the "prettified" version of Whitman then current, and in 1918, under Gide's aegis, selections from Whitman were published with translations by Gide, Larbaud, Laforgue, Fabulet, Schlumberger, and Vielé-Griffin, with an introduction by Valery Larbaud.

The essay that follows, written by Stuart Merrill (1863–1915), the American-born French Symbolist, is a moving testimony to Whitman in his old age and recounts as well Whitman's pleasure upon being discovered by the French.

It should be noted that the essay was dedicated to Léon Bazalgette and bears evidence of Bazalgette's influence (though it also mentions Laforgue's translations). Bazalgette's habit of blending lines from the works of his subjects into a narrative account and his somewhat rhapsodic approach also influenced Van Wyck Brooks, whose *The Flowering of New England* (New York: 1936) reflects his reading of Bazalgette.

Bibliography: Whitman's reputation and influence in France are traced in a brief introductory chapter by Gay Wilson Allen in his compilation of critical essays, *Walt Whitman Abroad* (Syracuse, N. Y.: 1955), which also contains a valuable bibliography on the subject, pp. 267–69. The bibliography, however, does not include the Merrill essay reproduced here.

Merrill's essay, translated from the French by "Aeon," appeared in *Masque*, series II, nos. 9–11 (1922), 303–7. A few sentences have been omitted from the text given here.

WALT WHITMAN
To Leon Bazalgette
(1912)

I MET WALT WHITMAN in New York four or five years before his death. He had come, according to his touching custom, on the day of the anniversary of Abraham Lincoln's assassination, to deliver a lecture on the great president . . . .

We were at that happy age, (and for my part I have not gone beyond it), where literary respect carries all the force of a religious emotion.

The Advertisement stated that the lecture would take place early in the afternoon; they wished to thus spare the strength of "Old Walt," as his intimate friends called him. I will never forget our long wait in the huge, cold theatre, dimly lighted, musty smelling, a thinly scattered audience of devotees whose whispering made more perceptible the silence inside, and the deafening hubbub without.

Outside! . . . Vain noises! absurd agitation, concern of a day! We knew that in this cold theatre, silent and obscure, we were going to hear the poor, weak, trembling voice of an old man, a voice that the crowd would not hear, because it would not take the trouble to listen to it. The voice of a prophet, who moved in advance of his race and beyond his own time. We were, in short, going to hear the word which enclosed in its rhythm the history of the future, the lyric song of holy democracy.

Walt Whitman! Here he is, half paralyzed, hardly able to walk, leaning with his right hand upon a cane, and heavily with his left arm on that of the poet [Edmund Clarence] Stedman. With the aid of his friend he was installed in a great armchair, before papers which he scarcely used, allowing himself to slowly improvise. And how affecting this was! He related the death of Abraham Lincoln quite simply, as though the event had taken place the evening before. . . .

At the end of the lecture, some-one asked that Walt Whitman should recite "O Captain! My Captain!" the ode, dedicated by him to the memory of Lincoln. The poor voice of the old man exerted itself anew, a little before sunset, sobbing, rather than chanting, the funeral verses. I was in the presence of the sublime, and I could only weep, listening to this threnody, which Francis Vielé-Griffin has so admirably translated into French.

When the voice died in the noise of applause, which appeared to me an outrage to the grief of the poet, Stedman came forward on the stage, and told us Walt Whitman would be happy to receive his friends, that evening, known and unknown, at the hotel where he was staying, the name of which I have forgotten.

Timid, in spite of the invitation, my two friends and I sought for some pretext to be presented, blending our homage to the master with a small gathering of the faithful. I remembered, in this connection, I had just received from Paris several numbers of Vogue, one of which contained a translation of "Children of Adam" by Jules Laforgue. I hurried to my lodgings, and armed with the precious magazine, went with my friends to see Walt Whitman.

. . . I believe that never has so fine or beautiful an old man appeared among men. Certainly Tennyson, Longfellow, Tolstoy, were beautiful, but with a beauty spiritual rather than plastic, while with Walt Whitman the physical harmony was equal to that of the soul. The face was of perfect proportions, the brow rounded, domelike, recalled that of Shakespeare; under the noble arch of his eyebrows his eyes, candid and blue, as those of a little child, sparkled with mischief and goodness; the full red lips described an arc with charming delicacy. This face, the sweetness of which tempered its majesty, was framed with a head of hair and a beard still abundant in spite of the extreme age of the poet. His complexion suggested exactly that of a fair young man a little excited from exertion. The shoulders were broad, the neck round and very graceful, his linen exquisite. Never have I seen a man so fresh, so clean, so immaculate. A young woman would have liked him for a lover, this old man was so inviting, she would have said. He seemed to be nourished by the purest substance of the earth. . . . He wore, on this day a loose jacket of black velvet, and a large turned-down collar of unstarched linen,—for he was very stylish in his own fashion.

When my turn came to be presented to him, I held out to him, stammeringly, my copy of Vogue. I do not know how I succeeded in making him understand that it contained a translation of one of his poems by a young French poet, Jules Laforgue. A sudden light in his glance, a smile spreading over his face, and a sudden animation of interest proved to me that my offering had given him pleasure.

"Ah! how happy I am that they are translating me into French," he cried.

And I recalled the magnificent poem that he had addressed to France after the terrible year.

He asked me for information about Jules Laforgue, of whose genius he had otherwise no knowledge.

"And what poem of mine has he translated?" he asked.

"The 'Children of Adam'," I answered.

It is in this section of Leaves of Grass that are found the passages that most shock American modesty, and which caused the masterpiece of Walt Whitman to be ranked by I do not know how many postmasters, "drunk with virtue," among . . . obscene writings. . . .

Walt Whitman wore a smile half pleased and half roguish, in answering me:

"I was certain that a Frenchman would hit upon those poems."

The day declined; the old man was weary; we took no further advantage of his patience, and went out quickly, touched by his good, patriarchal reception.

VALERY LARBAUD

(1881–1957)

Thoreau

VALERY LARBAUD, poet, novelist, and student of comparative literature, manifested a cosmopolitan spirit, traveling frequently throughout Europe, many localities of which provided settings for his
creative work, and reading in and writing on American, English,
Spanish, and Italian, as well as French literature. Larbaud did
yeoman service in promoting contemporary French literature abroad
and foreign literature in France.

From the time he received his *licence-ès-lettres* in English literature
at the Sorbonne in 1907, he was especially active in familiarizing his
countrymen with English writers, among them Samuel Butler, Francis Thompson, Joseph Conrad, and James Joyce. His second edition
of *Domaine anglais* (1936), in addition to essays on English authors,
includes essays on Poe and Whitman, of whom he was an ardent
admirer, and his preface to the first French translation (1934) of
William Faulkner's *As I Lay Dying.* He was also a close reader of
Hawthorne and, of course, Thoreau (1817–1862).

In 1913 his *A. O. Barnabooth: Ses Oeuvres complètes* appeared,
comprising the journal and poetry of Larbaud's *persona,* Barnabooth, a South American millionaire who journeys through
Europe in search of *self-sapience* (Larbaud's term), trying to separate
his true self from fortuitous circumstances. Finally Barnabooth
admits defeat and goes home. No wonder that Larbaud was attracted, in *Walden,* to Thoreau's escape from society and to
Thoreau's attempt to discover the realities of self and the universal
apart from social life; at the same time, in reviewing *Walden,* Larbaud
sounds a pessimistic note about Thoreau's endeavor.

The occasion of Larbaud's review-article of *Walden* was the first
French translation, in 1922, by Louis Fabulet. That *Walden* (1854)
had to wait so long for its translation indicates the French lack of

74

interest before that time in Thoreau despite his pregnant influence in
other countries and on other figures like Mohandas Gandhi and Leo
Tolstoy. As Larbaud suggests, Poe, Emerson, and Whitman exercised vital effects in France before the First World War; Hawthorne,
Thoreau, and Melville had little or no influence. Written comments
on Thoreau before 1922 were few. Thérèse Bentzon, who first drew
attention to Mark Twain in France, praised Thoreau in the *Revue des
Deux Mondes,* September 15, 1887. In 1904, Marcel Proust, also a
social historian and critic of society, advised the Comtesse de Noail-
les in a letter to read Thoreau, who, he wrote, speaks to the depths of
one's being.

   Bibliography: French scholarly activity on Thoreau since Larbaud's article includes: Léon Bazalgette's fictionalized biography in
1924; Andrée Bruel's impressive dissertation, *Emerson et Thoreau,*
1924; Régis Michaud's translation of selections from Thoreau in 1930
and his discussion of Thoreau as disciple in nature in *Vie des Peuples,*
1924. Walter Harding, *A Thoreau Handbook* (New York: 1959),
throws light on Thoreau's reputation abroad. Vincent Mulligan's
unpublished dissertation, *Valery Larbaud: Anglicist* (Columbia
University: 1953), examines Larbaud's studies in Anglo-American
literature. Frida Weissman, *L'Exotisme de Valery Larbaud* (Paris:
1966), discusses Larbaud's interest in numerous literatures.

   Larbaud's review appeared in *La Revue de France,* 4 (Aug., 1922),
658–62. It is here translated, except for a few omissions from the text,
by the editors.

THOREAU'S *WALDEN*

(1922)

THE OTHER BOOK, recently translated and published, is of an entirely
different sort. It is *Walden,* by the American classic author, H. D.
Thoreau, and its translator is Louis Fabulet. . . .

   A book of this importance should have been translated into French
thirty years ago, at a period when, since it had already fallen into
public domain, not only American editors, but particularly English
editors reprinted it in their collections of classics and in their series of
"masterworks of world literature." The Germans and, I believe, the
Danes translated it some twenty years ago, and it would be interest-

ing to study what influence it has had in these countries. In France I know for a fact that some young people knew and read it, in the original, between 1899 and 1902 and that it exerted a moral influence on them and, on their own writings, a rather profound literary influence. It was these young authors who had just discovered Walt Whitman and who, in the enthusiasm of their first contact with the American poet, started to study American literature from E. A. Poe to those writers who were the most recent; and thus, midway, they came across, first, R. W. Emerson and soon after H. D. Thoreau and *Walden*.

Now, for a young man of twenty, the reading of *Walden* is an incomparable treat. It is a poetic commentary on the biblical exhortation: Leave your childhood and live! With a captivating passion and intrepidity, with an irresistible richness of imagery and power of irony, the author seems to tell the reader: "Believe in yourself; do not heed the counsels of your elders; have faith only in your own experience. The duties which tradition and current opinion would impose upon you are snares: disobey! The conveniences of modern life are snares: learn to do without them! You do not need the house which your father, who had toiled all his life to enrich himself and who has led a life not of a free man but a slave, has had built. And not only have you no need of it, but it would hamper you; it is your prison. It is, indeed, a trunk ridiculously large and heavy, and not one railroad company would transport it when you should wish to travel. It obliges you to live constantly in the same town, whereas you were born a citizen of the world and of the universe. What a strange occupation, what folly, for a man to take account of his possessions or to work in his office! A master of slaves, and a slave himself! . . . Give up also the rights that your title of citizen gives you and free yourself of the duties which that title imposes upon you. Beware of the state; it is your natural enemy. Do not arm this tyrant; reject taxes, military service, jury duty. Boycott society, boycott the state: the salvation of your immortal soul will be the recompense which an energetic resistance to these tyrants will gain for you. I, who speak to you, have dared to do so. I have acted in consonance with that profound disaffection, that innermost and complete detachment from the low and utilitarian society in the midst of which I lived, that spirit of revolt which was in me and which is in all of you; but you are weak, full of greed, cowardly, and you let yourself sometimes be easily seduced or intimidated. I have succeeded in setting myself off from society, and from opinion, and from the state, and for two years I have lived in the woods, near a lovely pond, in a cabin which I had built myself with borrowed tools and on a terrain which I did not have, legally, the right to occupy. I provided for my needs by myself, these being reduced to the minimum in order that I might avoid almost completely the law of labor. The spectacle of, and constant association with, open nature, some visits from friends or passersby, the reading of sacred books of India and China, of the Bible and Homer, hunting, fishing, and a little kitchen gardening—behold my sole occupations and my principal distractions. Indeed, these two years were for me two years of health, of happiness, of plenitude: two years of liberty. I had renounced the alleged pleasures which injure our bodies. I had broken all the shackles, moral and social, which injure our spiritual health and the integrity of our 'self'; I had found myself. Afterwards, it seemed to me rather comic that when, by chance, I returned among men, I was put in prison for not paying my taxes."

The effect of such discourses on a young and ardent spirit is beyond question, especially when they conclude with a peroration of this kind: ". . . Do not create any bond, do not undertake any career, but dream solely of becoming one of the glories of the world." Prolonged applause! It is academic and filial disobedience raised to the height of a principle; it is the philosophical and religious justification of rebellion—and even of simple "ragging." In any event, it is precisely harangues like these that a young man has need of to fortify the frame of his personality and of his character. . . .

The man of experience who reads *Walden* will readily discriminate between the true and false ideas which jostle against each other ceaselessly. He knows that social life, like life in general, is, above all, a matter of adaptation, that is to say, of exchanges and compromises. Thoreau, because he sees that society is imperfect,—and indeed the image of society which New England and the United States, still tributary, intellectually, of England, presented him, and of that which was most mean, hypocritically and sentimentally utilitarian in the Anglo-Saxon public mind of that period, must have seemed monstrous to that noble and delicate spirit,—Thoreau, we say, denounces the social contract and preaches a kind of asceticism which is in reality an obstacle to all adaptation and which renders his doctrine sterile and impracticable as that famous "simple life" of which he was one of the first apostles, and which is like a fashion that reappears from time to time. But, on the other hand, he makes a passionate appeal to everything that is most noble, elevated, and capable of happiness within man. That great poetic theme which became, a little after Thoreau, the Dionysian rapture and the advent of the superman in Nietzsche, and which is perhaps of purely and uniquely Christian origin: *Fatti non foste a viver come brutti* and: "Renounce everything and follow Christ." A theologian would say here: "Yes, but what do you mean by Christ?" and it does seem to me that to such a question Thoreau would make a response which would be a heresy, some old heresy of the first centuries, which was thought to be long dead. Unless he should respond: "The same Christ as you" and then let him extricate himself with the assistance of the Church doctors.

With all that, *Walden* is a very beautiful book. "It is of such captivating music that one is astonished that institutions can resist it." This saying applies perfectly to Thoreau's eloquence, which is not a political eloquence, but a highly poetic one. But there is also in him, and in this book (as in his other books, such as *Cape Cod* and the four which have for titles the names of the seasons) the great poet of nature, the incomparable landscapist of New England. And he is also an essayist in the manner of Montaigne, the man who studies and talks intimately about himself. The kinship between the *Essais* and *Walden* had not struck us with as much force upon a first reading twenty years ago. R. W. Emerson and the whole New England group (that is to say, all American philosophy in the first two-thirds of the nineteenth century) seemed, at first view, to be attached particularly to German romantic philosophy. Since then, thanks to the studies of Régis Michaud, it is clearly apparent that the influence of Montaigne on Emerson was at least as great as the influence of Fichte and Hegel. His influence on H. D. Thoreau is undeniable. . . . The reader will be grateful to Louis Fabulet for having had the courage to preface his translation and for writing, at the head of his French *Walden*, a magnificent defence of Thoreau.

ALBERT CAMUS

(1913–1960)

Herman Melville

HERMAN MELVILLE'S REPUTATION in France languished until the 1930's—not so strange a fact, since, even in his own country until after the First World War, Melville had sunk into virtual oblivion. Among those French critics who wrote studies of American authors from the 1830s through the 1850s Philarète Chasles (1798–1893) wrote an unsympathetic review of Melville's *Mardi* (1849) in the *Revue des Deux Mondes* (1849), part of which appeared, in translation, in the *Literary World* (Aug. 4, 1849), pp. 89–90; and (Aug. 11, 1849), pp. 101–3. Calling *Mardi* a "bizarre work," Chasles declared: "I did not understand it after I read it, I understood it still less after I had re-read it," and he characterized it as "the dream of an ill-educated cabin boy." An added reference to two of Melville's earlier works, *Typee* (1846) and *Omoo* (1847), is no more complimentary. They exhibit, he states, "vigorous power of imagination and grand hardihood in lying."

The turn in Melville's favor took place with the publication of the first full-length study—a significant work—by Jean Simon (1939), followed by the novelist Jean Giono's *Pour Saluer Melville* (1943), which employed fictional devices. (Giono also labored on a translation of *Moby Dick* from 1936 to 1939; the completed translation, by Giono, Lucien Jacques, and Joan Smith was published in 1941). A biography of Melville by Pierre Frédérix appeared in 1950. Among men of letters, André Gide stated that he was one of the first in France to admire Melville, having urged his friends to read *Moby Dick* before Giono undertook his translation (see the Gide essay, "The New AmericanNovelists," in this volume).

Albert Camus, novelist, man of letters, and Nobel Prize winner, apparently regarded Melville for a long time as a favorite author. His first mention of Melville in his *Notebooks* appears in April, 1938. In his essay on Melville reprinted here, Camus places him "among the greatest geniuses of the West." He finds Melville engaged in a quest for meaning in the sea of existence, and considers him as superior to Kafka, engaged in a similar quest, because Melville's works are less disembodied, having "more flesh and blood." In contrast to Chasles, who proclaimed Melville a liar, Camus sees Melville as a mythmaker.

Bibliography: Camus, *Lyrical and Critical Essays* (see below), includes three selections (pp. 311–20) on Faulkner's *Requiem for a Nun* (1951), which Camus adapted for the stage.

"Herman Melville" appeared first in *Les écrivains célèbres,* III (Paris: 1953), pp. 128–29. This translation by Ellen Conroy Kennedy is from *The Lyrical and Critical Essays of Camus,* ed. Philip Thody (New York: Alfred A. Knopf, 1968), pp. 288–94.

HERMAN MELVILLE

(1953)

BACK IN THE DAYS when Nantucket whalers stayed at sea for several years at a stretch, Melville, at twenty-two, signed on one, and later on a man-of-war, to sail the seven seas. Home again in America, his travel tales enjoyed a certain success while the great books he published later were received with indifference and incomprehension.[1] Discouraged after the publication and failure of *The Confidence Man* (1857), Melville "accepted annihilation." Having become a custom's officer and the father of a family, he began an almost complete silence (except for a few infrequent poems) which was to last some thirty years. Then one day he hurriedly wrote a masterpiece, *Billy Budd* (completed in April 1891), and died, a few months later, forgotten (with a three-line obituary in *The New York Times*). He had to wait until our own time for America and Europe to finally give him his place among the greatest geniuses of the West.

It is scarcely easier to describe in a few pages a work that has the tumultuous dimensions of the oceans where it was born than to summarize the Bible or condense Shakespeare. But in judging Melville's genius, if nothing else, it must be recognized that his works

---

[1]For a long time, *Moby Dick* was thought of as an adventure story suitable for school prizes.

trace a spiritual experience of unequaled intensity, and that they are
to some extent symbolic. Certain critics[2] have discussed this obvious
fact, which now hardly seems open anymore to question. His
admirable books are among those exceptional works that can be read
in different ways, which are at the same time both obvious and
obscure, as dark as the noonday sun and as clear as deep water. The
wise man and the child can both draw sustenance from them. The
story of captain Ahab, for example, flying from the southern to the
northern seas in pursuit of Moby Dick, the white whale who has
taken off his leg, can doubtless be read as the fatal passion of a
character gone mad with grief and loneliness. But it can also be seen as
one of the most overwhelming myths ever invented on the subject of
the struggle of man against evil, depicting the irresistible logic that
finally leads the just man to take up arms first against creation and the
creator, then against his fellows and against himself.[3] Let us have no
doubt about it: if it is true that talent recreates life, while genius has
the additional gift of crowning it with myths, Melville is first and
foremost a creator of myths.

I will add that these myths, contrary to what people say of them,
are clear. They are obscure only insofar as the root of all suffering and
all greatness lies buried in the darkness of the earth. They are no more
obscure than Phèdre's cries, Hamlet's silences, or the triumphant
songs of Don Giovanni. But it seems to me (and this would deserve
detailed development) that Melville never wrote anything but the
same book, which he began again and again. This single book is the
story of a voyage, inspired first of all solely by the joyful curiosity of
youth (*Typee, Omoo,* etc.), then later inhabited by an increasingly
wild and burning anguish. *Mardi* is the first magnificent story in
which Melville begins the quest that nothing can appease, and in
which, finally, "pursuers and pursued fly across a boundless ocean."
It is in this work that Melville becomes aware of the fascinating call
that forever echoes in him: "I have undertaken a journey without
maps." And again: "I am the restless hunter, the one who has no
home." *Moby Dick* simply carries the great themes of *Mardi* to
perfection. But since artistic perfection is also inadequate to quench

[2]In passing, let me advise critics to read page 449 of *Mardi* in the French translation.

[3]As an indication, here are some of the obviously symbolic pages of *Moby Dick.*
(French translation, Gallimard): pp. 120, 121, 123, 173–7, 191–3, 203, 209, 241, 310,
313, 339, 373, 415, 421, 452, 457, 460, 472, 485, 499, 503, 517, 520, 522.

the kind of thirst with which we are confronted here, Melville will start once again, in *Pierre: or the Ambiguities,* that unsuccessful masterpiece, to depict the quest of genius and misfortune whose sneering failure he will consecrate in the course of a long journey on the Mississippi that forms the theme of *The Confidence Man.*

This constantly rewritten book, this unwearying peregrination in the archipelago of dreams and bodies, on an ocean "whose every wave is a soul," this Odyssey beneath an empty sky, makes Melville the Homer of the Pacific. But we must add immediately that his Ulysses never returns to Ithaca. The country in which Melville approaches death, that he immortalizes in *Billy Budd,* is a desert island. In allowing the young sailor, a figure of beauty and innocence whom he dearly loves, to be condemned to death, Captain Vere submits his heart to the law. And at the same time, with this flawless story that can be ranked with certain Greek tragedies, the aging Melville tells us of his acceptance for the first time of the sacrifice of beauty and innocence so that order may be maintained and the ship of men may continue to move forward toward an unknown horizon. Has he truly found the peace and final resting place that earlier he had said could not be found in the Mardi archipelago? Or are we, on the contrary, faced with a final shipwreck that Melville in his despair asked of the gods? "One cannot blaspheme and live," he had cried out. At the height of consent, isn't *Billy Budd* the worst blasphemy? This we can never know, any more than we can know whether Melville did finally accept a terrible order, or whether, in quest of the spirit, he allowed himself to be led, as he had asked, "beyond the reefs, in sunless seas, into night and death." But no one, in any case, measuring the long anguish that runs through his life and work, will fail to acknowledge the greatness, all the more anguished in being the fruit of self-conquest, of his reply.

But this, although it had to be said, should not mislead anyone as to Melville's real genius and the sovereignty of his art. It bursts with health, strength, explosions of humor, and human laughter. It is not he who opened the storehouse of sombre allegories that today hold sad Europe spellbound. As a creator, Melville is, for example, at the furthest possible remove from Kafka, and he makes us aware of this writer's artistic limitations. However irreplaceable it may be, the spiritual experience in Kafka's work exceeds the modes of expression and invention, which remain monotonous. In Melville, spiritual experience is balanced by expression and invention, and constantly finds flesh and blood in them. Like the greatest artists, Melville constructed his symbols out of concrete things, not from the material of dreams. The creator of myths partakes of genius only insofar as he inscribes these myths in the denseness of reality and not in the fleeting clouds of the imagination. In Kafka, the reality that he describes is created by the symbol, the fact stems from the image, whereas in Melville the symbol emerges from reality, the image is born of what is seen.[4] This is why Melville never cut himself off from flesh or nature, which are barely perceptible in Kafka's work. On the contrary, Melville's lyricism, which reminds us of Shakespeare's, makes use of the four elements. He mingles the Bible with the sea, the music of the waves with that of the spheres, the poetry of the days with the grandeur of the Atlantic. He is inexhaustible, like the winds that blow for thousands of miles across empty oceans and that, when they reach the coast, still have strength enough to flatten whole villages. He rages, like Lear's madness, over the wild seas where Moby Dick and the spirit of evil crouch among the waves. When the storm and total destruction have passed, a strange calm rises from the primitive waters, the silent pity that transfigures tragedies. Above the speechless crew, the perfect body of Billy Budd turns gently at the end of its rope in the pink and grey light of the approaching day.

T. E. Lawrence ranked *Moby Dick* alongside *The Possessed* or *War and Peace*. Without hesitation, one can add to these *Billy Budd, Mardi, Benito Cereno*, and a few others. These anguished books in which man is overwhelmed, but in which life is exalted on each page, are inexhaustible sources of strength and pity. We find in them revolt and acceptance, unconquerable and endless love, the passion for beauty, language of the highest order—in short, genius. "To perpetuate one's name," Melville said, "one must carve it on a heavy stone and sink it to the bottom of the sea; depths last longer than heights." Depths do indeed have their painful virtue, as did the unjust silence in which Melville lived and died, and the ancient ocean he unceasingly ploughed. From their endless darkness he brought forth his works, those visages of foam and night, carved by the waters, whose mysterious royalty has scarcely begun to shine upon us, though already they help us to emerge effortlessly from our continent of shadows to go down at last toward the sea, the light, and its secret.

---

[4]In Melville, the metaphor suggests the dream, but from a concrete, physical starting point. In *Mardi*, for example, the hero comes across "huts of flame." They are built, simply, of red tropical creepers, whose leaves are momentarily lifted by the wind.

FRANÇOIS MAURIAC
(1885–1970)

Hawthorne's *The Scarlet Letter*
James's *The Bostonians*

IN ADDITION TO his fiction (*Le Noeud de Vipères,* 1932, perhaps his best novel), François Mauriac maintained a voluminous production of essays, articles, and criticism. It is easy to understand his interest in Hawthorne's *The Scarlet Letter* (1850). Like Hawthorne's masterpiece, Mauriac's novels reflect the simultaneous attraction of religion and physical desire, the subtle interplay of sexual feeling, guilt, and conscience. Although Hawthorne writes about Puritanism, Mauriac reveals in his reading of the novel his own Catholic concern for sin, confession, and redemption.

Mauriac's striking essay contrasts the false pharisaism of the Puritan community of Boston with the sainthood, achieved by remorse and confession, finally arrived at by the sinner and adulterer Dimmesdale. (Mauriac's approach to Hawthorne's ambiguous novel differs from D. H. Lawrence's treatment [see *Studies in Classic American Literature, 1923*]. Lawrence reads *The Scarlet Letter* as a disguised affirmation of sexual love and elevates Hester Prynne's acceptance of love over Dimmesdale's inability—as Lawrence sees it—to renounce his religious training for the sake of his love for Hester.)

Hawthorne, it should be stated, did not have the influence in France during the nineteenth century that Poe and Emerson had, though he was the subject of six penetrating articles written by Émile Montégut in the *Revue des Deux Mondes* and the *Moniteur Universel,* mostly in the 1850s. In "Un romancier pessimiste" (*Revue des*

Deux Mondes, 1860), Montégut accredited Hawthorne with a pitiless analysis of character and an unflaggingly somber outlook. Hawthorne, for Montégut, was the misanthropic victim of his Puritan mentality. (For discussion of Montégut on Hawthorne and of Henry James's critical reaction to Montégut's essay, see Lionel Trilling's "Hawthorne in Our Time" in *Beyond Culture,* 1965).) Julien Green (1900–   ), the French novelist born of American parents, whom Mauriac mentions as the translator of *The Scarlet Letter,* in his *Un Puritain Homme de Lettres* (1927), a slender pamphlet of fifty pages, drew a more tender portrait of Hawthorne, but also saw Hawthorne as suffering the debilitating effects of a Puritan upbringing. Mauriac, with the broader perspective of later twentieth-century critics, recognizes Hawthorne's objective mastery over his Puritan subject matter.

Mauriac's essay on *The Bostonians* (1886), one of Henry James's early novels, is an uncommon instance of interest in James among French writers. Mauriac's comments in his first paragraph seem to agree with Sartre's (in the Sartre essay reprinted in this collection) that James holds little value to the French, since they possess Marcel Proust. An obstacle, one surmises, to the French novelist's appreciation of James, especially the later James, is the almost insurmountable task of translation.

Mauriac discusses *The Bostonians* as a comprehensive study of a sexual triangle, a man and woman fighting to engross a second woman's affections, with sex left out. The French novelist thinks of James as still bound in Victorian reticence. On the other hand, Mauriac writes, modern fiction often reveals sexual obsessions that their authors cannot manage artistically.

Bibliography: An excellent discussion of Mauriac appears in Henri Peyre, *French Novelists of Today* (New York: 1967), pp. 101–21.

Mauriac's essays on Hawthorne and James appear in *Mémoires Intérieures,* translated from the French by Gerard Hopkins (New York: Farrar, Straus and Cudahy, 1960), pp. 114–18, 227–30.

HAWTHORNE'S *THE SCARLET LETTER*

(1959)

I HAVE RECENTLY BEEN RE-READING Hawthorne's *The Scarlet Letter.*

Julien Green, who made the translation of this book, assures us that Nathaniel Hawthorne at eighteen was so beautiful that a gipsy-woman once asked him whether he was an angel or a man. Julien Green, at the same age, had a sombrely angelic look, and that is not the only point of resemblance between the translator and his author. Hawthorne, like Green, lived in a world which was not altogether the one we know, and when in his Introduction to *The Scarlet Letter* he tells us of the mysterious torpor of the life he led, peopled by the persons of his invention:—"late at night, I sat in the deserted parlour, lighted only by the glimmering coal-fire and the moon . . ."—the picture conjured up might be that of Julien Green at twenty, with his face showing clearly, or fading away, according as the room is drowned in shadow or touched by a brief flicker of firelight, which sets the mahogany armchairs gleaming.

Truth gone mad, and savagely mad, is the best description of the republic of bitter hypocrites who inhabit Hawthorne's story— hypocrites who look backwards to the farther side of the incarnations of the Son of Man, instead of taking it as their terminal point. It was the God of the Jews: not the loving and compassionate God of whom Abraham, our father, spoke, and whose loving-kindness overflows in the Psalms, but the inexorable Being, re-created in their own image by the hair-splitting Jews who abode by the letter of the law whom they worshipped; the God of the bad pharisees—for there were some who were just—the only men whom Christ denounced with a sort of despairing fury. For He who knew all things, knew that the pharisees were, no less than Himself, immortal. He saw them making use of Him down the centuries for the purpose of establishing their reign. *The Scarlet Letter* provides a sinister illustration of how the spirit can be exploited by the pitiless letter.

In the little town, which later grew into Boston, a young woman, whose husband has been absent on a journey for a year, becomes pregnant. Found guilty of the capital crime of adultery, she escapes the death sentence, but not the shame of having to stand in the pillory on the main square of the town. She is also condemned to wear on her breast, for the remainder of her life, a large "A" which will expose her to the scorn of her fellow-citizens, and be the symbol of a shame from which there can be no escaping. Her seducer had been the most saintly pastor in the community. He lives choked by the secret he cannot reveal, until finally he confesses it and dies. Though it has been a torment, it has also sanctified and transfigured him.

What gives this terrible story its true significance is that, in it, the letter of the law gone mad not only takes no account of the spirit, but flouts the very word of God. For, in the Gospel according to St. John, we are told of Christ's meeting with an adulteress. On this incident the Puritans were the less free to put their own interpretation, since the Lord's teaching was perfectly clear and admitted of no ambiguity. Who can fail to remember the eternal lesson delivered to us there? The woman has been taken in adultery, and the scribes and the pharisees bring her to the Master. "Now, Moses in the law commanded us that such should be stoned: but what sayest thou?" But Jesus, making no answer, wrote on the ground with his finger. Then He uttered the saying which has, ever since, sounded in the ears of men: "He that is without sin among you, let him first cast a stone at her." And again he stooped down and wrote on the ground. And they that heard it, being convicted by their own conscience, went out one by one, beginning at the eldest even unto the last. When Jesus had lifted up himself, and saw none but the woman, he said unto her, "Woman, where are those thy accusers? hath no man condemned thee?" She said, "No man, Lord." And Jesus said unto her, "neither do I condemn thee: go and sin no more."

So what the pharisees had not dared to do, the Puritans in *The Scarlet Letter* did, and gloried in it. But what is even worse is that this falsification of the Gospel, though in the Puritanism described by Hawthorne it may have reached its extreme limit, is still to be seen in all the Christian sects, and even in the old Mother Church. We can follow its ravages from century to century. Which of us has not suffered from it, whether at the hands of the posterity of Port-Royal or at those of the disciples of Calvin?

How strange a mystery that men should reject, in the Gospel, the very thing that constitutes the good news, and should be the very heart of hearts of human hope: the pardon indefinitely renewed, the remission of sins declared anew each time that Christ saw a human being prostrate before him. "Thy sins are forgiven thee." Whence comes this hatred of good fortune? In *The Scarlet Letter* we can catch a glimpse of the answer. For the harsh law of Moses, Christian theology, in its madness, has substituted its own law, which is no less harsh, no less pitiless, since, fundamentally, it is the same. But I will not pursue the subject further here.

What is really astonishing is that Hawthorne's novel, which

stresses all the most odious distortions of the religious spirit, and should be a satire, carries a very different message. Unlike Molière's, this American Tartuffe initiates us into one of the least known secrets of true religion. The pharisaism of the Puritans creates, not only in the heroine who wears the scarlet letter, but also in the guilty young pastor, condemned to live a lie by reason of his cowardly silence, a genuine sanctity. I do not use that word only in the sense of Augustin's *etiam peccata*. That even our faults are an element in our sanctification is a commonplace with every writer of sermons. But *The Scarlet Letter* goes much deeper.

Here I touch on what, to my mind, gives so great a value to *The Scarlet Letter*. This book furnishes us with a key to what seems the most impenetrable of all mysteries, especially to the believer: the mystery of evil. Evil is in the world, and in ourselves. Yet, "all is Grace." Those are the last words of Bernanos's country priest. The very principle of our regeneration is to be found in what is worst in us. From this point of view, *The Scarlet Letter* is a document of supreme importance which I have frequently brought to the attention of the troubled and despairing. In it we are shown a guilty pastor who passes for a saint: "To the high mountain peaks of faith and sanctity he would have climbed, had not the tendency been thwarted by the burden, whatever it might be, of crime or anguish, beneath which it was his doom to totter. It kept him down on the level of the lowest; him, the man of ethereal attributes, whose voice the angels might else have listened to and answered! But this very burden it was that gave him sympathies so intimate with the sinful brotherhood of mankind: so that his heart vibrated in unison with theirs, and sent its throb of pain through a thousand other hearts. . . ." What follows, must be read in its entirety.

It is not only because he humiliates himself, because he sees his own abjection and beats his breast, that the guilty pastor draws near to God: his very sin becomes in him a principle of total renewal before his brethren, but also before God. Similarly, the scarlet letter fastened to the breast of the young woman guilty of adultery, makes of her, in the eyes of the whole town, an authentic and venerated saint. What we are shown is pharisaism transmuted into the creative element of sanctity. Grace turns to its own purposes the worst canalizations invented by Tartuffe and Orgon. Its waters flow through them to reach and fertilize the hearts of men. The spirit makes use of the letter, no matter how despicable the letter may be. That is the moral of this sombre tale.

Some may hold that a novel which interests us mainly because of its theological implications can scarcely claim any very considerable degree of importance from the literary point of view. But the fact that, in spite of an outmoded technique, it still, after a century, has so great a power of suggestion, does, so it seems to me, bear witness to the richness of a literary form on which certain modern practitioners would impose their own narrow code. The genuine novel can afford to laugh at their "art of fiction" just as the genuine poet can laugh at "the art of poetry." A novel can express anything and everything, and can achieve, as does *The Scarlet Letter*, the remarkable triumph of turning a cruel caricature of Christianity into an apologia which opens a door upon the mystery of evil.

JAMES'S *THE BOSTONIANS*
(1959)

The Bostonians, the most recently translated of James's novels, is an early work, which though it is extremely attractive (it is, in fact, more approachable than the books of his maturity) is not, or it seems to me, one of those which can help us to form a true estimate of his very personal output as a whole. So far as I know Marcel Proust never tackled any of James's fictions, though his *oeuvre* does, to some extent, form an outer bastion, in the nineteenth century, to the great Proustian mountain-range.

Reading *The Bostonians* has led me, once again, to wonder whether Freud can be said to have enriched the novel as a literary form. Do the books which were written and published before the coming of the Freudian cult, and before *A la recherche du temps perdu*, really seem so sketchy and superficial compared with later productions in which sexuality reigns supreme and every variant of love can be called by its name without a blush?

But to return to *The Bostonians*. In this novel James has been at pains to introduce us to a feminist group in the Boston society of the eighties, when it was fashionable to get excited over the emancipation of women. There is nothing in it, I agree, to hold the attention of the modern reader, and, if it has aroused my interest, that is for reasons which have nothing to do with feminism.

What is *The Bostonians* "about"? A woman of the upper middle-class, Olive Chancellor, by no means in her first youth, takes a great liking to a girl of a humbler social class, who happens to have a great gift for public speaking. Olive determines to exploit her young friend's talents in the service of the feminist cause. The novel tells the story of her jealous possessiveness. The girl, Verena, is caught in the toils of Olive who belongs to that rapacious type of female who hates men, and does all she can to keep her charming prey from falling into their clutches, those, in particular, of a broad-shouldered South-erner, who, in the long run, turns out to be the stronger of the two.

The strange thing about the book is that, never once in the whole course of the drama, is the sexual aspect of the situation dealt with, or even suggested. The question of a passionate friendship in itself, the manifestations of which cause no embarrassment either to the woman who feels it, or to the girl who is its object, never arises. It provides no occasion for scandal, and produces no malicious gossip either in Boston or New York. There are no unpleasant hints about the couple: in fact, the book might have been written by somebody who had never heard of Gomorrha, of somebody, I would go so far as to say, who had lived in a world where the existence of that vice had never even been heard of. It is true that the Victorian society to which Henry James belonged, had taken quite literally—not because it was virtuous but because it was hypocritical—the advice of the Apostle: "Let not these things be spoken of among you."

But would not the novel have gained in depth if the question *had* been raised, if Olive Chancellor had not been virtuous, or if, while abstaining from any actually criminal behaviour, she had been aware of the abnormal nature of her leanings? Whatever the answer to that question, the fact remains that *The Bostonians,* free though it is from any hint of physiological treatment, offers the most searching study I know, of an extremely unpleasant situation, that of a man and an Amazon at daggers drawn over a young woman. It is perfectly obvious that feminism is used as an alibi, not only for the characters in the novel, but for the author, too, and for his Anglo-Saxon readers of 1886. Under cover of this fiction we are told all there is to tell about this type of conflict between two women and a man—all of them equally high-minded—not in terms of the horrible things that might have been done but only of the feelings of those concerned.

It might well be argued that the uninhibited treatment of sexual problems, so far from enriching the novel-form, has actually im-poverished it, and that the invasion of fiction by sex is one of the reasons for its decadence. On the other hand, it might be maintained that this invasion has, in fact, destroyed only the psychological novel in its traditional form, the possibilities of which had already been exhausted, and has given a new lease of life to the art of fictional narrative.

This is a subject for debate. I, personally, am inclined to think that sexual obsession has over-simplified the novelist's task, and has attacked the art of fiction at its source, because it tends to destroy that barrier of prohibitions which, within and without the individual, in society and, especially, in the family has been erected against the passions, and this passion in particular.

"Speak for writers of your own age"—I shall be told by members of the younger generation: "we have changed all that. It is meaningless to say that sexuality has invaded the novel. It occupies a prominent place only in so far as it activates the characters of our novels. That does not depend upon us, the authors; we ought not even to be conscious of it, since all we know of those characters are the gestures they make, the things they see, the words they speak. All that *The Bostonians* entitles you to say is that within the structure of a carefully composed psychological novel, in which human beings are described both from the outside and the inside, within a framework which arbitrarily determines their nature, sexual considerations are what we most easily do without. The painter arranges the model in the pose which best suits him, is free to clothe him or her as he will and to choose the light in which the sitter is to be displayed. That done, he contrives the drama into which he has decided to precipitate his victim."

These words, which I have put into the mouth of a purely imaginary modern novelist, help to define the position occupied by Henry James on the frontier-line between two epochs. Graham Greene, writing of him, has said: "he was mainly concerned with dramatizing . . ."—which establishes the author of *The Bostonians* in the tradition of the classical novel. But he goes on: "he was especially careful never to intervene in his own person." In this James shows himself to have been a forerunner of the technique which is, today, in the ascendant.

But I have wandered away from the question which I asked a while back: has obsession with sex enriched or impoverished the novelist? It would be of considerable interest to limit the problem to the work of two significant writers, very different from one another, but both situated on the edge of the same Dead Sea.

It has always seemed to me that Proust's novel, *qua* novel, achieves perfection only when (from *La Prisonnière* onwards) the sexual cancer, long suppressed, is at last brought into the open, becomes generalized, and, ends by so debasing, not to say, destroying all the characters, as to leave none of them untouched except Proust himself, who is left standing erect among the ruins of his own work, and saves it.

Now that André Gide is no longer with us, and we can take in at a single glance the man and his work as a whole, we are in a position to judge more accurately to what extent his one and only preoccupation dominates them and narrows their scope. His ambition to be the French Goethe merely accentuates and makes ridiculous an impoverishment brought about by an insurmountable and base obsession.

The more I think about it, the more convinced do I become that an aesthetic system demands, also, an ethical one: mastery. The same law holds good for the artist and the man. He will dominate his work precisely to the extent that he dominates his life.

PART III

Critical Cross-Currents

RALPH WALDO EMERSON

(1803–1882)

Montaigne

AMERICAN AUTHORS of Emerson's time and of the preceding generation were generally more attuned to the French literature of the past
than to current French authors, to the classics rather than to contemporaries. Henry Wadsworth Longfellow's early work *Outre-Mer*
(1823), recounting his youthful travels abroad, was antiquarian in
spirit and showed a delight in Provençal poetry. He later lectured at
Harvard on Molière. Among other established figures, Washington
Irving, like Longfellow, was more comfortable with older literature,
and more with Spanish literature than French. Edgar Allan Poe, on
the other hand, made reference, in various works, to Victor Hugo,
Pierre-Jean de Béranger, and Alphonso de Lamartine, but left no
extended critical response to contemporary French writers.

Emerson, who read translations without apology, first
encountered Montaigne in Charles Cotton's translation (1685). His
own essay "Montaigne, or the Skeptic," a sympathetic assessment of
Montaigne's skepticism, appeared in *Representative Men* (1850).
What drew Emerson to Montaigne was the Frenchman's shrewd and
appraising spirit, to which Emerson's ingrained sagacity responded.
As early as 1847, as a matter of fact, Émile Montégut, in his long
critical essay on Emerson in the *Revue des Deux Mondes*, already
recognized in the American sage both the transcendentalist and the
skeptic, the mystic and the Yankee. James Russell Lowell, in *A Fable
for Critics* (1848), tagged Emerson "A Plotinus-Montaigne."

Emerson was drawn, also, to Montaigne's naturalness of style. He
called the *Essais* the least *written* of books, and marvelled: "Cut these
words, and they would bleed; they are vascular and alive." Emerson,
however, though attracted by these qualities, made of the essay as
genre a more formal literary composition, analytical and interpretive
in form rather than personal and discursive.

Bibliography: In a volume, *Emerson's Montaigne* (New York: 1941), dedicated to the essay, Charles Lowell Young plays down Montaigne's skepticism. He asserts that Montaigne's skepticism is limited, prevalent in one part of his life only. Accordingly, Young concludes that Emerson was more interestsd in Montaigne as moralist than as skeptic. In any event, Young states, "Montaigne, or the Skeptic" reveals Emerson at the height of his powers.

André Célières, in the *Prose Style of Emerson* (Paris: 1936), makes a case for Montaigne's influence on Emerson's prose style.

This selection is from Emerson's *Representative Men* (Boston: Phillips, Sampson and Co., 1850), pp. 149–84. Omitted here are the sections not directly concerned with Montaigne (the first 11 paragraphs and the last 16).

MONTAIGNE, OR THE SKEPTIC

(1850)

THIS THEN is the right ground of the skeptic,—this of consideration, of self-containing; not at all of unbelief; not at all of universal denying, nor of universal doubting,—doubting even that he doubts; least of all of scoffing and profligate jeering at all that is stable and good. These are no more his moods than are those of religion and philosophy. He is the considerer, the prudent, taking in sail, counting stock, husbanding his means, believing that a man has too many enemies than that he can afford to be his own foe; that we cannot give ourselves too many advantages in this unequal conflict, with powers so vast and unweariable ranged on one side, and this little conceited vulnerable popinjay that a man is, bobbing up and down into every danger, on the other. It is a position taken up for better defence, as of more safety, and one that can be maintained; and it is one of more opportunity and range: as, when we build a house, the rule is to set it not too high nor too low, under the wind, but out of the dirt.

The philosophy we want is one of fluxions and mobility. The Spartan and Stoic schemes are too stark and stiff for our occasion. A theory of Saint John, and of non-resistance, seems, on the other hand, too thin and aerial. We want some coat woven of elastic steel, stout as the first and limber as the second. We want a ship in these billows we inhabit. An angular, dogmatic house would be rent to chips and splinters in this storm of many elements. No, it must be tight, and fit to the form of man, to live at all; as a shell must dictate the architecture of a house founded on the sea. The soul of man must be the type of our scheme, just as the body of man is the type after which a dwelling-house is built. Adaptiveness is the peculiarity of human nature. We are golden averages, volitant stabilities, compensated or periodic errors, houses founded on the sea. The wise skeptic wishes to have a near view of the best game and the chief players; what is best in the planet; art and nature, places and events; but mainly men. Every thing that is excellent in mankind,—a form of grace, an arm of iron, lips of persuasion, a brain of resources, every one skilful to play and win,—he will see and judge.

The terms of admission to this spectacle are, that he have a certain solid and intelligible way of living of his own; some method of answering the inevitable needs of human life; proof that he has played with skill and success; that he has evinced the temper, stoutness and the range of qualities which, among his contemporaries and countrymen, entitle him to fellowship and trust. For the secrets of life are not shown except to sympathy and likeness. Men do not confide themselves to boys, or coxcombs, or pedants, but to their peers. Some wise limitation, as the modern phrase is; some condition between the extremes, and having, itself, a positive quality; some stark and sufficient man, who is not salt or sugar, but sufficiently related to the world to do justice to Paris or London, and, at the same time, a vigorous and original thinker, whom cities can not overawe, but who uses them,—is the fit person to occupy this ground of speculation.

These qualities meet in the character of Montaigne. And yet, since the personal regard which I entertain for Montaigne may be unduly great, I will, under the shield of this prince of egotists, offer, as an apology for electing him as the representative of skepticism, a word or two to explain how my love began and grew for his admirable gossip.

A single odd volume of Cotton's translation of the Essays remained to me from my father's library, when a boy. It lay long neglected, until, after many years, when I was newly escaped from college, I read the book, and procured the remaining volumes. I remember the delight and wonder in which I lived with it. It seemed to me as if I had myself written the book, in some former life, so sincerely it spoke to my thought and experience. It happened, when in Paris, in 1833, that, in the cemetery of Père Lachaise, I came to a tomb of Auguste Collignon, who died in 1830, aged sixty–eight years, and who, said the monument, "lived to do right, and had formed himself to virtue on the Essays of Montaigne." Some years later, I became acquainted with an accomplished English poet, John Sterling; and, in prosecuting my correspondence, I found that, from a love of Montaigne, he had made a pilgrimage to his chateau, still standing near Castellan, in Périgord, and, after two hundred and fifty years, had copied from the walls of his library the inscriptions which Montaigne had written there. That Journal of Mr. Sterling's, published in the Westminster Review, Mr. Hazlitt has reprinted in the *Prolegomena* to his edition of the Essays. I heard with pleasure that one of the newly-discovered autographs of William Shakespeare was in a copy of Florio's translation of Montaigne. It is the only book which we certainly know to have been in the poet's library. And, oddly enough, the duplicate copy of Florio, which the British Museum purchased with a view of protecting the Shakespeare autograph (as I was informed in the Museum), turned out to have the autograph of Ben Johnson in the fly-leaf. Leigh Hunt relates of Lord Byron, that Montaigne was the only great writer of past times whom he read with avowed satisfaction. Other coincidences, not needful to be mentioned here, concurred to make this old Gascon still new and immortal for me.

In 1571 [*sic*], on the death of his father, Montaigne, then thirty-eight years old, retired from the practice of law at Bordeaux, and settled himself on his estate. Though he had been a man of pleasure and sometimes a courtier, his studious habits now grew on him, and he loved the compass, staidness and independence of the country gentleman's life. He took up his economy in good earnest, and made his farms yield the most. Downright and plain-dealing, and abhorring to be deceived or to deceive, he was esteemed in the country for his sense and probity. In the civil wars of the League, which converted every house into a fort, Montaigne kept his gates open and his house without defence. All parties freely came and went, his courage and honor being universally esteemed. The neighboring lords and gentry brought jewels and papers to him for safe-keeping. Gibbon reckons, in these bigoted times, but two men of liberality in France,—Henry IV and Montaigne.

Montaigne is the frankest and honestest of all writers. His French freedom runs into grossness; but he has anticipated all censure by the bounty of his own confessions. In his times, books were written to

one sex only, and almost all were written in Latin; so that in a
humorist a certain nakedness of statement was permitted, which our
manners, of a literature addressed equally to both sexes, do not
allow. But though a biblical plainness coupled with a most uncanoni-
cal levity may shut his pages to many sensitive readers, yet the offence
is superficial. He parades it: he makes the most of it: nobody can
think or say worse of him than he does. He pretends to most of the
vices; and, if there be any virtue in him, he says, it got in by stealth.
There is no man, in his opinion, who has not deserved hanging five or
six times; and he pretends no exception in his own behalf. "Five or six
as ridiculous stories," too, he says, "can be told of me, as of any man
living." But, with all this really superfluous frankness, the opinion of
an invincible probity grows into every reader's mind. "When I the
most strictly and religiously confess myself, I find that the best virtue
I have has in it some tincture of vice; and I, who am as sincere and
perfect a lover of virtue of that stamp as any other whatever, am afraid
that Plato, in his purest virtue, if he had listened and laid his ear close
to himself, would have heard some jarring sound of human mixture;
but faint and remote and only to be perceived by himself."

Here is an impatience and fastidiousness a color or pretence of any
kind. He has been in courts so long as to have conceived a furious
disgust at appearances; he will indulge himself with a little cursing
and swearing; he will talk with sailors and gipsies, use flash and street
ballads; he has stayed in-doors till he is deadly sick; he will to the
open air, though it rain bullets. He has seen too much of gentlemen of
the long robe, until he wishes for cannibals; and is so nervous, by
factitious life, that he thinks the more barbarous man is, the better he
is. He likes his saddle. You may read theology, and grammar, and
metaphysics elsewhere. Whatever you get here shall smack of the
earth and of real life, sweet, or smart, or stinging. He makes no
hesitation to entertain you with the records of his disease, and his
journey to Italy is quite full of that matter. He took and kept this
position of equilibrium. Over his name he drew an emblematic pair
of scales, and wrote *Que sçais je?* under it. As I look at his effigy
opposite the title-page, I seem to hear him say, 'You may play old
Poz, if you will; you may rail and exaggerate,—I stand here for truth,
and will not, for all the states and churches and revenues and personal
reputations of Europe, overstate the dry fact, as I see it; I will rather
mumble and prose about what I certainly know,—my house and
barns; my father, my wife and my tenants; my old lean bald pate; my

knives and forks; what meats I eat and what drinks I prefer, and a hundred straws just as ridiculous,—than I will write, with a fine crow-quill, a fine romance. I like gray days, and autumn and winter weather. I am gray and autumnal myself, and think an undress and old shoes that do not pinch my feet, and old friends who do not constrain me, and plain topics where I do not need to strain myself and pump my brains, the most suitable. Our condition as men is risky and ticklish enough. One cannot be sure of himself and his fortune an hour, but he may be whisked off into some pitiable or ridiculous plight. Why should I vapor and play the philosopher, instead of ballasting, the best I can, this dancing balloon? So, at least, I live within compass, keep myself ready for action, and can shoot the gulf at last with decency. If there be anything farcical in such a life, the blame is not mine: let it lie at fate's and nature's door.'

The Essays, therefore, are an entertaining soliloquy on every random topic that comes into his head; treating every thing without ceremony, yet with masculine sense. There have been men with deeper insight; but, one would say, never a man with such abundance of thoughts: he is never dull, never insincere, and has the genius to make the reader care for all that he cares for.

The sincerity and marrow of the man reaches to his sentences. I know not anywhere the book that seems less written. It is the language of conversation transferred to a book. Cut these words, and they would bleed; they are vascular and alive. One has the same pleasure in it that he feels in listening to the necessary speech of men about their work, when any unusual circumstance gives momentary importance to the dialogue. For blacksmiths and teamsters do not trip in their speech; it is a shower of bullets. It is Cambridge men who correct themselves and begin again at every half sentence, and, moreover, will pun, and refine too much, and swerve from the matter to the expression. Montaigne talks with shrewdness, knows the world and books and himself, and uses the positive degree; never shrieks, or protests, or prays: no weakness, no convulsion, no superlative: does not wish to jump out of his skin, or play any antics, or annihilate space or time, but is stout and solid; tastes every moment of the day; likes pain because it makes him feel himself and realize things; as we pinch ourselves to know that we are awake. He keeps the plain; he rarely mounts or sinks; likes to feel solid ground and the stones underneath. His writing has no enthusiasms, no aspiration; contented, self-respecting and keeping the middle of the road. There is but one exception,—in his love for Socrates. In speaking of him, for once his cheek flushes and his style rises to passion.

Montaigne died of a quinsy, at the age of sixty, in 1592. When he came to die he caused the mass to be celebrated in his chamber. At the age of thirty-three, he had been married. "But," he says, "might I have had my own will, I would not have married Wisdom herself, if she would have had me: but 'tis to much purpose to evade it, the common custom and use of life will have it so. Most of my actions are guided by example, not choice." In the hour of death, he gave the same weight to custom. *Que sçais je?* What do I know?

This book of Montaigne the world has endorsed by translating in into all tongues and printing seventy-five editions of it in Europe; and that, too, a circulation somewhat chosen, namely among courtiers, soldiers, princes, men of the world and men of wit and generosity.

Shall we say that Montaigne has spoken wisely, and given the right and permanent expression of the human mind, on the conduct of life?

We are natural believers. Truth, or the connection between cause and effect, alone interests us. We are persuaded that a thread runs through all things: all worlds are strung on it, as beads; and men, and events, and life, come to us only because of that thread: they pass and repass only that we may know the direction and continuity of that line. A book or statement which goes to show that there is no line, but random and chaos, a calamity out of nothing, a prosperity and no account of it, a hero born from a fool, a fool from a hero—dispirits us. Seen or unseen, we believe the tie exists. Talent makes counterfeit ties; genius finds the real ones. We hearken to the man of science, because we anticipate the sequence in natural phenomena which he uncovers. We love whatever affirms, connects, preserves; and dislike what scatters or pulls down. One man appears whose nature is to all men's eyes conserving and constructive; his presence supposes a well-ordered society, agriculture, trade, large institutions and empire. If these did not exist, they would begin to exist through his endeavors. Therefore he cheers and comforts men, who feel all this in him very readily. The nonconformist and the rebel say all manner of unanswerable things against the existing republic, but discover to our sense no plan of house or state of their own. Therefore, though the town and state and way of living, which our counsellor contemplated, might be a very modest or musty prosperity, yet men rightly go for him, and reject the reformer so long as he comes only with axe and crowbar.

But though we are natural conservers and causationists, and reject a sour, dumpish unbelief, the skeptical class, which Montaigne represents, have reason, and every man, at some time, belongs to it. Every superior mind will pass through this domain of equilibration,—I should rather say, will know how to avail himself of the checks and balances in nature, as a natural weapon against the exaggeration and formalism of bigots and blockheads.

Skepticism is the attitude assumed by the student in relation to the particulars which society adores, but which he sees to be reverend only in their tendency and spirit. The ground occupied by the skeptic is the vestibule of the temple. Society does not like to have any breath of question blown on the existing order. But the interrogation of custom at all points is an inevitable stage in the growth of every superior mind, and is the evidence of its perception of the flowing power which remains itself in all changes.

The superior mind will find itself equally at odds with the evils of society and with the projects that are offered to relieve them. The wise skeptic is a bad citizen; no conservative, he sees the selfishness of property and the drowsiness of institutions. But neither is he fit to work with any democratic party that ever was constituted; for parties wish every one committed, and he penetrates the popular patriotism. His politics are those of the "Soul's Errand" of Sir Walter Raleigh; or of Krishna, in the Bhagavat, "There is none who is worthy of my love or hatred;" whilst he sentences law, physic, divinity, commerce and custom. He is a reformer; yet he is no better member of the philanthropic association. It turns out that he is not the champion of the operative, the pauper, the prisoner, the slave. It stands in his mind that our life in this world is not of quite so easy interpretation as churches and schoolbooks say. He does not wish to take ground against these benevolences, to play the part of devil's attorney, and blazon every doubt and sneer that darkens the sun for him. But he says, There are doubts.

PAUL ELMER MORE

(1864–1937)

The Centenary of Sainte-Beuve

IN THE LAST PART of the nineteenth century and until the first World
War, Charles-Augustin Sainte-Beuve (1804–1869) was considered,
in the United States and England, the peerless critic. In his mul-
titudinous literary portraits—he wrote a critical essay of twenty-odd
pages every week for about twenty years—he caught the essence of
the figures he examined through a study of their biographies, their
intimate psychologies, and their individualities of style. In America
James Huneker tried to incorporate, in his own impressionistic
criticism, Sainte-Beuve's curiosity and relativism of approach. The
biographer Gamaliel Bradford, in his psychological portraits, revealed his debt. Lafcadio Hearn and Henry James acknowledged
Sainte-Beuve's mastery.

The Humanists Irving Babbitt and Paul Elmer More found, in the
latter part of Sainte-Beuve's career, when Sainte-Beuve had shifted
from his original Romanticism to a more neo-classical position, a
congenial model. The school of Humanists, who included in their
number William Cary Brownell and Stuart R. Sherman, were critics
and men of letters, who, in the tradition of Matthew Arnold, upheld
classical and neo-classic standards against the extreme of Romantic
subjectivity, on the one hand, and scientific naturalism, on the other.
Their influence, strong until the 1920s, lost ground during that
decade.

Irving Babbitt's expansive, scholarly, and positive assessment of
Sainte-Beuve serves as the climax of Babbitt's *Masters of Modern
French Criticism* (1912). Babbitt, who taught French literature at
Harvard, produced in this volume an authoritative study, without

103

the dogmatism of his better-known *Rousseau and Romanticism* (1919)

We have chosen for this collection, in preference to Babbitt's essay, the more introductory and readable "Centenary of Sainte-Beuve" by Paul Elmer More. More, less combative and more insinuating than Babbitt, is best known for his Shelburne Essays (eleven volumes, 1904–1921). Like Babbitt, he sees Sainte-Beuve's work as a crux, where different aspects of nineteenth-century thought intersect, and views sympathetically Sainte-Beuve's endeavors to find values after admitting his religious doubts.

Bibliography: Sainte-Beuve's reputation has suffered in the mid-twentieth century, a decline exemplified by Proust's *Contre Sainte-Beuve* (published posthumously in 1954). Proust points to his lack of sufficient sympathy for contemporaries like Balzac and Stendhal, his vindictiveness toward Baudelaire, and the danger of his critical approach, close to confusing the artist and his work. More recently attempts have been made to arrive at a more balanced estimate of Sainte-Beuve. See, for example, René Wellek, *A History of Modern Criticism: 1750–1950,* III (New Haven and London: 1965), pp.34–72. Robert G. Mahieu, *Sainte-Beuve Aux États-Unis* (Princeton: 1945) traces in detail Sainte-Beuve's reputation in the United States at a more receptive time. A French assessment of the Humanists is Louis J. A. Mercier, *Le Movement Humaniste aux Etats-Unis: W. C. Brownell, Irving Babbitt, Paul Elmer More* (Paris: 1928).

This selection is from *Shelburne Essays, Third Series* (New York: G. P. Putnam's Sons, 1905), pp. 54–81. The essay is reprinted here with some excisions.

THE CENTENARY OF SAINTE-BEUVE

(1905)

IT IS A HUNDRED YEARS SINCE Sainte-Beuve was born in the Norman city that looks over toward England, and more than a generation has passed since his death just before the war with Germany.[1] Yesterday three countries—France, Belgium, and Switzerland—were celebrating his centenary with speeches and essays and dinners, and the singing of hymns. . . . He was a critic, and something more; he was,

[1]Charles Augustin Sainte-Beuve was born at Boulogne-sur-Mer, December 23, 1804, and died at Paris, October 13, 1869.

if any man may claim such a title, the *maître universel* of the century, as, indeed, he has been called.

And the time of his life contributed as much to this position of Doctor Universalis as did his own intelligence. France, during those years from the Revolution of 1830 to the fall of the Second Empire, was the seething-pot of modern ideas, and the impression left by the history of the period is not unlike that of watching the witch scenes in *Macbeth*. The eighteenth century had been earnest, mad in part, but its intention was comparatively single,—to tear down the fabric of authority, whether political or religious, and allow human nature, which was fundamentally good, though depraved by custom, to assert itself. And human nature did assert itself pretty vigorously in the French Revolution, proving, one might suppose, if it proved anything, that its foundation, like its origin, is with the beasts. To the men who came afterward that tremendous event stood like a great prism between themselves and the preceding age; the pillar of light toward which they looked for guidance was distorted by it and shattered into a thousand coloured rays. For many of them, as for Sainte-Beuve, it meant that the old humanitarian passion remained side by side with a profound distrust of the popular heart; for all, the path of reform took the direction of some individual caprice or ideal. There were democrats and monarchists and imperialists; there was the rigid Catholic reaction led by Bonald and de Maistre, and the liberal Catholicism of Lamennais; there was the socialism of Saint-Simon, mixed with notions of a religious hierarchy, and other schemes of socialism innumerable; while skepticism took every form of condescension or antagonism. Literature also had its serious mission, and the battle of the romanticists shook Paris almost as violently as a political revolution. Through it all science was marching with steady gaze, waiting for the hour when it should lay its cold hand on the heart of society.

And with all these movements Sainte-Beuve was more or less intimately concerned. As a boy he brought with him to Paris the pietistic sentiments of his mother and an aunt on whom, his father being dead, his training had devolved. Upon these sentiments he soon imposed the philosophy of the eighteenth century, followed by a close study of the Revolution. It is noteworthy that his first journalistic work on the *Globe* was a literary description of the places in Greece to which the war for independence was calling attention, and the reviewing of various memoirs of the French Revolution. From these influences he passed to the *cénacle* of Victor Hugo, and

became one of the champions of the new romantic school. Meanwhile literature was mingled with romance of another sort, and the
story of the critic's friendship for the haughty poet and of his love for
the poet's wife is of a kind almost incomprehensible to the Anglo-
Saxon mind. It may be said in passing that the letters of Sainte-Beuve
to M. and Mme. Hugo, which have only to-day been recovered and
published in the *Revue de Paris,* throw rather a new light on this
whole affair. They do not exculpate Sainte-Beuve, but they at least
free him from ridicule. His successful passion for Mme. Hugo, with
its abrupt close when Mme. Hugo's daughter came to her first
confession, and his tormented courtship of Mme. d'Arbouville in
later years, were the chief elements in that *éducation sentimentale*
which made him so cunning in the secrets of the feminine breast.

But this is a digression. Personal and critical causes carried him out
of the camp of Victor Hugo into the ranks of the Saint-Simonians,
whom he followed for a while with a kind of half-detached
enthusiasm. Probably he was less attracted by the hopes of a mysti-
cally regenerated society, with Enfantin as its supreme pontiff, than
by the desire of finding some rest for the imagination in this religion
of universal love. At least he perceived in the new brotherhood a
relief from the strained individualism of the romantic poets, and the
same instinct, no doubt, followed him from Saint-Simonism into the
fold of Lamennais. There at last he thought to see united the ideals of
religion and democracy, and some of the bitterest words he ever
wrote were in memory of the final defalcation of Lamennais, who, as
Sainte-Beuve said, saved himself but left his disciples stranded in the
mire. Meanwhile this particular disciple had met new friends in
Switzerland, and through their aid was brought at a critical moment
to Lausanne to lecture on *Port-Royal.* There he learned to know and
respect Vinet, the Protestant theologian and critic, who, with the
help of his good friends the Oliviers, undertook to convert the wily
Parisian to Calvinism. Saint-Beuve himself seems to have gone into
the discussion quite earnestly, but for one who knows the past
experiences of that subtle twister there is something almost ludicrous
in the way these anxious missionaries reported each accession and
retrogression of his faith. He came back to Paris a confirmed and
satisfied doubter, willing to sacrifice to the goddess Chance as the
blind deity of this world, convinced of materialism and of the
essential baseness of human nature, yet equally convinced that within
man there rules some ultimate principle of genius or individual
authority which no rationalism can explain, and above all things

determined to keep his mind open to whatever currents of truth may blow through our murky human atmosphere. He ended where he began, in what many be called a subtilised and refined philosophy of the eighteenth century, with a strain of melancholy quite peculiar to the baffled experience of the nineteenth. His aim henceforth was to apply to the study of mankind the analytical precision of science, with a scientific method of grouping men into spiritual families.

Much has been made of these varied twistings of Sainte-Beuve's, both for his honour and dishonour. Certainly they enabled him to insinuate himself into almost every kind of intelligence and report of each author as if he were writing out a phase of his own character; they made him in the end the spokesman of that eager and troubled age whose ferment is to-day just reaching America. France scarcely holds the place of intellectual supremacy once universally accorded her, yet to her glory be it said that, if we look anywhere for a single man who summed up within himself the life of the nineteenth century, we instinctively turn to that country. And more and more it appears that to Sainte-Beuve in particular that honour must accrue. His understanding was more comprehensive than Taine's or Renan's, more subtle than that of the former, more upright than that of the latter, more single toward the truth and more accurate than that of either. He never, as did Taine, allowed a preconceived idea to warp his arrangement of facts, nor did he ever, at least in his mature years, allow his sentimentality, as did Renan, to take the place of judgment. Both the past and the present are reflected in his essays with equal clearness.

On the other hand, this versatility of experience has not seldom been laid to lightness and inconsistency of character. I cannot see that the charge holds good, unless it be directed also against the whole age through which he passed. . . .

And in literature I find that same inconstancy on the surface, while at heart he suffered little change. Only here his experience ran counter to the times, and most of the opprobrium that has been cast on him is due to the fact that he never allowed the clamour of popular taste and the warmth of his sympathy with present modes to drown that inner critical voice of doubt. As a standard-bearer of Victor Hugo and the romanticists he still maintained his reserves, and, on the other hand, long after he had turned renegade from that camp he still spoke of himself as only *demi-converti*. The proportion changed with his development, but from beginning to end he was at bottom classical in his love of clarity and self-restraint, while intensely interested in the life and aspirations of his own day. There is in one of the recently published letters to Victor Hugo a noteworthy illustration of this steadfastness. It was, in fact, the second letter he wrote to the poet, and goes back to 1827, the year of *Cromwell*. On the twelfth of February, Hugo read his new tragi-comedy aloud, and Sainte-Beuve was evidently warm in expressions of praise. But in the seclusion of his own room the critical instinct reawoke in him, and he wrote the next day a long letter to the dramatist, not retracting what he had said, but adding certain reservations and insinuating certain admonitions. "Toutes ces critiques rentrent dans une seule que je m'étais déjà permis d'adresser à votre talent, l'excès, l'abus de la *force*, et passez-moi le mot, la *charge*." Is not the whole of his critical attitude toward the men of his age practically contained in this rebuke of excess, and over-emphasis, and self-indulgence? And Sainte-Beuve when he wrote the words was just twenty-three, was in the first ardour of his attachment to the giant—the Cyclops, he seemed to Sainte-Beuve later—of the century.

But after all, it is not the elusive seeker of these years that we think of when Sainte-Beuve is named, nor the author of those many volumes,—the *Portraits*, the *Chateaubriand*, even the *Port-Royal*,—but the writer of the incomparable *Lundis*. In 1849 he had returned from Liège after lecturing for a year at the University, and found himself abounding in ideas, keen for work, and without regular employment. He was asked to contribute a critical essay to the *Constitutionnel* each Monday, and accepted the offer eagerly. "It is now twenty-five years," he said, "since I started in this career; it is the third form in which I have been brought to give out my impressions and literary judgments." These first *Causeries* continued until 1860, and are published in fourteen solid volumes. There was a brief respite then, and in 1861 he began the *Nouveaux Lundis,* which continued in the *Moniteur* and the *Temps* until his last illness in 1869, filling thirteen similar volumes. . . .

In his earlier years he had been poor and anxious, living in a student's room, and toiling indefatigably to keep the wolf from the door. At the end he was rich, and had command of his time, yet the story of his labours while writing the latest *Lundis* is one of the herioc examples of literature. "Every Tuesday morning," he once wrote to a friend, "I go down to the bottom of a pit, not to reascend until Friday evening at some unknown hour." Those were the days of preparation and plotting. From his friend M. Chéron, who was librarian of the Bibliothèque Impériale, came memoirs and histories and manuscripts,—whatever might serve him in getting up his subject. Late in the week he wrote a rough draft of the essay, commonly about six thousand words long, in a hand which no one but himself could decipher. This task was ordinarily finished in a single day, and the essay was then dictated off rapidly to a secretary to take down in a fair copy. That must have been a strenuous season for the copyist, for Sainte-Beuve read at a prodigious rate, showing impatience at any delay, and still greater impatience at any proposed alteration. . . .

. . . The strain of living thus passionately in a new subject week after week was tremendous, and it is not strange that his letters are filled with complaints of fatigue, and that his health suffered in spite of his robust constitution. Nor was the task ended with the dictation late Friday night. Most of Saturday and Sunday was given up to proof-reading, and at this time he invited every suggestion, even contradiction, often practically rewriting an essay before it reached the press. Monday he was free, and it was on that day occurred the famous Magny dinners, when Sainte-Beuve, Flaubert, Renan, the Goncourts, and a few other chosen spirits, met and talked as only Frenchmen can talk. Every conceivable subject was passed under the fire of criticism; nothing was held sacred. Only one day a luckless guest, after faith in religion and politics and morals had been laughed away, ventured to intimate that Homer as a canon of taste was merely a superstition like another; whereupon such a hubbub arose as threatened to bring the dinners to an end at once and for all. The story is told in the *Journal* of the Goncourts, and it was one of the brothers, I believe, who made the perilous insinuation. Imagine, if you can, a party of Englishmen taking Homer, or any other question of literary faith, with tragic seriousness. Such an incident explains many things; it explains why English literature has never been, like the French, an integral part of the national life.

And the integrity of mind displayed in the *Lundis* is as notable as the industry. From the beginning Sainte-Beuve had possessed that inquisitive passion for the truth, without which all other critical gifts are as brass and tinkling cymbals. Nevertheless, it is evident that he did not always in his earlier writings find it expedient to express his whole thought. He was, for example, at one time the recognised herald of the romantic revolt, and naturally, while writing about Victor Hugo, he did not feel it necessary to make in public such frank reservations as his letters to that poet contain. His whole thought is there, perhaps, but one has to read between the lines to get it. And so it was with the other men and movements with which he for a while allied himself. With the *Lundis* came a change; he was free of all entanglements, and could make the precise truth his single aim. No doubt a remnant of personal jealousy toward those who had passed him in the race of popularity embittered the critical reservations which he felt, but which might otherwise have been uttered more genially. But quite as often this seeming rancour was due to the feeling that he had hitherto been compelled to suppress his full convictions, to a genuine regret for the corrupt ways into which French literature was deviating. . . .

. . . It might almost be said that the history of his intellect is summed up in his growth toward the sane and the simple; that, like Goethe, from whom so much of his critical method derives, his life was a long endeavour to supplant the romantic elements of his taste by the classical. What else is the meaning of his attack on the excesses of Balzac? or his defence of Erasmus *(le droit, je ne dis des tièdes, mais des neutres)*, and of all those others who sought for themselves a governance in the law or proportion? In one of his latest volumes he took the occasion of Taine's *History of English Literature* to speak out strongly for the admirable qualities of Pope:

I insist on this because the danger to-day is in the sacrifice of the writers and poets whom I will call the moderate. For a long time they had all the honours: one pleaded for Shakespeare, for Milton, for Dante, even for Homer; no one thought it necessary to plead for Virgil, for Horace, for Boileau, Racine, Voltaire, Pope, Tasso,—these were accepted and recognised by all. To-day the first have completely gained their cause, and matters are quite the other way about: the great and primitive geniuses reign and triumph; even those who come after them in invention, but are still naïve and original in thought and expression, poets such as Regnier and Lucretius, are raised to their proper rank; while the moderate, the cultured, the polished, those who were the classics to our fathers, we tend to make subordinate, and, if we are not careful, to treat a little too cavalierly. Something like disdain and contempt (relatively speaking) will soon be their portion. It seems to me that there is room for all, and that none need be sacrificed. Let us render full homage and complete reverence to those great human forces which are like the powers of nature, and which like them burst forth with something of strangeness and harshness; but still let us not cease to honour those other forces which are more restrained, and which, in their less explosive expression, clothe themselves with elegance and sweetness.

And this love of the golden mean, joined with the long wanderings of his heart and his loneliness, produced in him a preference for scenes near at hand and for the quiet joys of the hearth. So it was that the idyllic tales of George Sand touched him quickly with their strange romance of the familiar. Chateaubriand and the others of that school had sought out the nature of India, the savannahs of America, the forests of Canada. "Here," he says, "are discoveries for you,— deserts, mountains, the large horizons of Italy; what remained to discover? That which was nearest to us, here in the centre of our own France. As happens always, what is most simple comes at the last." In the same way he praised the refined charm of a poet like Cowper, and sought to throw into relief the purer and more homely verses of a Parny: "If a little knowledge removes us, yet greater knowledge brings us back to the sentiment of the beauties and graces of the hearth." Indeed, there is something almost pathetic in the contrast between the life of this laborious recluse, with his sinister distrust of human nature, and the way in which he fondles this image of a sheltered and affectionate home.

But the nineteenth century was not the seventeenth, neither was Sainte-Beuve a Boileau, to stem the current of exaggeration and egotism. His innate sense of proportion brought him to see the dangerous tendencies of the day, and, failing to correct them, he sank deeper into that disillusion from which his weekly task was a long and vain labour of deliverance. He took to himself the saying of the Abbé Galiani: "Continue your works; it is a proof of attachment to life to compose books." Yet it may be that this very disillusion was one of the elements of his success; for after all, the real passion of literature, that perfect flower of the contemplative intellect, hardly comes to a man until the allurement of life has been dispelled by many experiences, each bringing its share of disappointment. . . .

Nor is it to be supposed that Sainte-Beuve, because he was primarily a critic, drew his knowledge of life from books only, and wrote, as it were, at second hand. The very contrary is true. As a younger man, he had mixed much with society, and even in his later years, when, as he says, he lived at the bottom of a well, he still, through his friendship with the Princesse Mathilde and others of the great world, kept in close touch with the active forces of the Empire. As a matter of fact, every one knows, who has read at all in his essays, that he was first of all a psychologist, and that his knowledge of the human breast was quite as sure as his acquaintance with libraries. He might almost be accused of slighting the written word in order to get at the secret of the writer. What attracted him chiefly was that middle ground where life and literature meet, where life becomes self-conscious through expression, and literature retains the reality of association with facts. "A little poesy," he thought, "separates us from history and the reality of things; much of poesy brings us back." Literature to him was one of the arts of society. Hence he was never more at his ease, his touch was never surer and his eloquence more communicable, than when he was dealing with the great ladies who guided the society of the eighteenth century and retold its events in their letters and memoirs,—Mme. du Deffand, Mme. de Grafigny, Mlle. de Lespinasse, and those who preceded and followed. Nowhere does one get closer to the critic's own disappointment than when he says with a sigh, thinking of those irrecoverable days: "Happy time! all of life then was turned to sociability." And he was describing his own method as a critic, no less than the character of Mlle. de Lespinasse, when he wrote: "Her great art in society, one of the secrets of her success, was to feel the intelligence (*l'esprit*) of others, to make it prevail, and to seem to foget her own. Her conversation was never either above or below those with whom she spoke; she possessed measure, proportion, rightness of mind. She reflected so well the impressions of others, and received so visibly the influence of their intelligence, that they loved her for the success she helped them to attain. She raised this disposition to an art. 'Ah!' she cried one day, 'how I long to know the foible of every one!' " And this love of the social side of literature, this hankering after *la bella scuola* when men wrote under the sway of some central governance, explains Sainte-Beuve's feeling of desolation amidst the scattered, individualistic tendencies of his own day.

There lie the springs of Sainte-Beuve's critical art,—his treatment of literature as a function of social life, and his search in all things for the golden mean. There we find his strength, and there, too, his limitation. If he fails anywhere, it is when he comes into the presence of those great and imperious souls who stand apart from the common concerns of men, and who rise above our homely mediocrities, not by extravagence or egotism, but by the lifting wings of inspiration. He could, indeed, comprehend the ascetic grandeur of a Pascal or the rolling eloquence of a Bossuet, but he was distrustful of that fervid breath of poesy that comes and goes unsummoned and uncontrolled. It is a common charge against him that he was cold to the sublime, and he himself was aware of his defect, and sought to justify it. "Il ne faut donner dans le sublime," he said, "qu'à la dernière extrémité et à son corps défendant." Something of this, too, must be held to account for the haunting melancholy that he could forget, but never overcome. He might have lived with a kind of content in the society of those refined and worldly women of the eighteenth century, but, missing the solace of that support, he was unable amid the dissipated energies of his own age to rise to that surer peace that needs no communion with others for its fulfilment. Like the royal friend of Voltaire, he still lacked the highest degree of culture, which is religion. He strove for that during many years, but alone he could not attain to it. As early as 1839 he wrote, while staying at Aigues-Mortes: "My soul is like this beach, where it is said Saint Louis embarked: the sea and faith, alas! have long since drawn away." One may excuse these limitations as the "defect of his quality," as indeed they are. But more than that, they belong to him as a French critic, as they are to a certain degree inherent in French literature. That literature and language, we have been told by no less an authority than M. Brunetière, are pre-eminently social in their strength and their weakness. And Sainte-Beuve was indirectly justifying his own method when he pointed to the example of Voltaire, Molière, La Fontaine, and Rabelais and Villon, the great ancestors. "They have all," he said, "a corner from which they mock at the sublime." I am even inclined to think that these qualities explain why England has never had, and may possibly never have, a critic in any way comparable to Sainte-Beuve; for the chief glory of English literature lies in the very field where French is weakest, in the lonely and unsociable life of the spirit, just as the faults of English are due to its lack of discipline and uncertainty of taste. And after all, the critical temperament consists primarily in just this linking together of literature and life, and in the levelling application of common sense.

Yet if Sainte-Beuve is essentially French, indeed almost inconceivable in English, he is still immensely valuable, perhaps even more valuable, to us for that very reason. There is nothing more whole-

some than to dip into this strong and steady current of wise judgment. It is good for us to catch the glow of his masterful knowledge of
letters and his faith in their supreme interest. His long row of
volumes are the scholar's Summa Theologiae. As John Cotton loved
to sweeten his mouth with a piece of Calvin before he went to sleep,
so the scholar may turn to Sainte-Beuve, sure of his never-failing
abundance and his ripe intelligence.

JAMES GIBBONS HUNEKER

(1860–1921)

Rémy de Gourmont

JAMES G. HUNEKER, essayist on literature, art, and music, was the chief critical exponent of impressionism and cosmopolitanism in America from 1899 to the date of his death, a period when collections of his newspaper and magazine essays appeared regularly in book form. At eighteen, he had gone to Paris to become a professional musician, but upon his return to New York several years later he shifted his interests to criticism and journalism. He was to visit Europe again many times.

Like his critical heroes, Anatole France and Rémy de Gourmont (1858–1915), Huneker did not seek to develop a systematic critical doctrine. Paraphrasing Anatole France, Huneker declared that the critic's aim is "to spill his own soul." He valued conscious artistry, and faithful to his idea of relativism, disregarded labels and schools, such as Realism, Symbolism, and decadence. Liks his disciple, H. L. Mencken, he attacked Puritanism as an obstacle to the arts and espoused tolerance in the presence of beauty; he also assumed the role of iconoclast, writing damaging assessments of those he felt had been revered without cause. To the modern reader, he lacks real originality, though he is capable of pungent comment. In retrospect, his role as critic was to stimulate interest, particularly in as yet unknown Continental writers, rather than to offer profound assessment. Also, he combined broad learning and intensive preparation with a style that—despite an over-inclination for the striking phrase—is still very readable.

Especially in *Egoists* (1909), *Ivory, Apes and Peacocks* (1915), and *Unicorns* (1917), Huneker wrote appreciative essays on approximately twenty French writers, including Balzac, Stendhal, Flaubert, Maupassant, Zola, Baudelaire, Huysmans, Maeterlinck, and Bergson. One of his best, the first substantial study in English, is of

115

his critical master, Rémy de Gourmont, in which he clearly spells out the philosophic materialism that produced Gourmont's posture of critical impressionism based on classical principles.

The star of Rémy de Gourmont, essayist, critic, novelist, poet, and analyst of human and animal behavior, has dimmed. In the 1910s and 1920s, he seemed to both Americans and Englishmen the leading critic since Sainte-Beuve. The early T. S. Eliot referred to him as "the critical consciousness of a generation" (1917), and adopted from him the idea of poetry as a superior amusement. Ezra Pound, who also repudiated the idea of a systematic critical doctrine, extolled him, in an extended essay (from *Instigations*, 1920), as follows: "Gourmont prepared our era; behind him there stretches a limitless darkness . . . ."

Bibliography: Glenn S. Burne, *Rémy de Gourmont: His Ideas and Influences in England and America* (Carbondale, Ill.: 1963) discusses Gourmont's reputation abroad. Useful on Huneker is E. C. Fay, "Huneker's Criticism of French Literature," *French Review,* 14 (1940), 130–37, which remarks on his foresight in this area. (Of incidental interest is the full-length account of contemporary French poetry by Vance Thompson, Huneker's friend and colleague, in his *French Portraits* [1900]; unfortunately, however, it is vitiated by plagiarism.)

This selection, with one paragraph omitted, is reprinted from *Unicorns* (New York: Charles Scribner's Sons, 1917), pp. 18–32.

RÉMY DE GOURMONT

(1917)

I

THOSE were days marked by a white stone when arrived in the familiar yellow cover a new book, with card enclosed from "Rémy de Gourmont, 71, rue des Saints-Pères, Paris." Sometimes I received as many as two in a year. But they always found me eager and grateful, did those precious little volumes bearing the imprint of the *Mercure de France,* with whose history the name of De Gourmont is so happily linked. And there were post-cards too in his delicate hand-writing on which were traced sense and sentiment; yes, this man of genius possessed sentiment, but abhorred sentimentality. His personal charm transpired in a friendly salutation hastily pencilled. He played exquisitely upon his intellectual instrument, and knew the value of time and space. So his post-cards are souvenirs of his courtesy, and it was through one, which unexpectedly fell from the sky in 1897, I began my friendship with this distinguished French critic. His sudden death in 1915 at Paris (he was born 1858), caused by apoplexy, was the heroic ending of a man of letters. Like Flaubert he was stricken while at his desk. I can conceive no more fitting end for a valiant soldier of literature. He was a moral hero and the victim of his prolonged technical heroism.

De Gourmont was incomparable. Thought, not action, was his chosen sphere, but ranging up and down the vague and vast territory of ideas he encountered countless cerebral adventures; the most dangerous of all. An aristocrat born, he was, nevertheless, a convinced democrat. The latch was always lifted on the front door of his ivory tower. He did live in a certain sense a cloistered existence, a Benedictine of arts and letters; but he was not, as has been said, a sour hermit nursing morose fancies in solitude. De Gourmont, true pagan, enjoyed the gifts the gods provide, and had, despite the dualism of his nature, an epicurean soul. But of a complexity. He never sympathised with the disproportionate fuss raised by the metaphysicians about Instinct and Intelligence, yet his own magnificient cerebral apparatus was a battle-field over which swept the opposing hosts of Instinct and Intelligence, and in a half-hundred volumes the history of his conflict is faithfully set down. As personal as Maurice Barrès, without his egoism, as subtle as Anatole France, De Gourmont saw life steadier and broader than either of these two contemporaries. He was one who said "vast things simply." He was the profoundest philosopher of the three, and never, after his beginnings, exhibited a trace of the dilettante. Life soon became something more than a mere spectacle for him. He was a meliorist in theory and practice, though he asserted that Christianity, an Oriental-born religion, has not become spiritually acclimated among Occidental peoples. But he missed its consoling function; religion, the poetry of the poor, never had for him the prime significance that it had for William James; a legend, vague, vast, and delicious.

Old frontiers have disappeared in science and art and literature. We have Maeterlinck, a poet writing of bees, Poincaré, a mathematician opening our eyes to the mystic gulfs of space; solid matters resolved into mist, and the law of gravitation questioned. The new horizons beckon ardent youth bent on conquering the secrets of life. And there are more false beaconlights than true. But if this is an age of specialists a man occasionally emerges who contradicts the formula. De Gourmont was at base a poet; also a dramatist, novelist, raconteur, man of science, critic, moralist of erudition, and, lastly, a philosopher. Both formidable and bewildering were his accomplishments. He is a poet in his *Hieroglyphes, Oraisons mauvaises, Le Livre des Litanies, Les Saintes du Paradis, Simone, Divertissements*—his last appearance in singing robes (1914); he is a raconteur—and such tales—in *Histoires magiques, Prose moroses, Le Pèlerin du silence, D'un Pays lointain, Couleurs;* a novelist in *Merlette*—his first book—*Sixtine, Le Fantôme, les Chevaux de Diomède, Le Songe d'une Femme, Une Nuit au Luxembourg, Un Cœur virginal;* dramatist in *Théodat, Phénissa, Le vieux Roi, Lilith;* as master critic of the æsthetics of the French language his supremacy is indisputable; it is hardly necessary to refer here to *Le Livre des Masques,* in two volumes, the five volumes of *Promenades littéraires,* the three of *Promenades philosophiques;* as moralist he has signed such works as *l'Idéalisme, La Culture des Idées, Le Chemin de Velours;* historian and humanist, he has given us *Le Latin mystique;* grammarian and philologist, he displays his learning in *Le Problème du Style,* and *Esthétique de la Langue française,* and incidentally flays an unhappy pedagogue who proposed to impart the secret of style in twenty lessons. He edited many classics of French literature.

His chief contribution to science, apart from his botanical and entomological researches is *Physique de l'Amour,* in which he reveals himself as a patient, thorough observer in an almost new country. And what shall we say to his incursions into the actual, into the field of politics, sociology and hourly happenings of Paris life; his *Epilogues* (three volumes), *Dialogues des Amateurs,* the collected pages from his monthly contributions to *Mercure de France?* Nothing human was alien to him, nor inhuman, for he rejected as quite meaningless the latter vocable, as he rejected such clichés as "organic and inorganic." Years before we heard of a pluralistic universe De Gourmont was a pragmatist, though an idealist in his conception of the world as a personal picture. Intensely interested in ideas, as he was in words, he might have fulfilled Lord Acton's wish that some one would write a History of Ideas. At the time of his death the French thinker was composing a work entitled *La Physique des*

Moeurs, in which he contemplated a demonstration of his law of intellectual constancy.

A spiritual cosmopolitan, he was like most Frenchmen an ardent patriot. The little squabble in the early eighties over a skit of his, *Le Jou-jou—patriotisme* (1883), cost him his post at the National Library in Paris. As a philosopher he deprecated war; as a man, though too old to fight, he urged his countrymen to victory, as may be noted in his last book, *Pendant l'Orage* (1916). But the philosopher persists in such a sorrowful sentence as: "In the tragedy of man peace is but an entr'acte." To show his mental balance at a time when literary men, artists, and even philosophers, indulged in unseemly abuse, we read in *Jugements* his calm admission that the war has not destroyed for him the intellectual values of Goethe, Schopenhauer, or Nietzsche. He owes much to their thought as they owed much to French thought; Goethe has said as much; and of Voltaire and Chamfort, Schopenhauer was a disciple. Without being a practical musician, De Gourmont was a lover of Beethoven and Wagner. He paid his compliments to Romain Rolland, whose style, both chalky and mucilaginous, he dislikes in that overrated and spun-out series Jean-Christophe. Another little volume, *La Belgique littéraire,* was published in 1915, which, while it contains nothing particularly new about George Rodenbach, Emile Verhaeren, Van Lerberghe, Camille Lemonnier, and Maurice Maeterlinck, is excellent reading. The French critic was also editor of the *Revue des Idées,* and judging from the bibliography compiled by Pierre de Querlon as long ago as 1903, he was a collaborator of numerous magazines. He wrote on Emerson, English humour, or Thomas à Kempis with the same facility as he dissected the mystic Latin writers of the early centuries after Christ. Indeed, such versatility was viewed askance by the plodding crowd of college professors, his general adversaries. But his erudition could not be challenged; only two other men matched his scholarship, Anatole France and the late Marcel Schwob. And we have only skimmed the surface of his accomplishments. Rémy de Gourmont is the Admirable Crichton of French letters.

II

Prodigious incoherence might be reasonably expected from this diversity of interests, yet the result is quite the reverse. The artist in this complicated man banished confusion. He has told us that because of the diversity of his aptitudes man is distinguished from his fellow animals, and the variety in his labours is a proof positive of his superiority to such fellow critics as the mentally constipated Brunetière, the impressionistic Anatole France, the agile and graceful Lemaître, and the pedantic philistine Faguet. But if De Gourmont always attains clarity with no loss of depth, he sometimes mixes his genres; that is, the poet peeps out in his reports of the psychic life of insects, as the philosopher lords it over the pages of his fiction. A mystic betimes, he is a crystal-clear thinker. And consider the catholicity evinced in *Le Livre des Masques.* He wrote of such widely diverging talents as Maeterlinck, Mallarmé, Villiers de l'Isle Adam, and Paul Adam; of Henri de Regnier and Jules Renard; of Huysmans and Jules Laforgue; the mysticism of Francis Poictevin's style and the imagery of Saint-Pol-Roux he defined, and he displays an understanding of the first symbolist poet, Arthur Rimbaud, while disliking the personality of that abnormal youth. But why recite this litany of new talent literally made visible and vocal by our critic? It is a pleasure to record the fact that most of his swans remained swans and did not degenerate into tame geese. In this book he shows himself a profound psychologist.

Insatiably curious, he yet contrived to drive his chimeras in double harness and safely. His best fiction is *Sixtine* and *Une Nuit au Luxembourg*, if fiction they may be called. Never will their author be registered among best-sellers. *Sixtine* deals with the adventures of a masculine brain. Ideas are the hero. In *Un Cœur virginal* we touch earth, fleshly and spiritually. This story shocked its readers. It may be considered as a sequel to *Physique de l'Amour*. It shows mankind as a gigantic insect indulging in the same apparently blind pursuit of sex sensation as a beetle, and also shows us the "female of our species" endowed with less capacity for modesty than the lady mole, the most chaste of all animals. Disconcerting, too, is the psychology of the heroine's virginal soul, not, however, cynical; cynicism is the irony of vice, and De Gourmont is never cynical. But a master of irony.

Une Nuit au Luxembourg has been done into English. It handles with delicacy and frankness themes that in the hands of a lesser artist would be banished as brutal and blasphemous. The author knows that all our felicity is founded on a compromise between the dream and reality, and for that reason while he signals the illusion he never mocks it; he is too much an idealist. In the elaborately carved cups of his tales, foaming over with exquisite perfumes and nectar, there lurks the bitter drop of truth. He could never have said with Proudhon that woman is the desolation of the just; for him woman is often an obsession. Yet, captain of his instincts, he sees her justly; he is not subdued by sex. With a gesture he destroys the sentimental scaffolding of the sensualist and marches on to new intellectual conquests.

In Lilith, an Adamitic Morality, he reveals his Talmudic lore. The first wife of our common ancestor is a beautiful hell-hag, the accomplice of Satan in the corruption of the human race. Thus mediæval play is epical in its Rabelaisian-plainness of speech. Perhaps the Manichean in De Gourmont fabricated its revolting images. He had traversed the Baudelairian steppes of blasphemy and black pessimism; Baudelaire, a poet who was a great critic. Odi profanum vulgus! was De Gourmont's motto, but his soul was responsive to so many contacts that he emerged, as Barrès emerged, a citizen of the world. Anarchy as a working philosophy did not long content him, although he never relinquished his detached attitude of proud individualism. He saw through the sentimental equality of J.-J. Rousseau. Rousseau it was who said that thinking man was a depraved animal. Perhaps he was not far from the truth. Man is an affective animal more interested in the immediate testimony of his senses than in his intellectual processes. His metaphysic may be but the reverberation of his sensations on the shore of his subliminal self, the echo of the sounding shell he calls his soul. And our critic had his scientific studies to console him for the inevitable sterility of soul that follows egoism and a barren debauch of the sensations. He did not tarry long in the valley of excess. His artistic sensibility was his saviour.

Without being a dogmatist, De Gourmont was an antagonist of absolutism. A determinist, (which may be dogmatism à rebours), a relativist, he holds that mankind is not a specially favoured species of the animal scale; thought is only an accident, possibly the result of rich nutrition. An automaton, man has no free will, but it is better for him to imagine that he has; it is a sounder working hypothesis for the average human. The universe had no beginning, it will have no end. There is no first link or last in the chain of causality. Everything must submit to the law of causality; to explain a blade of grass we must dismount the stars. Nevertheless, De Gourmont no more than Renan, had the mania of certitude. Humbly he interrogates the sphinx. There are no isolated phenomena in time or space. The mass of matter is eternal. Man is an animal submitting to the same laws that govern crystals or brutes. He is the expression of matter in physique and chemistry. Repetition is the law of life. Thought is a physiological product; intelligence the secretion of matter and is amenable to the law of causality. (This sounds like Taine's famous definition of virtue and vice.) And who shall deny it all in the psychochemical laboratories? It is not the rigid old-fashioned materialism, but a return to the more plastic theories of Lamarck and the transformism of the Dutch botanist, Hugo de Vries. For De Gourmont the Darwinian notion that man is at the topmost notch of creation is as antique and absurd as most cosmogonies; indeed, it is the Asiatic egocentric idea of creation. Jacob's ladder repainted in Darwinian symbols. Voilà l'ennemi! said De Gourmont and put on his controversial armour. What blows, what sudden deadly attacks were his! . . .

III

A synthetic brain is De Gourmont's, a sower of doubts, though not a No-Sayer to the universe. He delights in challenging accepted "truths." Of all modern thinkers a master of Vues d'ensembles, he smiles at the pretensions, usually a mask for poverty of ideas, of so-called "general ideas." He dissociates such conventional grouping of ideas as Glory, Justice, Decadence. The shining ribs of disillusion shine through his pyschology; a psychology of nuance and finesse. Disillusioning reflections, these. Not to be put in any philosophical pigeonhole, he is as far removed from the eclecticism of Victor Cousin as from the verbal jugglery and metaphysical murmurings of Henri Bergson. The world is his dream; but it is a tangible dream, charged with meaning, order, logic. The truest reality is thought. Action spoils. (Goethe said: "Thought expands, action narrows.") Our abstract ideas are metaphysical idols, says Jules de Gaultier. The image of the concrete is De Gourmont's touchstone. Théophile Gautier declared that he was a man for whom the visible world existed. He misjudged his capacity for apprehending reality. The human brain, excellent instrument in a priori combinations is inept at perceiving realities. The "Sultan of the Epithet," as De Goncourt nicknamed "le bon Théo," was not the "Emperor of Thought," according to Henry James, and for him it was a romantic fiction spun in the rich web of his fancy. A vaster, greyer world is adumbrated in the books of De Gourmont. He never allowed symbolism to deform his representation of sober, every-day life. He pictured the future domain of art and ideas as a fair and shining landscape no longer a series of little gardens with high walls. A hater of formulas, sects, schools, he teaches that the capital crime of the artist, the writer, the thinker, is conformity. (Yet how serenely this critic swims in classic currents!) The artist's work should reflect his personality, a magnified reflection. He must create his own æsthetic. There are no schools, only individuals. And of consistency he might have said that it is oftener a mule than a jewel.

Sceptical in all matters, though never the fascinating sophist that is Anatole France, De Gourmont criticised the thirty-six dramatic situations, reducing the number to four. Man as centre in relation to himself; in relation to other men; in relation to the other sex; in relation to God, or Nature. His ecclesiastical *fond* may be recognised in *Le Chemin de Velours* with its sympathetic exposition of Jesuit doctrine, and the acuity of its judgments on Pascal and the Jansenists. The latter section is as an illuminating foot-note to the history of Port-Royal by Sainte-Beuve. The younger critic has the supple intellect of the supplest-minded Jesuit. His bias toward the order is unmistakable. There are few books I reread with more pleasure than this Path of Velvet. Certain passages in it are as silky and sonorous as the sound of Eugène Ysaye's violin.

The colour of De Gourmont's mind is stained by his artistic sensibility. A maker of images, his vocabulary astounding as befits both a poet and philologist, one avid of beautiful words, has variety. The temper of his mind is tolerant, a quality that has informed the finer intellects of France since Montaigne. His literary equipment is unusual. A style as brilliant, sinuous, and personal as his thought; flexible or massive, continent or coloured, he discourses at ease in all the gamuts and modes major, minor, and mixed. A swift, weighty style, the style of a Latinist; a classic, not a romantic style. His formal sense is admirable. The tenderness of Anatole France is absent, except in his verse, which is less spontaneous than volitional. A pioneer in new æsthetic pastures, De Gourmont is a poet for poets. He has virtuosity, though the gift of tears nature—possibly jealous because of her prodigality—has denied him. But in the curves of his overarching intellect there may be found wit, gaiety, humour, the Gallic attributes, allied with poetic fancy, profundity of thought, and a many-sided comprehension of life, art, and letters. He is in the best tradition of French criticism only more versatile than either Sainte-Beuve or Taine; as versatile as Doctor Brandes or Arthur Symons, and that is saying much. With Anatole France he could have exclaimed: "The longer I contemplate human life, the more I believe that we must give it, for witnesses and judges, Irony and Pity. . . ."

PART IV

French Realism and Naturalism: American Perspectives

JOHN LOTHROP MOTLEY
(1814–1877)

The Novels of Balzac

IN THE 1830s and 1840s, American reviewers, like those writing for the *North American Review,* a leading critical journal of the time, tended to regard French fiction, such as the novels of Balzac, Hugo, and George Sand, as immoral. Doubtless, the strain of Puritanism in the New England fiber contributed to this tendency. Claude C. Spiker writes: "Frequently the reviewer burned with righteous wrath as he denounced the wickedness of French sex morality" (in "The *North American Review* and French Morals," *Philological Studies,* vol. 4, West Virginia University, September 1943, p. 6).

Even superior reviewers, like Margaret Fuller and Orestes Brownson, could not shake themselves completely free of this attitude. Margaret Fuller (1810–1850), associated with the Transcendental movement and a crusader for women's rights, on February 1, 1845 wrote, as literary editor of the *New York Tribune,* an essay "French Novelists of the Day" in which, attempting to defend the French authors, she mingled an appreciation of their artistry with a condemnation of their morals. Orestes Brownson (1803–1876), devoted largely to social and religious problems, in an essay "Modern French Literature" (1842)—found in his *Works,* vol. 19, ed. Henry F. Brownson (1885)—applied the criterion of "normalcy" and classified French fiction as inferior to the British, with Hugo given too much to the grotesque and Balzac lacking the warmth of Charles Dickens and Bulwer-Lytton.

What proved the most forceful defense of Balzac in this period— the French novelist who succeeded George Sand in attracting most American attention in the nineteenth century—was written by John Lothrop Motley (1814–1877), who was to develop into an important historian, with his *Rise of the Dutch Republic* (1856). His article of July, 1847, in the *North American Review* commended Balzac for his realism, his social perception, and his artistic detachment. Van Wyck Brooks, in his *Flowering of New England*, writes that the article "made a great stir. It was a lively defense of the artist as man of letters, the sort of defense that Poe was making, and that Hawthorne might have made, but that, in fact, had not been made by any other writer in New England. . . . He praised the detachment of Balzac as the proper attitude of the artist as a man of letters, and he uttered a phrase that resounded through New England, 'Certainly the world should be reformed, but not by novel-writing' " (New York: 1952, pp. 347–48). Despite Motley's eloquent praise of Balzac, the French realism Balzac represented did not find common acceptance in the United States until the 1870s.

Bibliography: Claude C. Spiker includes a bibliography of reviews of French writing as they appear in the *North American Review*, 1815–1861. Helen MacMahon, in *Criticism of Fiction: A Study of Trends in the* Atlantic Monthly: *1857–1898* (New York: 1952), traces the rising reputation of French realism in America. She provides as well a register of reviews and critical essays on French fiction in the *Atlantic Monthly* from 1857 to 1898. Benjamin Griffith, in *Balzac aux États-Unis* (Paris: 1931), offers a bibliography of essays and references to Balzac in the United States beginning with Motley and continuing through the 1920s.

This essay, reprinted here only in excerpted form, first appeared in the *North American Review, 65* (July, 1847), 85–108.

THE NOVELS OF BALZAC
(1847)

• • • •

With all his faults, Balzac is essentially an artist, and not a mechanic. It is, perhaps, a result of this very quality that he has found himself growing less popular. He has been unable to sympathize with the sudden moral movement of the French mind. The late rush into morality has been terrific in Paris. Those volatile gentlemen, the *feuilletonistes,* have, as it were, discovered it all at once. Morality is like the mines of Mexico to them, and they are all hammering, digging, and picking, with might and main. The sudden demand for works of an elevating, humanizing, intensely moral fabric, which has sprung up in Paris since the great success of Mr. Dickens in English literature, has been partially supplied by Eugene Sue, George Sand, and others; but Balzac has not set himself to the work. Nothing, by the way, illustrates more aptly the great fertility and versatility of the French literary mind of the present day, than this sudden change in their style of writing and thinking. The *feuilletonistes*, like manufacturers, watch the popular taste, and they are all at this moment working double speed, and turning off morality, and democracy, and philanthropy, and articles of that nature, by the yard, like so much *mousseline de laine*, because they happen just now to be popular. After publishing legions of books of the most unblushing immorality, they are all at once grown as unblushingly moral. There is a change in the fashion.

Now it strikes us that Balzac has been writing out of himself all his life, working up the stuff which is in him, but that he is too idiosyncratic to fall in with this sudden revolution in literature. He has been very popular in France, but he has been little translated, and is but little known in England or America. We are not surprised at this, but upon the whole, if there is to be so large an infusion of French novels into our literature, we should rather recommend Balzac than either Sue or Sand. The writers who have been naturalized in this country are worse, because they are both socially and politically disorganizing. Balzac, on the contrary, is an artist. He is neither moral nor immoral, but a calm and profound observer of human society and human passions, and a minute, patient, and powerful delineator of scenes and characters in the world before his eyes. His readers must moralize for themselves. There is no doubt that the audacity of the modern French literature gives an author an advantage which the squeamishness of the English denies. French imaginative literature, that portion of it, for example, which may be represented by Balzac, is able to anatomize society more boldly and scientifically, because less trammelled by prudery. The strict administration of justice in the concluding portions of every English novel, where the characters are all drawn up, as on the day of judgment, in two lines, the vicious all whipped and the virtuous all married (that being considered the highest earthly reward of virtue); where, in the last chapter, a great Christmas pie is regularly served up to the meritorious, each one of whom puts in his thumb and pulls out a plum, and says, What a good boy am I! while the villains look on and gnash their teeth in despair,—this sort of romantic jurisprudence, with which even Scott, while he ridiculed it, was often forced to comply, has been out of date in France since the days of the Grand Cyrus.

It is odd, and a good subject to be pondered upon, if we had the time and space,—the striking contrast sometimes presented between the character of an age and its literature. Ninon de l'Enclos, Bussy, Maréchal de Bassompierre, would hardly be cited for their austere morality; Cardinal de Retz was not exclusively addicted to the practice of all the cardinal virtues; yet De Retz, Bassompierre, Ninon, and their friends and contemporaries, would tolerate no romances but the "severely proper" and ponderous productions of Scudéry. They order matters differently in France at the present day. It is very certain, that De Balzac has not yet, like Charles Lamb, found himself a disreputable personage. Nobody in Paris ever dreamed of his being immoral. He is, as we before observed, essentially an artist, and deals with materials which society affords him. If his pictures be dark, they are none the less truthful copies from human nature. If they reveal a vicious or disorderly condition of society, society, and not the artist, is reprehensible. An author is not responsible for the disorders which he depicts. . . .

The three romances upon which Balzac may most securely rest his fame are *Le Père Goriot, Eugenie Grandet,* and *La Recherche de l'Absolu.* These are all less disfigured by his characteristic faults, and more distinguished by masterly portraiture of passion and minutely accurate delineation of character and scenery, than any of his other productions. We have no time nor inclination to analyze these novels. *Père Goriot* is the history of a Lear in private life, a rich maccaroni-maker, who divides his fortune between his two daughters, the Baronne de Nucingen, and the Comtesse de Restaud, and who, although cruelly neglected by them, and allowed almost to starve to death, is unfaltering and sublime in his passionate affection for his unworthy offspring. The boarding-house where he lives, the *"Maison Vauquer, pension bourgeoise des deux sexes et autres,"* is also the residence of several prominent characters, some of which are the most striking and finished pictures which his pencil has ever drawn. The old maccaroni-maker, the *forçat* Vautrin, otherwise Trempe la Mort, the Demoiselle Michonneau, and Madame Vauquer née de Conflans, the mistress of the boarding-house, are all conceived and executed with consummate skill. The boarding-house itself is a character,—nay, the very street where it is situated has a physiognomy of its own. No one who has read *Père Goriot* can ever forget the extraordinary power with which that *pension bourgeoise,* the odor of the house, the character of its furniture, the color of its walls, the locks of its doors, are presented to the imagination, blended with the various but minutely depicted portraits of the inmates, the sound of their voices, the expression of their features, the strain of their general conversation at table, their meagre *table-d'hôte* fare, their boarding-house jokes, their conventional witticisms, their petty plots, their interior heart-burnings. Nor is less to be admired the artful manner in which the counterpart to this musty fusty *pension* life is managed, the magic-lantern style in which suddenly flash upon the view the brilliant ball-rooms of the Faubourg St. Germain, with all their soft crush, and flutter, and glitter, their beauty, music, flowers, their diamonds, dalliance, and dance. The obscure Maison Vauquer is connected by two links with the dazzling scenes of Parisian life; the Père Goriot and the hero Eugène de Rastignac are both inmates of the boarding-house.

The two masterpieces of Balzac, however, are unquestionably *Eugenie Grandet* and *La Recherche de l'Absolu;* both of which are included in the *Scènes de la Vie de Province.* The story of *Eugenie Grandet* is nothing, a mere narrative of every-day life, in which the self-abnegation of woman and the egotism of man are depicted in a series of interior, exquisitely finished scenes, which inevitably suggest, to be sure, the works of the Flemish painters, but to which we are disposed to assign a much higher rank in literature than those pictures occupy in art. Moreover, there are passages of passion, strokes of nature, scenes of light and shadow, which reveal so broad and profound a knowledge of nature and of the heart, that we consider this comparison as an undervaluation of Balzac.

Eugenie Grandet is the daughter of a provincial miser, whose life is wasted in devotion to an inhuman father and a worthless lover. It is a story without a catastrophe, and therefore the more lifelike. The father, a miser, whose picture is admirably drawn, and well illustrates the effect which may be produced by the accumulation of delicate touches, after having kept all his family upon the rack during his whole life, dies at last with his money-bags in his arms, and leaves many millions to his daughter. The lover has, however, in the mean time, deserted her and married another. There is no need of making an analysis of the story, for it would disappear in the attempt. So meagre and minute are the incidents, so slight is the framework of the novel, that it would seem impossible that the interest could be sustained; and yet it is hardly possible to conceive of a work of more absorbing and enchaining interest. The consummate skill with which petty and every-day events are handled, and the lifelike portraiture of the characters, constitute the charm of the book. In the heroine, Balzac has, for once at least, approached the ideal. Eugenie is the perfection of the moral-beautiful evolved from the true; a type of woman which to the vulgar mind might be vulgar, but to the moralist, as well as to the artist, is one of inestimable beauty and sublimity. In the author's own words, "Eugenie Grandet among women will be a type,—that of devotions thrown into the tempests of the world, and buried there, as a noble statue taken from Greece, which, upon the passage, falls into the ocean, where it will for ever remain unknown."

• • • •

WALT WHITMAN

(1819–1892)

Taine's *History of English Literature:* A Lesson for America

Hippolyte Taine (1828–1893), French critic and historian of art and literature, expounded the naturalistic doctrine that *race, milieu,* and *moment* (national character, environment, and historical moment) determine the essence of the artist and his work. Though his doctrine has limitations (he has always been assailed for neglecting the subjective or inherently imaginative aspects of literature), it contains an important truth which he often brilliantly exploited.

In the 1870s, Taine, along with the French novelists, helped stimulate the development of Realism in American fiction. Edward Eggleston, author of *The Hoosier Schoolmaster* (1871), a book often cited as an early landmark in the history of American Realism, was directly inspired by Taine. After reading Taine's *Art in the Netherlands* (1869), which he briefly reviewed in the *Independent* in 1870, Eggleston applied Taine's notion of the importance of environment to his own writing. Of *The Hoosier Schoolmaster,* Eggleston wrote: "I am often asked in regard to the immediate impetus to the writing of this story, and the answer seems paradoxical enough. I had just finished Taine's 'Art in the Netherlands'. Applying his maxim, that an artist ought to paint what he has seen, I tried my hand on the dialect and other traits of the more illiterate people of Southern Indiana" (*Forum,* 3 [1887], 578–84). Incidentally, in the same article, Eggleston credits Sainte-Beuve—"to whose writings I owe a hundred debts"—with encouraging him to relinquish his religious training and to take the path that led to Darwinism.

133

In the 1890s Hamlin Garland, author of *Main-Travelled Roads* (1891), the bitter picture of midwestern farm lives, read Taine's *History of English Literature* (1871; English trans. 1871–72) and copied into his notebooks Taine's analysis of the duties of a writer in an age of science. In *Crumbling Idols* (1899), his literary credo and an attack on literary genteelism, Garland often refers to Taine.

Reciprocally, Taine displayed a realist's interest and appreciation of the United States. In his *Vie et opinions de M. Frédéric-Thomas Graindorge* (1867), Paris is observed and shrewdly appraised by a fictitious American-trained businessman, M. Graindorge. Taine describes Graindorge as follows: "His learning was not extensive, but he had travelled, and his mind was well stored with facts. . . . There was nothing of the man-of-letters in his conversation, save its cold irony. But as he was fond of reading, and had received a classical education, he could and did write very much as other people do." Apparently Taine approved, to some degree, of Graindorge's toughmindedness and was willing to accept his strictures on Paris. Similarly, Taine appreciated William Dean Howells's *Rise of Silas Lapham* (1885), a sympathetic, but not uncritical, account of a Yankee businessman, and recommended the translation of Howells's novel to a French publisher as follows: "I have read it in English with the greatest pleasure and admiration; it is the best novel written by an American, the most like those of Balzac, the most profound, and the most comprehensive. Silas, his wife and two daughters are new types to us, very solid and complete." (Quoted in the original French in a letter by John Durand, Taine's American translator, to Howells, April 13, 1888.)

Walt Whitman's review (unpublished until 1957) of Taine's *History of English Literature* was probably written between 1871 and 1873. Unlike Eggleston and Garland, Whitman does not extract from Taine a program for Realism so much as a prophetic lesson for all American literature. In the lesson he derives from Taine, Whitman reaffirms the theory he had recently exhorted in *Democratic Vistas* (1871), that a vital American literature would grow only from a burgeoning democracy and that the national poet would perfectly embody these democratic principles.

Bibliography: For a modern account of Taine, see Harry Levin, "Literature as an Institution," *Accent,* 5 (1946), 159–68. Everett Carter, *Howells and the Age of Realism* (Boston: 1964), has interesting references to Taine in America. Norman Foerster's chapter on Whitman as critic in *American Criticism* (New York: 1928) is still good.

Whitman's "Taine's *History of English Literature*" was first published from manuscript by Roger Asselineau in *Etudes Anglaises, 2* (1957), 128–38. The essay, which appears here in extracted form, is reprinted with the kind permission of Charles E. Feinberg of Detroit, who owns the original manuscript. For a textual examination of the manuscript, see Asselineau's edition. The italicized words and phrases indicate the underlining in the original manuscript.

TAINE'S *HISTORY OF ENGLISH LITERATURE:* A LESSON FOR AMERICA

(ca. 1871)

THIS is the first *elaborated* History, comprehending many centuries, of a concrete and consecutive National Literature, *written* according to the school of modern criticism born in France of Ste Beuve, and which, *after being accepted by the best intellects of Europe,* has already *crossed the Channel* & settled in the British Islands—though *it would seem hardly* visible in the literary organs of the United States.

The author begins by saying that History, (*i.e.,* the science or writing of History,) has been revolutionized in our time by the study of nations' literatures. Concerning his theme in this book, he says, If it were asked, why not leave the narration of English literature to the English themselves, who stand in the midst thereof, & must know best, the answer is, A stranger still possesses some marked advantages—association has not blunted his perceptions—he is more open to & struck by the principal characteristics—he stands off, and is *uncommitted &* impartial. It will be an advantage also to judge from the outside, from the points of view of universal, and even *from opposite and* foreign standards.

He selects English Literature, for reasons. Most nations, the ancient Latins, modern Germany, Spain, Italy, &c., are in *their* literary development, more or less defective, and the consecutiveness broken. Only ancient Greece and modern France & England offer a complete series of great significant *continued* monuments.

After an Introduction critically giving his general views, Taine *presents,* (Book I, Chapter I, "The Source") the old Saxon & Scandinavian ancestry of the race whose literature he is to *call up &* review. He brings forward & describes the birth-fountains, the *pre-Christian* Germans and Norsemen, savage, self-willed, piratical, murderous with certain instincts *of* nobility,—half-heroes half-felons, with crude ideas of freedom, with the institutions of the family and monogamy & *strong in* fealty & friendship. All those *far-back* tribes in their hardihood, revelry *brutal appetite* for blood, are *set* before us—*and not only the persons but places.* The soil, sea, sky, climate—characteristics incidents & scraps from their history—are outlined, *the race brought forward* step by step. The poems, Pagan on to Christian—the Edda, Beowulf, *the* Chronicles, Hymns of Caedmon—are noted. . . .

And now having given the foregoing *abregé* I would say that, *above all the narrative & fine writing,* the main matter of the volumes is this master-critic's new philosophy and presentation of national Literature. For it is to be deliberately said that the difference between Taine's theory, of the body, the *corpus* of a nation's Literature, and the theory & treatment even of the best of the orthodox critics and writers of its "Histories", so far, is *substantially* the difference between the theory & treatment of a first-class anatomist or sculptor, and those of a first-class tailor or milliner.

Note, *indeed,* the direct & indirect answer by the Frenchman to the question, What is a nation's literature? A nation says Taine, is analogous to a *Man*—only it lives centuries, thousands of years, instead of sixty or 70 years. Suppose of any famous man we had a succession of authentic *identical* portraits of him, & similar pictures of the principal events of his life,—Well, the *literature* of a nation is such a series of pictures and portraits of *it.* Inside of all literature, he sees the *individual or aggregate* living human being, or *community,* yearning to *deposit* some record of his *or its idiosyncratic self,* his *day & surroundings* his developement, [sic] his sense of beauty or [illegible].

With respect to the past, a book, a poem, a religious treatise, a code of laws, is as the mould, the shell, left by an animal which itself has lived & perished. The animal under and behind the shell, the poem, the book, was *Man.* You must study the shell to find out what kind of man. You do not investigate in it an isolated thing, a mere abstract curiosity or beautiful object, to be judged by itself, but in reference to

its antecedents, and in connection, place, time, the race, the surroundings, the epoch. Only in such amplitude of ever expanding
radiations and references do you get at any fine literary production's
real character and meaning. Men & women, the suggestion and
certificates of them, their customs, beliefs, physiologies, vices,
virtues, in Greece, Syria, Egypt, India, Rome—such are the animals
you seek to restore to life, however long gone, by these fossils.

The more a book represents important sentiments, & artistically
expresses (however indirectly) the characteristic facts & spirit of its
author, age, and land, the higher, *according to Taine,* its place in
literature. To a grand literature, bracing, exhilarating, breathing the
breath, the nourishment, of proud, active, free, religious, joyous,
sympathetic, clean-bodied races of men & women, all their political
constitutions, worldly prosperity, sectarian churches, & *even their
erudition,* are comparatively of inferior importance. Following Taine
to his conclusions, there is no real & *lasting* history for any nation
except *what is in due time educed* out of its *original* literature, its *own
native* works of art, poems, bibles, *schools of philosophy,* tragedies,
comedies, fables, *legends, songs, oration.* &c.

After the method laid down, Taine gives, (Introduction, Sec. VII,)
a profound analysis of the sects & religions of different races & eras,
in their connection with the literature of those races. He is very
vivacious all through the *work* & skips from theme to theme, without
attempting connection. But there is nevertheless the largest & most
comprehensive connection. He illustrates *as* copiously, *as* Buckle
and Darwin.

It is almost superfluous to add that according to this treatment, the
question of the literature of a nation expands to hitherto unknown
proportions, & comprehends all. It does not *only not* stand *separate,*
any more than one limb of the body but is *little or nothing unless*
connected with & *has reference to* every part of Humanity—and all
that goes to make up civilization, *nationality* & progress. Politics, the
human physiology, religion, the emotions, the race-stock, language,
the peculiar meanings, genius of a people, all their idiopathies and
local influences, whether they *tend to* gravity or gayety, *to independence or servility*—and a hundred other *facts* & considerations, are
embraced *in it, & underlie it.*

A national dogma or poem is little or nothing abstractly in itself;
look at the people who have made it. When we read a Greek tragedy
we lose *all that is vital about it* unless we realize & *resume* to ourselves

the Greeks—that is men who live half naked in the gymnasia, or in the public squares, under a glowing sky, face to face with the most noble landscapes, bent on making their bodies nimble & strong, on conversing, discussing, voting, carrying on patriotic piracies, but for the rest lazy and temperate with three urns for their furniture, two anchovies in a jar of oil for their food, waited on by slaves, so as to give them leisure to cultivate their understanding & exercise their limbs, with no desire beyond that of having the most beautiful town, the most beautiful processions, the most beautiful ideas, the most beautiful men. And so of an Indian Purana, *you must* imagine the antecedents, *perhaps* the present facts, customs, the chant, the catechism: *the motif, the* basis, is the man who acts, the man corporeal and visible who eats, walks, fights, labors. *The ostent is always deceptive.* Beneath the *real* thing, the person visible, is a more *real* thing, person, invisible. That is what we are after.

There is only one work to be mentioned with this of Taine, namely Ticknor's *History of Spanish Literature.* That is equally truthful, & consecutive, & full in its material presentations—has all the corporeal body—a great work—yet lacks the philosophic plan, the vital fusion, that breathes the breath of life through Taine's *volumes* & makes them an electric entirety, a living soul.

Finally, it is to be said of these Volumes, that they & the theories out of which they arise, contain lessons of incalculable value to the United States, lighting up the present, & full of significant warning for the future.

FRANK NORRIS

(1870–1902)

Zola as a Romantic Writer

NATURALISM as a literary movement, with its debt to Taine's theories and its stress on scientific determinism, found its foremost French exponent in Émile Zola (1840–1902). Zola, in his *Rougon-Macquart* series (1871–1893), attempted to trace, from novel to novel, the hereditary and environmental influences on five successive genera-tions. His naturalistic theories, not always consistent with his artistic practice, were incorporated in several essays, chiefly *Le Roman Expérimental* (1880), written after reading a scientific study, Claude Bernard's *Introduction à l'étude de la médecine expérimentale* (1865). Zola wrote that the novelist, like the scientist, must employ the laboratory methods of observation and experiment.

Zola's novels met with hostile resistance in the United States during the 1870s and 1880s, not so much because of his scientific approach as because of his seeming devotion to the seamy and passionate. The generation that accepted Balzac was not yet prepared to approve of Zola. Thomas Sergeant Perry, whose notices in the *Atlantic Monthly* during the 1870s had helped the cause of realistic fiction (Turgenev was the novelist he most admired), nevertheless opposed Zola's work because he regarded it as animalistic and vulgar. Henry James, in an 1880 review of *Nana*, likewise displayed his antagonism: "On what authority does M. Zola represent nature to us as a combination of the cesspool and the house of prostitution?" James referred to Zola's "singular foulness of imagination." Oliver Wendell Holmes, physician, novelist, and "Autocrat of the Breakfast Table," in *Over the Teacups* (1891), attacked both Flaubert's *Madame Bovary* (1857) and Zola as sensationalistic, lacking the proper modesty of science. In the 1890s, however, Zola and the Naturalism he represented began to win favor. In his extended essay of 1903 on Zola, Henry James, reversing himself almost completely, termed Zola's work "one of the few most constructive achievements of our time."

Among the young naturalistic writers of the 1890s, which included Stephen Crane and Theodore Dreiser, Frank Norris was most indebted to Zola. Even as an undergraduate at the University of California, he would stroll across ths campus with a copy of Zola under his arm. In his brief but active literary career, the influence of Zola often revealed itself. Similarities have been drawn betweeen *McTeague* (1899) and *L'Assommoir* (1877), between *Vandover and the Brute* (1914) and *La Bête Humaine* (1890), between *The Octopus* (1901) and *Germinal* (1885). Leon Howard has called *McTeague* "the best example of French naturalism in nineteenth-century American literature."

In the selection that follows, "Zola as a Romantic Writer," Norris interprets Zola as transcending the realism exemplified by Howells because Zola adds to Realism the romantic and colorful qualities associated with Hugo. Though Zola's settings are often lower-class, his novels vibrate with romantic excitement. Clearly, Norris recognized in Zola not only a new science but a new vividness that the realistic school in America did not provide. Norris, in a sense, turns around the argument put forth by Holmes and the earlier James—that Zola was more sensationalistic than realistic.

Of course, Naturalism in American fiction did not derive simply from Zola. Stephen Crane never professed an allegiance to Zola, though some scholars have seen resemblances between *La Débâcle* (1892) and *The Red Badge of Courage* (1895), between Zola's streetwalkers and Maggie. Dreiser wrote *Sister Carrie* (1900) before reading Zola, and generally was more affected by Balzac.

Bibliography: On Zola's general influence, see Albert J. Salvan's *Zola aux Etats-Unis* (Providence, R.I.: 1943). Studies of Norris's debts to Zola are Lars Ahnebrink, *The Influence of Emile Zola on Frank Norris* (English trans., Cambridge, Mass.: 1947) and Marius Biencourt, *Une Influence du Naturalisme Français en Amerique: Frank Norris* (Paris: 1933). Pertinent, too, are *The Literary Criticism of Frank Norris,* ed. Donald Pizer (Austin: 1964) and Charles C. Walcutt, *American Literary Naturalism, A Divided Stream* (Minneapolis: 1956). Ahnebrink, in *The Beginnings of Naturalism in American Fiction: 1891–1903* (New York: 1961) stresses foreign influences. The question of Zola's influence on Crane is discussed in R. W. Stallman's *Stephen Crane: A Biography* (New York: 1968).

Norris's essay appeared in the San Francisco *Wave*, 15 (June 27, 1896), 3.

ZOLA AS A ROMANTIC WRITER
(1896)

IT IS CURIOUS to notice how persistently M. Zola is misunderstood. How strangely he is misinterpreted even by those who conscientiously admire the novels of the "man of the iron pen." For most people Naturalism has a vague meaning. It is a sort of inner circle of realism—a kind of diametric opposite of romanticism, a theory of fiction wherein things are represented "as they really are," inexorably, with the truthfulness of a camera. This idea can be shown to be far from right, that Naturalism, as understood by Zola, is but a form of romanticism after all.

Observe the methods employed by the novelists who profess and call themselves "realists"—Mr. Howells, for instance. Howells's characters live across the street from us, they are "on our block." We know all about them, about their affairs, and the story of their lives. One can go even further. We ourselves are Mr. Howells's characters, so long as we are well behaved and ordinary and bourgeois, so long as we are not adventurous or not rich or not unconventional. If we are otherwise, if things commence to happen to us, if we kill a man or two, or get mixed up in a tragic affair, or do something on a large scale, such as the amassing of enormous wealth or power or fame, Mr. Howells cuts our acquaintance at once. He will have none of us if we are out of the unusual.

This is the real Realism. It is the smaller details of every-day life, things that are likely to happen between lunch and supper, small passions, restricted emotions, dramas of the reception-room, tragedies of an afternoon call, crises involving cups of tea. Every one will admit there is no romance here. The novel is interesting—which is after all the main point—but it is the commonplace tale of commonplace people made into a novel of far more than commonplace charm. Mr. Howells is not uninteresting; he is simply not romantic. But that Zola should be quoted as a realist, and as a realist of realists, is a strange perversion.

Reflect a moment upon his choice of subject and character and episode. The Rougon-Macquart live in a world of their own; they are not of our lives any more than are the Don Juans, the Jean Valjeans, the Gil Blases, the Marmions, or the Ivanhoes. We, the bourgeois, the commonplace, the ordinary, have no part nor lot in the *Rougon-Macquart*, in *Lourdes*, or in *Rome*; it is not our world, not because our social position is different, but because we are *ordinary*. To be noted of M. Zola we must leave the rank and file, either run to the fore-front of the marching world, or fall by the roadway; we must separate ourselves; we must become individual, unique. The naturalist takes no note of common people, common in so far as their interests, their lives, and the things that occur in them are common, are ordinary. Terrible things must happen to the characters of the naturalistic tale. They must be twisted from the ordinary, wrenched out from the quiet, uneventful round of every-day life, and flung into the throes of a vast and terrible drama that works itself out in unleashed passions, in blood, and in sudden death. The world of M. Zola is a world of big things; the enormous, the formidable, the terrible, is what counts; no teacup tragedies here. Here Nana holds her monstrous orgies, and dies horribly, her face distorted to a frightful mask; Etienne Lantier, carried away by the strike of coal miners of *Le Voreux*, (the strike that is almost war), is involved in the vast and fearful castastrophe that comes as a climax of the great drama; Claude Lantier, disappointed, disillusioned, acknowledging the futility of his art after a life of effort, hangs himself to his huge easel; Jacques Lantier, haunted by an hereditary insanity, all his natural desires hideously distorted, cuts the throat of the girl he loves, and is ground to pieces under the wheels of his own locomotive; Jean Macquart, soldier and tiller of the fields, is drawn into the war of 1870, passes through the terrible scenes of Sedan and the Siege of Paris only to bayonet to death his truest friend and sworn brother-at-arms in the streets of the burning capital.

Everything is extraordinary, imaginative, grotesque even, with a vague note of terror quivering throughout like the vibration of an ominous and low-pitched diapason. It is all romantic, at times unmistakably so, as in *Le Rêve* or *Rome*, closely resembling the work of the greatest of all modern romanticists, Hugo. We have the same huge dramas, the same enormous scenic effects, the same love of the extraordinary, the vast, the monstrous, and the tragic.

Naturalism is a form of romanticism, not an inner circle of realism. Where is the realism in the *Rougon-Macquart*? Are such things likely to happen between lunch and supper? That Zola's work is not purely romantic as was Hugo's, lies chiefly in the choice of Milieu. These great terrible dramas no longer happen among the personnel of a feudal and Renaissance nobility, those who are in the fore-front of the marching world, but among the lower—almost the lowest—classes; those who have been thrust or wrenched from the ranks, who are falling by the roadway. This is not romanticism—this is drama of the people, working itself out in blood and ordure. It is not realism. It is a school by itself, unique, somber, powerful beyond words. It is naturalism.

WILLIAM DEAN HOWELLS

(1837–1920)

Emile Zola

WILLIAM DEAN HOWELLS, in a long and productive career, remained the chief American advocate of Realism, both in the example set in his own fiction and in his writings on fiction. His encouragement of many American writers, as diverse as Abraham Cahan and Hamlin Garland, was both generous and far-sighted. True, he was particularly attuned to the "smiling aspects of life" (see, as a good example, his review of Jean François Marmontel's *Memoirs* in the *Atlantic Monthly*, 41 [1878], 332–43); and a seeming timidity in facing the uglier realities has marred his later reputation. Leslie Fiedler remarks that, in forty realistic novels, Howells never set up an adulterous relationship. He preferred a realism devoted to the ordinary, in the manner of Jane Austin or Turgenev, and untouched by an unnatural excitement. Thus, in *Criticism and Fiction* (1891), he takes Balzac's *Le Père Goriot* to task for being "full of a malarial restlessness, wholly alien to healthful art."

Yet Howells's social conscience and his literary sensitivity made him respond affirmatively, and sometimes enthusiastically, to a later generation of writers who went beyond the limitations of his own practice and personal preference, including the young American naturalistic writers Crane and Norris, and international figures of controversy like Ibsen and Zola. In 1902 both Zola and his young American disciple, Frank Norris, died within a month of each other, and Howells wrote successive literary estimates in the *North American Review*, vol. 175; the essay of Zola appeared in November, 1902; the one on Norris a month later.

Whereas Norris thought of Zola's "Romanticism," his more vivid qualities, as lending Zola's realism a greater excitement (indeed, this excitement seemed to Norris the essence of Naturalism), Howells thinks of these "Romantic" qualities, in realistic contexts, as

144

paradoxical, contributing an inconsistency to Zola's work. Typically, Howells is moved by Zola's humanitarianism. In addition, Howells faces earlier charges leveled against Zola for immorality, and asserts that Zola seems indecent to him at times, but never immoral. In fact, Howells continues, Zola ultimately is sternly moralistic. Although Howells defended Zola in this essay, even with fervor, he did not permit Zola's novels to appear in his living room, for fear that minors would peruse them.

Bibliography: A number of studies place Howells in the context of the battle for Realism and Naturalism, notably Edwin H. Cady's biographies: *The Road to Realism* and *The Realist at War* (Syracuse, N.Y.: 1956 and 1958, respectively).

This essay, reprinted here in its entirety, first appeared in the *North American Review*, 175 (November, 1902), 587–96.

ÉMILE ZOLA

(1902)

IN THESE TIMES of electrical movement, the sort of construction in the moral world for which ages were once needed, takes place almost simultaneously with the event to be adjusted in history, and as true a perspective forms itself as any in the past. A few weeks after the death of a poet of such great epical imagination, such great ethical force, as Émile Zola, we may see him as clearly and judge him as fairly as posterity alone was formerly supposed able to see and to judge the heroes that antedated it. The present is always holding in solution the elements of the future and the past, in fact; and whilst Zola still lived, in the moments of his highest activity, the love and hate, the intelligence and ignorance, of his motives and his work were as evident, and were as accurately the measure of progressive and retrogressive criticism, as they will be hereafter in any of the literary periods to come. There will never be criticism to appreciate him more justly, to depreciate him more unjustly, than that of his immediate contemporaries. There will never be a day when criticism will be of one mind about him, when he will no longer be a question, and will have become a conclusion.

A conclusion is an accomplished fact, something finally ended, something dead; and the extraordinary vitality of Zola, when he was doing the things most characteristic of him, forbids the notion of this in his case. Like every man who embodies an ideal, his individuality partook of what was imperishable in that ideal. Because he believed with his whole soul that fiction should be the representation, and in no measure the misrepresentation, of life, he will live as long as any history of literature survives. He will live as a question, a dispute, an affair of inextinguishable debate; for the two principles of the human mind, the love of the natural and the love of the unnatural, the real and the unreal, the truthful and the fanciful, are inalienable and indestructible.

I

Zola embodied his ideal inadequately, as every man who embodies an ideal must. His realism was his creed which he tried to make his deed; but, before his fight was ended, and almost before he began to forebode it a losing fight, he began to feel and to say (for to feel, with that most virtuous and veracious spirit, implied saying) that he was too much a romanticist by birth and tradition, to exemplify realism in his work. He could not be all to the cause he honored that other men were—men like Flaubert and Maupassant, and Tourguenieff and Tolstoy, and Galdós and Valdés—because his intellectual youth had been nurtured on the milk of romanticism at the breast of his mother-time. He grew up in the day when the great novelists and poets were romanticists, and what he came to abhor he had first adored. He was that pathetic paradox, a prophet who cannot practise what he preaches, who cannot build his doctrine into the edifice of a living faith.

Zola was none the less, but all the more, a poet in this. He conceived of reality poetically and always saw his human documents, as he began early to call them, ranged in the form of an epic poem. He fell below the greatest of the Russians, to whom alone he was inferior, in imagining that the affairs of men group themselves strongly about a central interest to which they constantly refer, and after whatever excursions definitely or definitively return. He was not willingly an epic poet, perhaps, but he was an epic poet, nevertheless; and the imperfection of his realism began with the perfection of his form. Nature is sometimes dramatic, though never on the hard and fast terms of the theatre, but she is almost never epic; and Zola was always epic. One need only think over his books and his subjects to be convinced of this: *"L'Assommoir"* and drunkenness; *"Nana"* and harlotry; *"Germinale"* and strikes; *"L'Argent"* and money getting and losing in all its branches; *"Pot-Bouille"* and the cruel squalor of poverty; *"La Terre"* and the life of the peasant; *"Le Debâcle"* and the decay of imperialism. The largest of these schemes does not extend beyond the periphery described by the centrifugal whirl of its central motive, and the least of the Rougon-Macquart series is of the same epicality as the grandest. Each is bound to a thesis, but reality is bound to no thesis. You cannot say where it begins or where it leaves off; and it will not allow you to say precisely what its meaning or argument is. For this reason, there are no such perfect pieces of realism as the plays of Ibsen, which have all or each a thesis, but do not hold themselves bound to prove it, or even fully to state it; after these, for reality, come the novels of Tolstoy, which are of a direction so profound because so patient of aberration and exception.

We think of beauty as implicated in symmetry, but there are distinctly two kinds of beauty: the symmetrical and the unsymmetrical, the beauty of the temple and the beauty of the tree. Life is no more symmetrical than a tree, and the effort of art to give it balance and proportion is to make it as false in effect as a tree clipped and trained to a certain shape. The Russians and the Scandinavians alone seem to have risen to a consciousness of this in their imaginative literature, though the English have always unconsciously obeyed the law of our being in their generally crude and involuntary formulations of it. In the northern masters there is no appearance of what M. Ernest Dupuy calls the joiner-work of the French fictionists; and there is, in the process, no joiner-work in Zola, but the final effect is joiner-work. It is a temple he builds, and not a tree he plants and lets grow after he has planted the seed, and here he betrays not only his French school but his Italian instinct.

In his form, Zola is classic, that is regular, symmetrical, seeking the beauty of the temple rather than the beauty of the tree. If the fight in his day had been the earlier fight between classicism and romanticism, instead of romanticism and realism, his nature and tradition would have ranged him on the side of classicism, though, as in the later event, his feeling might have been romantic. I think it has been the error of criticism not to take due account of his Italian origin, or to recognize that he was only half French, and that this half was his superficial half. At the bottom of his soul, though not perhaps at the bottom of his heart, he was Italian, and of the great race which in every science and every art seems to win the primacy when it will. The

French, through the rhetoric of Napoleon III., imposed themselves on the imagination of the world as the representatives of the Latin race, but they are the least and the last of the Latins, and the Italians are the first. To his Italian origin Zola owed not only the moralistic scope of his literary ambition, but the depth and strength of his personal conscience, capable of the austere puritanism which underlies the so-called immoralities of his books, and incapable of the peculiar lubricity which we call French, possibly to distingiush it from the lubricity of other people rather than to declare it a thing solely French. In the face of all public and private corruptions his soul is as Piagnone as Savonarola's, and the vices of Arrabbiati, small and great, are always his text, upon which he preaches virtue.

II

Zola is to me so vast a theme that I can only hope here to touch his work at a point or two, leaving the proof of my sayings mostly to the honesty of the reader. It will not require so great an effort of his honesty now, as it once would, to own that Zola's books, though often indecent, are never immoral, but always most terribly, most pitilessly moral. I am not saying now that they ought to be in every family library, or that they could be edifyingly committed to the hands of boys and girls; one of our first publishing houses is about to issue an edition even of the Bible "with those passages omitted which are usually skipped in reading aloud"; and it is always a question how much young people can be profitably allowed to know; how much they do know, they alone can tell. But as to the intention of Zola in his books, I have no doubt of its righteousness. His books may be, and I suppose they often are, indecent, but they are not immoral; they may disgust, but they will not deprave; only those already rotten can scent corruption in them, and these, I think, may be deceived by effuvia from within themselves.

It is to the glory of the French realists that they broke, one and all, with the tradition of the French romanticists that vice was or might be something graceful, something poetic, something gay, brilliant, something superior almost, and at once boldly presented it in its true figure, its spiritual and social and physical squalor. Beginning with Flaubert in his "*Madame Bovary*," and passing through the whole line of their studies in morbid anatomy, as the "*Germinie Lacerteux*" of the Goncourts, as the "*Bel-Ami*" of Maupassant, and as all the books of Zola, you have portraits as veracious as those of the

Russians, or those of Defoe, whom, indeed, more than any other master, Zola has made me think of in his frankness. Through his epicality he is Defoe's inferior, though much more than his equal in the range and implication of his work.

A whole world seems to stir in each of his books; and, though it is a world altogether bent for the time being upon one thing, as the actual world never is, every individual in it seems alive and true to the fact. M. Brunetière says Zola's characters are not true to the French fact; that his peasants, working-men, citizens, soldiers are not French, whatever else they may be; but this is merely M. Brunetière's word against Zola's word, and Zola had as good opportunities of knowing French life as M. Brunetière, whose æsthetics, as he betrays them in his instances, are of a flabbiness which does not impart conviction. Word for word, I should take Zola's word as to the fact, not because I have the means of affirming him more reliable, but because I have rarely known the observant instinct of poets to fail, and because I believe that every reader will find in himself sufficient witness to the veracity of Zola's characterizations. These, if they are not true to the French fact, are true to the human fact; and I should say that in these the reality of Zola, unreal or ideal in his larger form, his epicality, vitally resided. His people live in the memory as entirely as any people who have ever lived; and, however devastating one's experience of them may be, it leaves no doubt of their having been.

III

It is not much to say of a work of literary art that it will survive as a record of the times it treats of, and I would not claim high value for Zola's fiction because it is such a true picture of the Second Empire in its decline; yet, beyond any other books I just now think of, his books have the quality that alone makes novels historical. That they include everything, that they do justice to all sides and phases of the period, it would be fatuous to expect, and ridiculous to demand. It is not their epical character alone that forbids this; it is the condition of every work of art, which must choose its point of view, and include only the things that fall within a certain scope. One of Zola's polemical delusions was to suppose that a fiction ought not to be selective, and that his own fictions were not selective, but portrayed the fact without choice and without limitation. The fact was that he was always choosing, and always limiting. Even a map chooses and limits, far more a picture. Yet this delusion of Zola's and its affirmation resulted in no end of misunderstanding. People said the noises of the streets, which he supposed himself to have given with graphophonic fulness and variety, were not music; and they were quite right. Zola, as far as his effects were voluntary, was not giving them music; he openly loathed the sort of music they meant just as he openly loathed art, and asked to be regarded as a man of science rather than an artist. Yet, at the end of the ends, he was an artist and not a man of science. His hand was perpetually selecting his facts, and shaping them to one epical result, with an orchestral accompaniment, which, though reporting the rudest noises of the street, the vulgarest, the most offensive, was, in spite of him, so reporting them that the result was harmony.

Zola was an artist, and one of the very greatest, but even before and beyond that he was intensely a moralist, as only the moralists of our true and noble time have been. Not Tolstoy, not Ibsen himself, has more profoundly and indignantly felt the injustice of civilization, or more insistently shown the falsity of its fundamental pretentions. He did not make his books a polemic for one cause or another; he was far too wise and sane for that; but when he began to write them they became alive with his sense of what was wrong and false and bad. His tolerance is less than Tolstoy's, because his resignation is not so great; it is for the weak sinners and not for the strong, while Tolstoy's, with that transcendent vision of his race, pierces the bounds where the shows of strength and weakness cease and become of a solidarity of error in which they are one. But the ethics of his work, like Tolstoy's, were always carrying over into his life. He did not try to live poverty and privation and hard labor, as Tolstoy does; he surrounded himself with the graces and the luxuries which his honestly earned money enabled him to buy; but when an act of public and official atrocity disturbed the working of his mind and revolted his nature, he could not rest again till he had done his best to right it.

IV

The other day Zola died (by a casualty which one fancies he would have liked to employ in a novel, if he had thought of it), and the man whom he had befriended at the risk of all he had in the world, his property, his liberty, his life itself, came to his funeral in disguise, risking again all that Zola had risked, to pay the last honors to his incomparable benefactor.

It was not the first time that a French literary man had devoted himself to the cause of the oppressed, and made it his personal affair, his charge, his inalienable trust. But Voltaire's championship of the persecuted Protestant had not the measure of Zola's championship of the persecuted Jew, though in both instances the courage and the persistence of the vindicator forced the reopening of the case and resulted in final justice. It takes nothing from the heroism of Voltaire to recognize that it was not so great as the heroism of Zola, and it takes nothing from the heroism of Zola to recognize that it was effective in the only country of Europe where such a case as that of Dreyfus would have been reopened; where there was a public imagination generous enough to conceive of undoing an act of immense public cruelty. At first this imagination was dormant, and the French people conceived only of punishing the vindicator along with the victim, for daring to accuse their processes of injustice. Outrage, violence, and the peril of death greeted Zola from his fellow-citizens, and from the authorities ignominy, fine, and prison. But nothing silenced or deterred him, and, in the swift course of moral adjustment characteristic of our time, an innumerable multitude of those who were ready a few years ago to rend him in pieces joined in paying tribute to the greatness of his soul, at the grave which received his body already buried under an avalanche of flowers. The government has not been so prompt as the mob, but with the history of France in mind, remembering how official action has always responded to the national impulses in behalf of humanity and justice, one cannot believe that the representatives of the French people will long remain behind the French people in offering reparation to the memory of one of the greatest and most heroic of French citizens. It is a pity for the government that it did not take part in the obsequies of Zola; it would have been well for the army, which he was falsely supposed to have defamed, to have been present to testify of the real service and honor he had done it. But, in good time enough, the reparation will be official as well as popular, and when the monument to Zola, which has already risen in the hearts of his countrymen, shall embody itself in enduring marble or perennial bronze, the army will be there to join in its consecration.

V

There is no reason why criticism should affect an equal hesitation. Criticism no longer assumes to ascertain an author's place in literature. It is very well satisfied if it can say something suggestive concerning the nature and quality of his work, and it tries to say this with as little of the old air of finality as it can manage to hide its poverty in.

After the words of M. Chaumie at the funeral, "Zola's life work was dominated by anxiety for sincerity and truth, an anxiety inspired by his great feelings of pity and justice," there seems nothing left to do but to apply them to the examination of his literary work. They unlock the secret of his performance, if it is any longer a secret, and they afford its justification in all those respects where without them it could not be justified. The question of immorality has been set aside, and the indecency has been admitted, but it remains for us to realize that anxiety for sincerity and truth, springing from the sense of pity and justice, makes indecency a condition of portraying human nature so that it may look upon its image and be ashamed.

The moralist working imaginatively has always had to ask himself how far he might go in illustration of his thesis, and he has not hesitated, or if he has hesitated, he has not failed to go far very far. Defoe went far. Richardson went far, Ibsen has gone far, Tolstoy has gone far, and Zola went farther than any of these, still he did not go so far as the immoralists have gone in the portrayal of vicious things to allure where he wished to repel. There is really such a thing as high motive and such a thing as low motive, though the processes are often so bewilderingly alike in both cases. The processes may confound us, but there is no reason why we should be mistaken as to motive, and as to Zola's motive I do not think M. Chaumie was mistaken. As to his methods, they by no means always reflected his intentions. He fancied himself working like a scientist who has collected a vast number of specimens, and is deducing principles from them. But the fact is, he was always working like an artist, seizing every suggestion of experience and observation, turning it to the utmost account, piecing it out by his invention, building it up into a structure of fiction where its origin was lost to all but himself, and often even to himself. He supposed that he was recording and classifying, but he was creating and vivifying. Within the bounds of his epical scheme, which was always, factitious, every person was so natural that his characters seemed like the characters of biography rather than of fiction. One does not remember them as one remembers the characters of most novelists. They had their being in a design which was meant to represent a state of things, to enforce an opinion of certain conditions; but they themselves were free agencies, bound by no allegiance to the general frame, and not apparently acting in behalf of the author, but only from their own individuality. At the moment of reading, they make the impression of an intense reality, and they remain real, but one recalls them as one recalls the people read of in last week's or last year's newspaper. What Zola did was less to import science and its methods into the region of fiction, than journalism and its methods; but in this he had his will only so far as his nature of artist would allow. He was no more a journalist than he was a scientist by nature; and, in spite of his intentions and in spite of his methods, he was essentially imaginative and involuntarily creative.

VI

To me his literary history is very pathetic. He was bred if not born in the worship of the romantic, but his native faith was not proof against his reason, as again his reason was not proof against his native faith. He preached a crusade against romanticism, and fought a long fight with it, only to realize at last that he was himself too romanticistic to succeed against it, and heroically to own his defeat. The hosts of romanticism swarmed back over him and his followers, and prevailed, as we see them still prevailing. It was the error of the realists whom Zola led, to suppose that people like truth in fiction better than falsehood; they do not; they like falsehood best; and if Zola had not been at heart a romanticist, he never would have cherished his long delusion, he never could have deceived with his vain hopes those whom he persuaded to be realistic, as he himself did not succeed in being.

He wished to be a sort of historiographer writing the annals of a family, and painting a period: but he was a poet, doing far more than this, and contributing to creative literature as great works of fiction as have been written in the epic form. He was a paradox on every side but one, and that was the human side, which he would himself have held far worthier than the literary side. On the human side, the civic side, he was what he wished to be, and not what any perversity of his elements made him. He heard one of those calls to supreme duty, which from time to time select one man and not another for the response which they require; and he rose to that duty with a grandeur which had all the simplicity possible to a man of French civilization. We may think that there was something a little too dramatic in the manner of his heroism, his martyry, and we may smile at certain turns of rhetoric in the immortal letter accusing the French nation of intolerable wrong, just as, in our smug Anglo-Saxon conceit, we laughed at the procedure of the emotional courts which he compelled to take cognizance of the immense misdeed other courts had as emotionally committed. But the event, however indirectly and involuntarily, was justice which no other people in Europe would have done, and perhaps not any people of this more enlightened continent.

The success of Zola as a literary man has its imperfections, its phases of defeat, but his success as a humanist is without flaw. He triumphed as wholly and as finally as it has ever been given a man to triumph, and he made France triumph with him. By his hand, she added to the laurels she had won in the war of American Independence, in the wars of the Revolution for liberty and equality, in the campaigns for Italian Unity, the imperishable leaf of a national acknowledgement of national error.

HENRY JAMES
(1843–1916)

The Lesson of Balzac
Gustave Flaubert
Guy de Maupassant

HENRY JAMES, novelist, critic, and man of letters, maintained that his earliest memory, in his second year of life, was of the Place Vendôme in Paris. When he was twelve, the great Galerie d'Apollon in the Louvre introduced him to the idea of style and to a "general sense of glory," a vision to haunt him later in dream and nightmare. As a young man of thirty-two, after having already written on French literature in American journals, James spent a year (1875–76) in Paris, contemplating permanent residence there, and, with a ready command of French, was present at gatherings attended by Ivan Turgenev, Gustave Flaubert, Alphonse Daudet, Guy de Maupassant, and Emile Zola. A frequenter of the French theater, too, he seems to have had a busy and productive time, and he corresponded on the Parisian scene for the New York *Tribune*. (Leon Edel and Ilse D. Lind have assembled these letters in *Parisian Sketches*, New York: 1957.)

But after his year's stay he elected to live in London instead of Paris. In the French capital, his admiration for French literary life notwithstanding, he felt he would remain a permanent outsider. One French literary shortcoming, it seemed to him, was the French interest in subjects that were morally reprehensible or superficial. But his stay in Paris confirmed his notions that French novelists took their craft more seriously than did their Anglo-American counterparts and that a novelist's profession was of the most serious import.

155

Even after moving to London, he was to give the greater part of his critical attention to the contemporary French novel. In his lifetime he wrote over ninety reviews and essays on French literature, particularly on fiction (seven on George Sand, an early literary affection), and these constitute probably the most impressive body of criticism on French literature written by an American.

Like his friends, William Dean Howells and Thomas Sergeant Perry, James learned to overcome his American-bred repugnance in dealing with the subject matter of French novels, despite their praiseworthy form and style. The moral objections recorded in his first volume of criticism, *French Poets and Novelists* (1878), tend to disappear in his later collections: *Partial Portraits* (1888), *Notes on London and Elsewhere* (1893), and his most mature critical volume, *Notes on Novelists* (1914). On what grounds, then, did he, in his later criticism, judge his French contemporaries? The later James stressed craft in fiction, but, even more, he emphasized the idea that the novelist must convey a complete "illusion of life." Fiction, for James, should not merely mirror external reality, but project the writer's intense awareness, his deepest knowledge, of characters and situations. Balzac, "the father of us all," James implied, painted reality more richly than other French novelists; this density of texture was paid for dearly, for it was the product of Balzac's mind, heart, and imagination. And so James probed Balzac's realism more deeply than did John Lothrop Motley, who had seen Balzac simply as the detached observer of society.

Employing the same criteria in rigorous fashion, James saw Flaubert's *Madame Bovary* (1857) as falling short of Balzacian excellence, for the main character embodies too limited a conception and therefore has too limited a life. Madame Bovary, diagrammed from the start, lacks the perceptive capacities the really intelligent human being possesses. At the same time, James recognized that Flaubert, with his absolute dedication to his art, had raised the status of the novelist to its highest dignity. Similarly, Maupassant, master of the concise statement, neglected the reflective side of human nature, and thus failed, according to James, to transmit a complete illusion of life. Zola, who created a splendid picture of late nineteenth-century France, nevertheless let his novels sometimes run beyond the boundaries of his experience. In his essay on Zola in *Notes on Novelists,* James recounted a conversation with Zola, in which Zola said he was going to make Rome the subject of his next work. However, Zola confessed he had never visited Italy except for a brief excursion to Genoa. The fiction that resulted, the Roman section of *Three Cities* (1896), James claimed, revealed Zola's lack of specific knowledge. Thus Zola seemed to violate one of James's chief tenets, that a true realism could emerge only from an author's deeply felt observation or experience.

James could point to these weaknesses, as he saw them, of the French masters because he loved their work yet wished to apply the highest critical standards.

Bibliography: In addition to his own collections, further essays on French literature by James can be found in *Literary Reviews and Essays by Henry James*, ed. Albert Modell (New York: 1957). A good study is Morris Roberts, *Henry James's Criticism* (Cambridge, Mass.: 1929). A documented study is Marie R. Garnier, *Henry James et la France* (Paris: 1927).

"The Lesson of Balzac" is from *The Questions of Our Speech* by Henry James (Boston: Houghton Mifflin, 1905), pp. 55–116; "Gustave Flaubert" first appeared as the Preface to an edition of *Madame Bovary* (New York: D. Appleton and Co., 1902); "Guy de Maupassant" first appeared in the *Fortnightly Review*, 49 (March, 1888), 364–86, and was reprinted in *Partial Portraits* (London: Macmillan, 1888), pp. 243–87. The three essays are reprinted here in excerpted form.

THE LESSON OF BALZAC

(1905)

. . . LET ME meanwhile frankly say that I speak of him, and can only speak, as a man of his own craft, an emulous fellow-worker, who has learned from him more of the lessons of the engaging mystery of fiction than from any one else, and who is conscious of so large a debt to repay that it has had positively to be discharged in installments; as if one could never have at once all the required cash in hand. . . .

He died, as we sufficiently remember, at fifty—worn out with work and thought and passion; the passion, I mean, that he had put into his mighty plan and that had ridden him like an infliction of the gods. He began, a friendless and penniless young provincial, to write early, and to write very badly, and it was not till well toward his thirtieth year, with the conception of the *Comédie Humaine,* as we all again remember, that he found his right ground, found his feet and his voice. This huge distributed, divided and subdivided picture of the life of France in his time, a picture bristling with imagination and information, with fancies and facts and figures, a world of special and general insight, a rank tropical forest of detail and specification, but with the strong breath of genius forever circulating through it and shaking the treetops to a mighty murmur, got itself hung before us in the space of twenty short years. The achievement remains one of the most inscrutable, one of the unfathomable, final facts in the history of art, and if, as I have said, the author himself has his own surpassing objectivity, it is just because of this challenge his figure constitutes for any other painter of life, inflamed with ingenuity, who should feel the temptation to represent or explain him. How represent, how explain him, as a concrete active energy? How depict him, we ask ourselves, *at* his huge conceived and accepted task, how reconcile such dissemination with such intensity, the collection and possession of so vast a number of facts with so rich a presentation of each? The elements of the world he set up before us, with all its insistent particulars, these elements were not, for him, a direct revelation—of so large a part of life is it true that we can know it only by living, and that living is the process that, in our mortal span, makes the largest demand on our time. How could a man have lived at large so much if, in the service of art, he had so much abstracted and condensed himself? How could he have so much abstracted and condensed himself if, in the service of life, he had felt and fought and acted, had labored and suffered, so much as a private in the ranks? The wealth and strength of his temperament indeed partly answer the question and partly obscure it. He could so extend his existence partly because he vibrated to so many kinds of contact and curiosity. To vibrate intellectually was his motive, but it magnified, all the while, it multiplied his experience. He could live at large, in short, because he was always living in the particular necessary, the particular intended connection—was always astride of his imagination, always charging, with his heavy, his heroic lance in rest, at every object that sprang up in his path. But as he was at the same time always fencing himself in against the personal adventure, the personal experience, in order to preserve himself for converting it into history, how did experience, in the immediate sense, still get itself saved?—or, to put it as simply as possible, where, with so strenuous a conception of the use of

material, was material itself so strenuously quarried? Out of what
mines, by what innumerable tortuous channels, in what endless
winding procession of laden chariots and tugging teams and marching elephants, did the immense consignments required for his work
reach him?. . . .

It is a question, you see, of *penetrating* into a subject; his corridors
always went further and further and further; which is but another
way of expressing his inordinate passion for detail. It matters
nothing—nothing for my present contention—that this extravagance
is also his great fault; in spite, too, of its all being detail vivified and
related, characteristic and constructive, essentially prescribed by the
terms of his plan. The relations of parts to each other are at moments
multiplied almost to madness—which is at the same time just why
they give us the measure of his hallucination, make up the greatness
of his intellectual adventure. His plan was to handle, primarily, not a
world of ideas, animated by figures representing these ideas; but the
packed and constituted, the palpable, provable world before him, by
the study of which ideas would inevitably find themselves thrown
up. If the happy fate is accordingly to *partake* of life, actively,
assertively, not passively, narrowly, in mere sensibility and suffer-
ance, the happiness has been greatest when the faculty employed has
been largest. We employ different faculties—some of us only our
arms and our legs and our stomach; Balzac employed most what he
possessed in largest quantity. This is where his work ceases in a
manner to mystify us—this is where we make out how he did quarry
his material: it is the sole solution to an otherwise baffling problem.
He collected his experience within himself; no other economy explains his achievement; this thrift alone, remarkable yet thinkable,
embodies the necessary miracle. His system of cellular confinement,
in the interest of the miracle, was positively that of a Benedictine
monk, leading his life within the four walls of his convent and bent,
the year round, over the smooth parchment on which, with won-
drous illumination and enhancement of gold and crimson and blue, he
inscribed the glories of the faith and the legends of the saints. Balzac's
view of himself was indeed in a manner the monkish one; he was most
at ease, while he wrought, in the white gown and cowl—an image of
him that the friendly art of his time has handed down to us. Only, as
happened, his subject of illumination was the legends not merely of
the saints, but of the much more numerous uncanonized strugglers

and sinners, an acquaintance with whose attributes was not all to be gathered in the place of piety itself; not even from the faintest ink of old records, the mild lips of old brothers, or the painted glass of church windows.

This is where envy does follow him, for to have so many other human cases, so many other personal predicaments to get into, up to one's chin, is verily to be able to get out of one's own box. And it was up to his chin, constantly, that he sank in his illusion—not, as the weak and timid in this line do, only up to his ankles or his knees. The figures he sees begin immediately to bristle with all their characteristics. Every mark and sign, outward and inward, that they possess; every virtue and every vice, every strength and every weakness, every passion and every habit, the sound of their voices, the expression of their eyes, the tricks of feature and limb, the buttons on their clothes, the food on their plates, the money in their pockets, the furniture in their houses, the secrets in their breasts, are all things that interest, that concern, that command him, and that have, for the picture, significance, relation and value. It is a prodigious multiplication of values, and thereby a prodigious entertainment of the vision—on the condition the vision can bear it. Bearing it—that is *our* bearing it—is a serious matter; for the appeal is truly to that faculty of attention out of which we are educating ourselves, as hard as we possibly can; educating ourselves with such complacency, with such boisterous high spirits, that we may already be said to have practically lost it—with the consequence that any work of art or of criticism making a demand on it is by that fact essentially discredited. It takes attention not only to thread the labyrinth of the *Comédie Humaine,* but to keep our author himself in view, in the relations in which we thus image him. But if we can muster it, as I say, in sufficient quantity, we thus walk with him in the great glazed gallery of his thought; the long, lighted and pictured ambulatory where the endless series of windows, on one side, hangs over his revolutionized, ravaged, yet partly restored and reinstated garden of France, and where, on the other, the figures and the portraits we fancy stepping down to meet him climb back into their frames, larger and smaller, and take up position and expression as he desired they shall look out and compose.

We have lately had a literary case of the same general family as the case of Balzac, and in presence of which some of the same speculations come up: I had occasion, not long since, after the death of Émile

Zola, to attempt an appreciation of *his* extraordinary performance—his series of the *Rougon-Macquart* constituting in fact, in the library of the fiction that can hope in some degree to live, a monument to the idea of plenitude, of comprehension and variety, second only to the *Comédie Humaine*. The question presented itself, in respect to Zola's ability and Zola's career, with a different proportion and value. I quite recognize, and wearing a much less distinguished face; but it was there to be met, none the less, on the very threshold, and all the more because this was just where he himself had placed it. His idea had been, from the first, in a word, to lose no time—as if one could have experience, even the mere amount requisite for showing others as having it, *without* losing time!—and yet the degree in which he too, so handicapped, has achieved valid expression is such as still to stagger us. He had had inordinately to simplify—had had to leave out the life of the soul, practically, and confine himself to the life of the instincts, of the more immediate passions, such as can be easily and promptly caught in the fact. He had had, in a word, to confine himself almost entirely to the impulses and agitations that men and women are possessed by in common, and to take them as exhibited in mass and number, so that, being writ larger, they might likewise be more easily read. He met and solved, in this manner, his difficulty—the difficulty of knowing, and of showing, of life, only what his "notes" would account for. But it is in the *waste*, I think, much rather—the waste of time, of passion, of curiosity, of contact—that true initiation resides; so that the most wonderful adventures of the artist's spirit are those, immensely quickening for his "authority," that are yet not reducible to his notes. It is exactly here that we get the difference between such a solid, square, symmetrical structure as *Les Rougon-Macquart*, vitiated, in a high degree, by its mechanical side, and the monument left by Balzac—without the example of which, I surmise, Zola's work would not have existed. The mystic process of the crucible, the transformation of the material under aesthetic heat, is, in the *Comedie Humaine*, thanks to an intenser and more submissive fusion, completer, and also finer; for if the commoner and more wayside passions and conditions are, in the various episodes there, at no time gathered into so large and so thick an illustrative bunch, yet on the other hand they are shown much more freely at play in the individual case—and the individual case it is that permits of supreme fineness. It is hard to say where Zola is fine; whereas it is often, for pages together, hard to say where Balzac is, even under the weight of his too ponderous personality, not. The most fundamental and general sign of the novel, from one desperate experiment to another, is its being everywhere an effort at *representation*—this is the beginning and the end of it: wherefore it was that one could say at last, with account taken of everything, that Zola's performance, on his immense scale, was an extraordinary show of representation imitated. The imitation, in places—notably and admirably, for instance, in *L'Assommoir*—breaks through into something that we take for reality; but, for the most part, the separating rift, the determining difference, holds its course straight, prevents the attempted process from becoming the sound, straight, whole thing that is given us by those who have really *bought* their information. This is where Balzac remains unshaken,—in our feeling that, with all his faults of pedantry, ponderosity, pretentiousness, bad taste and charmless form, his spirit has somehow paid for its knowledge. His subject is again and again the complicated human creature or human condition; and it is with these complications as if he knew them, as Shakespeare knew them, by his charged consciousness, by the history of his soul and the direct exposure of his sensibility. This source of supply he found, forever—and one may indeed say he mostly left—sitting at his fireside; where it constituted the company with which I see him shut up, and his practical intimacy with which, during such orgies and debauches of intellectual passion, might earn itself that name of high personal good fortune that I have applied. . . .

He at all events robustly loved the sense of another explored, assumed, assimilated identity—enjoyed it as the hand enjoys the glove when the glove ideally fits. My image indeed is loose; for what he liked was absolutely to get into the constituted consciousness, into all the clothes, gloves and whatever else, into the very skin and bones, of the habited, featured, colored, articulated form of life that he desired to present. How do we know given persons, for any purpose of demonstration, unless we know their situation for themselves, unless we see it from their point of vision, that is, from their point of pressing consciousness or sensation?—without our allowing for which there is no appreciation. Balzac loved his Valérie then as Thackeray did not love his Becky, or his Blanche Amory in *Pendennis*. But his prompting was not to expose her; it could only be, on the contrary,—intensely aware as he was of all the lengths she might go to, and paternally, maternally alarmed about them—to cover her up and protect her, in the interest of her special genius and freedom. All his impulse was to *la faire valoir,* to give her all her value, just as Thackeray's attitude was the opposite one, a desire positively to expose and desecrate poor Becky—to follow her up, catch her in the act, and bring her to shame: though with a mitigation, an admiration, an inconsequence, now and then wrested from him by an instinct finer, in his mind, than the so-called "moral" eagerness. The English writer wants to make sure, first of all, of your moral judgment; the French is willing, while it waits a little, to risk, for the sake of his subject and its interest, your spiritual salvation. Madame Marneffe, detrimental, fatal as she is, is "exposed," so far as anything in life, or in art, may be, by the working-out of the situation and the subject themselves; so that when they have done what they would, what they logically had to, with her, we are ready to take it from them. We do not feel, very irritatedly, very lecturedly, in other words with superfluous edification, that she has been sacrificed. Who can say, on the contrary, that Blanche Amory, in *Pendennis,* with the author's lash about her little bare white back from the first—who can feel that she has *not* been sacrificed, or that her little bareness and whiteness, and all the rest of her, have been, by such a process, presented as they had a right to demand?

It all comes back, in fine, to that respect for the liberty of the subject which I should be willing to name as *the* great sign of the painter of the first order. . . .

GUSTAVE FLAUBERT

(1902)

. . .Madame Bovary has a perfection that not only stamps it, but that makes it stand almost alone; it holds itself with such a supreme unapproachable assurance as both excites and defies judgment. For it deals not in the least, as to unapproachability, with things exalted or refined; it only confers on its sufficiently vulgar elements of exhibition a final unsurpassable form. The form is in *itself* as interesting, as active, as much of the essence of the subject as the idea, and yet so close is its fit and so inseparable its life that we catch it at no moment on any errand of its own. That verily is to *be* interesting—all round; that is to be genuine and whole. The work is a classic because the thing, such as it is, is ideally *done,* and because it shows that in such doing eternal beauty may dwell. A pretty young woman who lives, socially and morally speaking, in a hole, and who is ignorant, foolish, flimsy, unhappy, takes a pair of lovers by whom she is successively deserted; in the midst of the bewilderment of which, giving up her husband and her child, letting everything go, she sinks deeper into duplicity, debt, despair, and arrives on the spot, on the small scene itself of her poor depravities, at a pitiful tragic end. In especial she does these things while remaining absorbed in romantic intention and vision while fairly rolling in the dust. That is the triumph of the book as the triumph stands, that Emma interests us by the nature of her consciousness and the play of her mind, thanks to the reality and beauty with which those sources are invested. It is not only that they represent *her* state; they are so true, so observed and felt, and especially so shown, that they represent the state, actual or potential, of all persons like her, persons romantically determined. Then her setting, the medium in which she struggles, becomes in its way as important, becomes eminent with the eminence of art; the tiny world in which she revolves, the contracted cage in which she flutters, is hung out in space for her, and her companions in captivity there are as true as herself.

I have said enough to show what I mean by Flaubert's having in this picture expressed something of his intimate self, given his heroine something of his own imagination: a point precisely that brings me back to the restriction at which I just now hinted, in which M. Faguet fails to indulge and yet which is immediate for the alien reader. Our complaint is that Emma Bovary, in spite of the nature of her consciousness and in spite of her reflecting so much that of her creator, is really too small an affair. This, critically speaking, is in view both of the value and the fortune of her history, a wonderful circumstance. She associates herself with Frédéric Moreau in *L'Education* to suggest for us a question that can be answered, I hold, only to Flaubert's detriment. Emma taken alone would possibly not so directly press it, but in her company the hero of our author's second study of the "real" drives it home. Why did Flaubert choose, as special conduits of the life he proposed to depict, such inferior and in the case of Frédéric such abject human specimens? I insist only in respect of the latter, the perfection of Madame Bovary scarce leaving one much warrant for wishing anything other. Even here, however, the general scale and size of Emma, who is small even of her sort, should be a warning to hyperbole. If I say that in the matter of Frédéric at all events the answer is inevitably detrimental I mean that it weighs heavily on our author's general credit. He wished in each case to make a picture of experience—middling experience, it is true—and of the world close to him; but if he imagined nothing better for his purpose than such a heroine and such a hero, both such limited reflectors and registers, we are forced to believe it to have been by a defect of his mind. And that sign of weakness remains even if it be objected that the images in question were addressed to his purpose better than others would have been: the purpose itself then shows as inferior. L'Éducation sentimentale is a strange, an indescribable work, about which there would be many more things to say than I have space for, and all of them of the deepest interest. It is moreover, to simplify my statement, very much less satisfying a thing, less pleasing whether in its unity or its variety, than its specific predecessor. But take it as we will, for a success or a failure—M. Faguet indeed ranks it, by the measure of its quantity of intention, a failure, and I on the whole agree with him—the personage offered us as bearing the weight of the drama, and in whom we are invited to that extent to interest ourselves, leaves us mainly wondering what our entertainer could have been thinking of. He takes Frédéric Moreau on the threshold of life and conducts him to the extreme of maturity without apparently suspecting for a moment either our wonder or our protest—"Why, why him?" Frédéric is positively too poor for his part, too scant for his change; and we feel with a kind of embarrassment, certainly with a kind of compassion, that it is somehow the business of a protagonist to prevent in his designer an excessive waste of faith. When I speak of the faith in Emma Bovary as proportionately wasted I reflect on M. Faguet's judgment that she is from the point of view of deep interest richly or at least roundedly representative. Representative of what? he makes us ask even while granting all the grounds of misery and tragedy involved. The plea for her is the plea made for all the figures that live without evaporation under the painter's hand—that they are not only particular persons but types of their kind, and as valid in one light as in the other. It is Emma's "kind" that I question for this responsibility, even if it be inquired of me why I then fail to question that of Charles Bovary, in its perfection, or that of the inimitable, the immortal Homais. If we express Emma's deficiency as the poverty of her consciousness for the typical function, it is certainly not, one must admit, that she is surpassed in this respect either by her platitudinous husband or by his friend the pretentious apothecary. The difference is none the less somehow in the fact that they are respectively studies but of their character and office, which function in each expresses adequately *all* they are. It may be, I concede, because Emma is the only woman in the book that she is taken by M. Faguet as *femininely* typical, typical in the larger illustrative way, whereas the others pass with him for images specifically conditioned. Emma is the same for myself, I plead; she is conditioned to such an excess of the specific, and the specific in her case leaves out so many even of the commoner elements of conceivable life in a woman when we are invited to see that life as pathetic, as dramatic agitation, that we challenge both the author's and the critic's scale of importances. The book is a picture of the middling as much as they like, but does Emma attain even to *that*? Hers is a narrow middling even for a little imaginative person whose "social" significance is small. It is greater on the whole than her capacity of consciousness, taking this all round; and so, in a word, we feel her less illustrational that she might have been not only if the world had offered her more points of contact, but if she had had more of these to give it.

We meet Frédéric first, we remain with him long, as a *moyen,* a provincial bourgeois of the mid-century, educated and not without fortune, thereby with freedom, in whom the life of his day reflects itself. Yet the life of his day, on Flaubert's showing, hangs together with the poverty of Frédéric's own inward or for that matter outward life; so that, the whole thing being, for scale, intention and extension, a sort of epic of the usual (with the Revolution of 1848 introduced indeed as an episode), it affects us as an epic without air, without wings to lift it; reminds us in fact more than anything else of a huge balloon, all of silk pieces strongly sewn together and patiently blown up, but that absolutely refuses to leave the ground. The discrimination I here make as against our author is, however, the only one inevitable in a series of remarks so brief. What it really represents—and nothing could be more curious—is that Frédéric enjoys his position not only without the aid of a single "sympathetic" character of consequence, but even without the aid of one with whom we can directly communicate. Can we communicate with the central personage? or would we really if we could? A hundred times no, and if he himself can communicate with the people shown us as surrounding him this only proves him of their kind. Flaubert on his "real" side was in truth an ironic painter, and ironic to a tune that makes his final accepted state, his present literary dignity and "classic" peace, superficially anomalous. There is an explanation to which I shall immediately come; but I find myself feeling for a moment longer in presence of *L'Éducation* how much more interesting a writer may be on occasion by the given failure than by the given success. Successes pure and simple disconnect and dismiss him; failures—though I admit they must be a bit qualified—keep him in touch and in relation. Thus it is that as the work of a "grand écrivain" *L'Éducation,* large, labored, immensely "written," with beautiful passages and a general emptiness, with a kind of leak in its stored sadness, moreover, by which its moral dignity escapes—thus it is that Flaubert's ill-starred novel is a curiosity for a literary museum. Thus it is also that it suggests a hundred reflections, and suggests perhaps most of them directly to the intending laborer in the same field. If in short, as I have said, Flaubert is the novelist's novelist, this performance does more than any other toward making him so. . . .

It was a mistake, as I have already hinted, to propose to register in so mean a consciousness as that of such a hero so large and so mixed a quantity of life as *L'Éducation* clearly intends; and it was a mistake of the tragic sort that is a theme mainly for silence to have embarked on *Bouvard et Pécuchet* at all, not to have given it up sooner than be given up by it. But these were at the worst not wholly compromising blunders. What *was* compromising—and the great point is that it remained so, that nothing has an equal weight against it—is the unconsciousness of error in respect to the opportunity that would have counted as his finest. We feel not so much that Flaubert misses it, for that we could bear; but that he doesn't *know* he misses it is what stamps the blunder. . . .

May it not in truth be said that we practice our industry, so many of us, at relatively little cost just *because* poor Flaubert, producing the most expensive fictions ever written, so handsomely paid for it? It is as if this put it in our power to produce cheap and thereby sell dear; as if, so expressing it, literary honor being by his example effectively secure for the firm at large and the general concern, on its whole esthetic side, floated once for all, we find our individual attention free for literary and esthetic indifference. All the while we thus lavish our indifference the spirit of the author of *Madame Bovary,* in the

cross-light of the old room above the Seine, is trying to the last
admiration for the thing itself. That production puts the matter into a
nutshell: *Madame Bovary,* subject to whatever qualification, as
absolutely the most literary of novels, so literary that it covers us with
its mantle. It shows us once for all that there is no *intrinsic* call for a
debasement of the type. The mantle I speak of is wrought with
surpassing fineness, and we may always, under stress of whatever
charge of illiteracy, frivolity, vulgarity, flaunt it as the flag of the
guild. Let us therefore frankly concede that to surround Flaubert
with our consideration is the least return we can make for such a
privilege. . . .

GUY DE MAUPASSANT
(1888)

. . . M. DE MAUPASSANT neglects nothing that he possesses; he
cultivates his garden with admirable energy; and if there is a flower
you miss from the rich parterre, you may be sure that it could not
possibly have been raised, his mind not containing the soil for it. He
is plainly of the opinion that the first duty of the artist, and the thing
that makes him most useful to his fellow-men, is to master his
instrument, whatever it may happen to be.

His own is that of the senses, and it is through them alone, or
almost alone, that life appeals to him; it is almost alone by their help
that he describes it, that he produces brilliant works. They render
him this great assistance because they are evidently, in his constitution, extraordinarily alive; there is scarcely a page in all his twenty
volumes that does not testify to their vivacity. Nothing could be
further from his thought than to disavow them and to minimize their
importance. He accepts them frankly, gratefully, works them, re-
joices in them. If he were told that there are many English writers
who would be sorry to go with him in this, he would, I imagine,
staring, say that that is about what was to have been expected of the
Anglo-Saxon race, or even that many of them probably could not go
with him if they would. Then he would ask how our authors can be so
foolish as to sacrifice such a *moyen,* how they can afford to, and
exclaim, "They must be pretty works, those they produce, and give a
fine, true, complete account of life, with such omissions, such
lacunæ!" . . .

As regards the other sense, the sense *par excellence,* the sense which we scarcely mention in English fiction, and which I am not very sure I shall be allowed to mention in an English periodical, M. de Maupassant speaks for that, and of it, with extraordinary distinctness and authority. To say that it occupies the first place in his picture is to say too little; it covers in truth the whole canvas, and his work is little else but a report of its innumerable manifestations. These manifestations are not, for him, so many incidents of life; they are life itself, they represent the standing answer to any question that we may ask about it. He describes them in detail, with a familiarity and a frankness which leave nothing to be added; I should say with singular truth, if I did not consider that in regard to this article he may be taxed with a certain exaggeration. M. de Maupassant would doubtless affirm that where the empire of the sexual sense is concerned, no exaggeration is possible; nevertheless it may be said that whatever depths may be discovered by those who dig for them, the impression of the human spectacle for him who takes it as it comes has less analogy with that of the monkeys' cage than this admirable writer's account of it. I speak of the human spectacle as we Anglo-Saxons see it—as we Anglo-Saxons pretend we see it, M. de Maupassant would possibly say.

At any rate, I have perhaps touched upon this peculiarity sufficiently to explain my remark that his point of view is almost solely that of the senses. If he is a very interesting case, this makes him also an embarrassing one, embarrassing and mystifying for the moralist. I may as well admit that no writer of the day strikes me as equally so. To find M. de Maupassant a lion in the path—that may seem to some people a singular proof of want of courage; but I think the obstacle will not be made light of by those who have really taken the measure of the animal. We are accustomed to think, we of the English faith, that a cynic is a living advertisement of his errors, especially in proportion as he is a thoroughgoing one; and M. de Maupassant's cynicism, unrelieved as it is, will not be disposed of off-hand by a critic of a competent literary sense. Such a critic is not slow to perceive, to his no small confusion, that though, judging from usual premises, the author of *Bel-Ami* ought to be a warning, he somehow is not. His baseness, as it pervades him, ought to be written all over him; yet somehow there are there certain aspects—and those commanding, as the house agents—in which it is not the least to be perceived. It is easy to exclaim that if he judges life only from the point of view of the senses, many are the noble and exquisite things that he must leave out. What he leaves out has no claim to get itself considered till after we have done justice to what he takes in. It is this positive side of M. de Maupassant that is more remarkable—the fact that his literary character is so complete and edifying. . . .

II

He has produced a hundred short tales and only four regular novels; but if the tales deserve the first place in any candid appreciation of his talent it is not simply because they are so much the more numerous: they are also more characteristic; they represent him best in his originality, and their brevity, extreme in some cases, does not prevent them from being a collection of masterpieces. (They are very unequal, and I speak of the best.) The little story is but scantily relished in England, where readers take their fiction rather by the volume than by the page, and the novelist's idea is apt to resemble one of those old-fashioned carriages which require a wide court to turn round. In America, where it is associated pre-eminently with Hawthorne's name, with Edgar Poe's, and with that of Mr. Bret Harte, the short tale has had a better fortune. France, however, has been the land of its great prosperity, and M. de Maupassant had from the first the advantage of addressing a public accustomed to catch on, as the modern phrase is, quickly. In some respects, it may be said, he encountered prejudices too friendly, for he found a tradition of indecency ready made to his hand. I say indecency with plainness, though my indication would perhaps please better with another word, for we suffer in English from a lack of roundabout names for the *conte leste*—that element for which the French, with their *grivois,* their *gaillard,* their *égrillard,* their *gaudriole,* have so many convenient synonyms. It is an honored tradition in France that the little story, in verse or in prose, should be liable to be more or less obscene (I can think only of that alternative epithet), though I hasten to add that among literary forms it does not monopolize the privilege. Our uncleanness is less producible—at any rate it is less produced. . . .

It may seem that I have claimed little for M. de Maupassant, so far as English readers are concerned with him, in saying that after publishing twenty improper volumes he has at last published a twenty-first, which is neither indecent nor cynical. It is not this circumstance that has led me to dedicate so many pages to him, but the circumstance that in producing all the others he yet remained, for those who are interested in these matters, a writer with whom it was impossible not to reckon. This is why I called him, to begin with, so many ineffectual names: a rarity, a "case," an embarrassment, a lion in the path. He is still in the path as I conclude these observations, but I think that in making them we have discovered a legitimate way round. If he is a master of his art and it is discouraging to find what low views are compatible with mastery, there is satisfaction, on the other hand, in learning on what particular condition he holds his strange success. This condition, it seems to me, is that of having totally omitted one of the items of the problem, an omission which has made the problem so much easier that it may almost be described as a short cut to a solution. The question is whether it be a fair cut. M. de Maupassant has simply skipped the whole reflective part of his men and women—that reflective part which governs conduct and produces character. He may say that he does not see it, does not know it; to which the answer is, "So much the better for you, if you wish to describe life without it. The strings you pull are by so much the less numerous, and you can therefore pull those that remain with greater promptitude, consequently with greater firmness, with a greater air of knowledge." Pierre Roland, I repeat, shows a capacity for reflection, but I cannot think who else does, among the thousand figures who compete with him—I mean for reflection addressed to anything higher than the gratification of an instinct. We have an impression that M. d'Apreval and Madame de Cadour reflect, as they trudge back from their mournful excursion, but that indication is not pushed very far. An aptitude for this exercise is a part of disciplined manhood, and disciplined manhood M. de Maupassant has simply not attempted to represent. I can remember no instance in which he sketches any considerable capacity for conduct, and his women betray that capacity as little as his men. I am much mistaken if he has once painted a gentleman, in the English sense of the term. His gentlemen, like Paul Brétigny and Gontran de Ravenel, are guilty of the most extraordinary deflections. For those who are conscious of this element in life, look for it and like it, the gap will appear to be immense. It will lead them to say, "No wonder you have a contempt if that is the way you limit the field. No wonder you judge people roughly if that is the way you see them. Your work, on your premises, remains the admirable thing it is, but is your 'case' not adequately explained?"

The erotic element in M. de Maupassant, about which much more might have been said, seems to me to be explained by the same limitation, and explicable in a similar way wherever else its literature occurs in excess. The carnal side of man appears the most characteristic if you look at it a great deal; and you look at it a great deal if you do not look at the other, at the side by which he reacts against his weaknesses, his defeats. The more you look at the other, the less the whole business to which French novelists have ever appeared to English readers to give a disproportionate place—the business, as I may say, of the senses—will strike you as the only typical one. Is not this the most useful reflection to make in regard to the famous question of the morality, the decency, of the novel? It is the only one, it seems to me, that will meet the case as we find the case today. Hard and fast rules, *a priori* restrictions, mere interdictions (you shall not speak of this, you shall not look at that) have surely served their time, and will in the nature of the case never strike an energetic talent as anything but arbitrary. A healthy, living and growing art, full of curiosity and fond of exercise, has an indefeasible mistrust of rigid prohibitions. Let us then leave this magnificent art of the novelist to itself and to its perfect freedom, in the faith that one example is as good as another, and that our fiction will always be decent enough if it be sufficiently general. Let us not be alarmed at this prodigy (though prodigies are alarming) of M. de Maupassant, who is at once so licentious and so impeccable, but gird ourselves up with the conviction that another point of view will yield another perfection.

PART V

Paul Bourget Viewed By Two American Writers

Mark Twain: What Paul Bourget Thinks of Us (1895)
Edith Wharton: Souvenirs du Bourget d'Outre Mer (1936)

MARK TWAIN

(1835–1918)

What Paul Bourget
Thinks of Us

IT IS INTERESTING to compare Mark Twain's and Edith Wharton's
attitudes toward Paul Bourget, especially toward Bourget's *Outre-
Mer* (1895).

Paul Bourget (1852–1935), a French novelist, essayist,
and psychologist, demonstrated, in his best known novel, *The Disciple* (1889), the unsatisfactory moral consequences of scientific determinism. Several years later, at the invitation and expense of James
Gordon Bennett, publisher of the *New York Herald*, Bourget toured
the United States and recorded his impressions in *Outre-Mer*. This
book of travel and social comment registered, with aristocratic
dismay, American methods of dealing with the major issues of the
day, as Bourget saw them—science, democracy, and race. Bourget
witnessed in America the triumph of technology, the partial ascen-
dance of democracy, and a melting pot of the races. Democracy in the
United States, Bourget stated, though marked by individualism,
energy, and intensity of social life, is vitiated by materialism, the
growing disparity between rich and poor, the economic power of the
robber barons. Bourget thought that America revealed the wave of
the future, but, to this man of culture and of a traditional moral code,
the prospect was not entirely pleasant.

Outre-Mer irritated many American readers, including Mark
Twain; Edith Wharton, reminiscing years later, viewed the work
more favorably.

Twain's purpose is to defend the United States against Bourget's
strictures, even to claim its superiority. Thus, for Twain, American
materialism is the natural extension of the greater economic oppor-

175

tunities America offers its citizens. In addition, he asserts that Bourget's abstract, theoretical approach cannot help but miss its target; only novelists, and especially regional novelists, can convey insights into the various particulars that constitute American life. Twain, in his customary manner, also champions American Womanhood.

Twain's relations with the French defy expectations. Though the French, earlier in the nineteenth-century and periodically thereafter, sought the original, the intrinsic, the least European, in American authors, they have shown no great appreciation of Twain, one of the most inherently American of American authors. This lack of appreciation probably stems from the attitude held by many Frenchmen that Twain, like Whitman, partook of the "vulgar realism" that the French detected in the American scene at this time. In his turn, Twain made no friendly response to French culture. In *Innocents Abroad* (1869), he praised the efficiency and cleanliness of Paris under Louis Napoleon, but his later writings reveal an animosity unusual in so tolerant a man. In his biography *Mr. Clemens and Mark Twain* (1966), Justin Kaplan suggests that Twain's hostile reactions to the French and to what he thought of as French morality were largely self-protective, to cover divisions in his own troubled psyche. Despite his general animosity, Twain, who read French easily, was impressed by Zola's *La Terre* (1887)—a work which threw light into a rural corner of human suffering and which confirmed Twain's growing pessimism.

Bibliography: On Twain in France, see Roger Asselineau, *The Literary Reputation of Mark Twain from 1910 to 1950: A Critical Essay and a Bibliography* (Paris: 1954), and E. Hudson Long, *Mark Twain Handbook* (New York: 1957), pp. 431–32.

"What Paul Bourget Thinks of Us," which first appeared in the *North American Review,* 160 (January, 1895), 48–62, is reprinted here with omissions.

WHAT PAUL BOURGET THINKS OF US
(1895)

HE REPORTS the American joke correctly. In Boston they ask, How much does he know? in New York, How much is he worth? in Philadelphia, Who were his parents? And when an alien observer turns his telescope upon us—advertisedly in our own special interest—a natural apprehension moves us to ask, What is the diameter of his reflector?

I take a great interest in M. Bourget's chapters, for I know by the newspapers that there are several Americans who are expecting to get a whole education out of them; several who foresaw, and also foretold, that our long night was over, and a light almost divine about to break upon the land.

"His utterances concerning us are bound to be weighty and well timed."

"He gives us an object-lesson which should be thoughtfully and profitably studied."

These well-considered and important verdicts were of a nature to restore public confidence, which had been disquieted by questionings as to whether so young a teacher would be qualified to take so large a class as 70,000,000, distributed over so extensive a schoolhouse as America, and pull it through without assistance.

I was even disquieted myself, although I am of a cold, calm temperament and not easily disturbed. I feared for my country. And I was not wholly tranquilized by the verdicts rendered as above. It seemed to me that there was still room for doubt. In fact, in looking the ground over I became more disturbed than I was before. Many worrying questions came up in my mind. Two were prominent. Where had the teacher gotten his equipment? What was his method?

He had gotten his equipment in France.

Then as to his method: I saw by his own intimations that he was an Observer, and had a System—that used by naturalists and other scientists. The naturalist collects many bugs and reptiles and butterflies and studies their ways a long time patiently. By this means he is presently able to group these creatures into families and subdivisions of families by nice shadings of differences observable in their characters. Then he labels all those shaded bugs and things with nicely descriptive group names, and is now happy, for his great work is completed, and as a result he intimately knows every bug and shade of a bug there, inside and out. It may be true, but a person who was not a naturalist would feel safer about it if he had the opinion of the bug. I think it is a pleasant System, but subject to error.

The Observer of Peoples has to be a Classifier, a Grouper, a Deducer, a Generalizer, a Psychologizer; and first and last, a

Thinker. He has to be all these, and when he is at home, observing his own folk, he is often able to prove competency. But history has shown that when he is abroad observing unfamiliar peoples, the chances are heavily against him. He is then a naturalist observing a bug; with no more than a naturalist's chance of being able to tell the bug anything new about itself, and no more than a naturalist's chance of being able to teach it any new ways which it will prefer to its own.

To return to that first question. M. Bourget, as teacher, would simply be France teaching America. It seemed to me that the outlook was dark; almost Egyptian, in fact. What would the new teacher, representing France, teach us? Railroading? No. France knows nothing valuable about railroading. Steamshipping? No. France has no superiorities over us in that matter. Steamboating? No. French steamboating is still of Fulton's date—1809. Postal service? No. France is a back number there. Telegraphy? No, we taught her that ourselves. Journalism? No. Magazining? No, that is our own specialty. Government? No; Liberty, Equality, Fraternity, Nobility, Democracy, Adultery—the system is too variegated for our climate. Religion? No, not variegated enough for our climate. Morals? No, we cannot rob the poor to enrich ourselves. Novel-writing? No. M. Bourget and the others know only one plan, and when that is expurgated there is nothing left of the book.

I wish I could think what he is going to teach us. Can it be Deportment? But he experimented in that at Newport and failed to give satisfaction, except to a few. Those few are pleased. They are enjoying their joy as well as they can. They confess their happiness to the interviewer. They feel pretty striped, but they remember with reverent recognition that they had sugar between the cuts. True, sugar with sand in it, but sugar. And true, they had some trouble to tell which was sugar and which was sand, because the sugar itself looked just like the sand, and also had a gravelly taste; still, they know that the sugar was there, and would have been very good sugar indeed if it had been screened. Yes, they are pleased; not noisily so, but pleased; invaded, or streaked, as one may say, with little recurrent shivers of joy—subdued joy, so to speak, not the overdone kind. And they commune together, these, and massage each other with comforting sayings, in a sweet spirit of resignation and thankfulness, mixing these elements in the same proportions as the sugar and the sand, as a memorial, and saying, the one to the other and to the interviewer: "It was severe—yes, it was bitterly severe; but oh, how true it was; and it will do us so much good!"

If it isn't Deportment, what is left? It was at this point that I seemed to get on the right track at last. M. Bourget would teach us to know ourselves; that was it: he would reveal us to ourselves. That would be an education. He would explain us to ourselves. Then we should understand ourselves; and after that be able to go on more intelligently.

It seemed a doubtful scheme. He could explain *us* to *him*self—that would be easy. That would be the same as the naturalist explaining the bug to himself. But to explain the bug to the bug—that is a quite different matter. The bug may not know himself perfectly, but he knows himself better than the naturalist can know him, at any rate.

A foreigner can photograph the exteriors of a nation, but I think that that is as far as he can get. I think that no foreigner can report its interior—its soul, its life, its speech, its thought. I think that a knowledge of these things is acquirable in only one way; not two or four or six—*absorption;* years and years of unconscious absorption; years and years of intercourse with the life concerned; of living it, indeed; sharing personally in its shames and prides, its joys and griefs, its loves and hates, its prosperities and reverses, its shows and shabbinesses, its deep patriotisms, its whirlwinds of political passion, its adorations—of flag, and heroic dead, and the glory of the national name. Observation? Of what real value is it? One learns peoples through the heart, not the eyes or the intellect.

There is only one expert who is qualified to examine the souls and the life of a people and make a valuable report—the native novelist. This expert is so rare that the most populous country can never have fifteen conspicuously and confessedly competent ones in stock at one time. This native specialist is not qualified to begin work until he has been absorbing during twenty-five years. How much of his competency is derived from conscious "observation"? The amount is so slight that it counts for next to nothing in the equipment. Almost the whole capital of the novelist is the slow accumulation of *un*conscious observation—absorption. The native expert's intentional observation of manners, speech, character, and ways of life can have value, for the native knows what they mean without having to cipher out the meaning. But I should be astonished to see a foreigner get at the right meanings, catch the elusive shades of these subtle things. Even the native novelist becomes a foreigner, with a foreigner's limitations, when he steps from the State whose life is familiar to him into a State whose life he has not lived. Bret Harte got his California and his Californians by unconscious absorption, and put both of them into his tales alive. But when he came from the Pacific to the Atlantic and tried to do Newport life from study—conscious observation—his failure was absolutely monumental. Newport is a disastrous place for the unacclimated observer, evidently.

To return to novel-building. Does the native novelist try to generalize the nation? No, he lays plainly before you the ways and speech and life of a few people grouped in a certain place—his own place—and that is one book. In time, he and his brethren will report to you the life and the people of the whole nation—the life of a group in a New England village; in a New York village; in a Texan village; in an Oregon village; in villages in fifty States and Territories; then the farm-life in fifty States and Territories; a hundred patches of life and groups of people in a dozen widely separated cities. And the Indians will be attended to; and the cowboys; and the gold and silver miners; and the negroes; and the Idiots and Congressmen; and the Irish, the Germans, the Italians, the Swedes, the French, the Chinamen, the Greasers; and the Catholics, the Methodists, the Presbyterians, the Congregationalists, the Baptists, the Spiritualists, the Mormons, the Shakers, the Quakers, the Jews, the Campbellites, the infidels, the Christian Scientists, the Mind-Curists, the Faith-Curists, the train-robbers, the White Caps, then Moonshiners. And when a thousand able novels have been written, *there* you have the soul of the people, the life of the people, the speech of the people; and not anywhere else can these be had. And the shadings of character, manners, feelings, ambitions, will be infinite.

• • • •

I spoke a moment ago of the existence of some superstitions that have been parading the world as facts this long time. For instance, consider the Dollar. The world seems to think that the love of money is "American"; and that the mad desire to get suddenly rich is "American." I believe that both of these things are merely and broadly human, not American monopolies at all. The love of money is natural to all nations, for money is a good and strong friend. I think that this love has existed everywhere, ever since the Bible called it the root of all evil.

I think that the reason why we Americans seem to be so addicted to trying to get rich suddenly is merely because the *opportunity* to make promising efforts in that direction has offered itself to us with a frequency out of all proportion to the European experience. For eighty years this opportunity has been offering itself in one new town or region after another straight westward, step by step, all the way from the Atlantic coast to the Pacific. When a mechanic could buy ten town lots on tolerably long credit for ten months' savings out of his wages, and reasonably expect to sell them in a couple of years for ten times what he gave for them, it was human for him to try the venture, and he did it, no matter what his nationality was. He would have done it in Europe or China if he had had the same chance.

In the flush times in the silver regions, a cook or any other humble worker stood a very good chance to get rich out of a trifle of money risked in a stock deal; and that person promptly took that risk, no matter what his or her nationality might be. I was there, and saw it.

But these opportunities have not been plenty in our Southern States; so there you have a prodigious region where the rush for sudden wealth is almost an unknown thing—and has been, from the beginning.

Europe has offered few opportunities for poor Tom, Dick, and Harry; but when she has offered one, there has been no noticeable difference between European eagerness and American. England saw this in the wild days of the Railroad King; France saw it in 1720—time of Law and the Mississippi Bubble. I am sure I have never seen in the gold and silver mines any madness, fury, frenzy to get suddenly rich which was even remotely comparable to that which raged in France in the Bubble day. If I had a cyclopaedia here I could turn to that memorable case, and satisfy nearly anybody that the hunger for the sudden dollar is no more "American" than it is French. And if I could furnish an American opportunity to staid Germany, I think I could wake her up like a house afire.

But I must return to the Generalizations, Psychologizings, Deductions. When M. Bourget is exploiting these arts, it is then that he is peculiarly and particularly himself. His ways are wholly original when he encounters a trait or a custom which is new to him. Another person would merely examine the find, verify it, estimate its value, and let it go; but that is not sufficient for M. Bourget: he always wants to know *why* that thing exists, he wants to know how it came to happen; and he will not let go of it until he has found out. And in every instance he will find that reason where no one but himself would have thought of looking for it. He does not seem to care for a reason that is not picturesquely located; one might almost say picturesquely and impossibly located.

He found out that in America men do not try to hunt down young married women. At once, as usual he wanted to know *why*. Any one could have told him. He could have divined it by the lights thrown by the novels of the country. But no, he preferred to find out for himself. He has a trustfulness as regards men and facts which is fine and unusual; he is not particular about the source of a fact, he is not particular about the character and standing of the fact itself; but when it comes to pounding out the reason for the existence of the fact, he will trust no one but himself.

In the present instance here was his fact: American young married women are not pursued by the corruptor; and here was the question: What is it that protects her?

It seems quite unlikely that that problem could have offered difficulties to any but a trained philosopher. Nearly any person would have said to M. Bourget: "Oh, that is very simple. It is very seldom in America that a marriage is made on a commercial basis; our marriages, from the beginning, have been made for love; and where love is there is no room for the corruptor."

• • • •

But I wish M. Bourget had read more of our novels before he came. It is the only way to thoroughly understand a people. When I found I was coming to Paris, I read *La Terre*.

EDITH WHARTON

(1862–1937)

Souvenirs du Bourget d'Outre-Mer

EDITH WHARTON's remarkable transformation from young society matron to a probing novelist of manners is the backdrop for her essay on Bourget. The French man of letters, whom she first met on his American tour, helped her form her decision to become an author. Through long years of friendship they shared many cultural and social values, though they differed, Mrs. Wharton later notes, on the subject of the techniques of fiction. Of *Outre-Mer,* she takes a view opposite to Twain's; it is not the native novelist who is best equipped to observe the American scene, but the cultured traveler, like Bourget, who can draw comparisons with other countries. In 1936 Mrs. Wharton seemed to raise no great objection to Bourget's condemnation of American materialism.

Always an admirer of French culture, Mrs. Wharton resided for many years in Paris. In her *French Ways and Their Meanings* (1919), interpreting French culture for Americans, she praised the French attempt to cultivate continuity with the past. Americans, on the other hand, granted their energy and daring, allow their inherited traditions to disintegrate. Her article on Bourget, written in French, attempts to render an American's impressions for a French audience.

Charles Cestre, in "American Literature Through French Eyes" (in *Yale Review,* Oct., 1920, 85–98), indicated that Edith Wharton's novels had a popular audience in France. "What is prized in them is the piquant combination of foreign manners, characters and surroundings with the French method of psychological analysis; society pictures and moral problems spiced with sexual allurements."

183

Mrs. Wharton's relations with the French, apparently, were altogether happier than Twain's.

Bibliography: An interesting sidelight on Bourget, as the correspondent who kept Henry James abreast of contemporary French literary developments, is revealed in I. D. McFarlane, "A Literary Friendship—Henry James and Paul Bourget," *Cambridge Journal*, 4 (1950), 144–61.

"Souvenirs du Bourget d'Outremer" was first published in French in *Revue Hebdomadaire*, 45 (June 21, 1936), 266–86. This essay, approximately half of which appears here, has been translated by the editors.

SOUVENIRS DU BOURGET D'OUTRE-MER

(1936)

IN READING THE OBITUARIES devoted to Paul Bourget in all the great French dailies, and also in the reviews, I have been struck by the uniformity of these "portraits" of the master. Whatever the judgments of these writers on his literary work and his political convictions, all, without exception, are in accord in representing the man as one too often sees him in his works: the intransigent moralist, the unsmiling pedagogue. Now I have known many men of letters in whom one immediately discovered a fundamental bond between the man and the work; but for those who knew Bourget intimately, it was indeed difficult to discover this bond; for the true, the living Bourget, as I knew him, extended beyond every aspect of the limited personality which his youthful admirers have constructed since his death with those elements drawn from his work.

At first, I was surprised by the uniformity of all these "portraits" of this great man; then I realized that many among the most intimate friends of his youth and his lustrous maturity have disappeared and that writers who comment on him today can only offer their readers the rigid effigy of the aged Bourget loaded with honors and prejudices, an image which little by little has replaced the one of the glittering and free-and-easy friend of my youth. Indeed, I knew Bourget well since his visit to the United States the year after his marriage; and nothing resembles less my dear comrade of long ago, so full of life and gaiety, the "older brother" who for years played so large a role in my life, than the severe and stately personage who is in the process of becoming the Bourget of the future.

Alas, all this is quite understandable, for there remain very few survivors of the period when Bourget truly attained the summit of his intellectual development without yet having lost his freedom of spirit. And so I have been moved to render my old friend a homage affected by these old memories—scattered and incomplete notes of a friendship which ceased only at that moment when, after the death of his wife, he separated himself voluntarily from most of those with whom he had until then shared an intimacy. . . .

II

It was 1893.

The year before, Bourget had married the sweet and exquisite Minnie David and had taken her on a honeymoon to Greece—a voyage which, with its beauty of landscape resembling no other and with the splendor of the works of art ornamenting that landscape, had enchanted them. Like all those who have made this pilgrimage, he dreamed only of beginning it again—when, the summer following, Gordon Bennett, publisher of the *New York Herald* and his old friend, proposed that Bourget undertake, at the expense of the great daily newspaper, a reportorial tour of the United States.

At that distant period the French were not extensive travelers. The idea of going to America would have given pause to an explorer more intrepid than Bourget, and I do not know really what made him decide, with his young wife, to make the great leap into the unknown. But he accepted the offer of the *Herald,* and when his friends in Paris learned that he had made his decision, they hastened to give him letters of introduction for New York, Boston, Washington, etc.

Since his first appearance in Paris, Bourget had been connected with the Ridgway family, originally from Philadelphia, but residing in Paris for a long time. Now, it happened that the elder Mrs. Ridgway, whose children had married in France, was a first cousin of my father-in-law, and my husband, consequently, was a relative of the marvelous Henry Ridgway who was the model of the elegant "man about town" in Bourget's early novels. Thus, when the latter embarked on his discovery of the New World, the young Mrs. Henry Ridgway, daughter of the banker Munroe of Paris, had the idea of offering him a letter of introduction to his cousins the Whartons.

At that time, my husband and I spent our summers at Newport, the most "fasionable" [sic] (as Bourget used to say) resort of the New World. Bourget wanted very much to see closely the social life of this

Deauville across the sea, and as soon as he arrived he presented to us the letter of introduction which our cousin Ridgway had given him.

What a storm of feeling for a young woman with a passion for literature, but who had not even dreamed of possibly being a part of the illustrious fraternity of writers! I had naturally read all Bourget's books, and although, even at that period, his novels did not please me very much, I had the liveliest admiration for his *Essais de Psychologie contemporaine,* of which the first volume had appeared.

At the moment of our meeting I knew practically no one from the world of letters. I had always been completely a woman of society, and the idea of receiving as guest an important French writer intimidated at least as much as it flattered me. Not sharing the taste of my husband for the frivolous and monotonous life in Newport, I did not realize the documentary interest that a style of life which seemed to me to possess a desperate banality might have for a foreigner as curious about new things as was Bourget. I did not know whom to invite to meet the illustrious author, and I was much too timid to imagine that he might perhaps have preferred to share a family repast rather than be present at a ceremonial service.

But I had to act, and, with some misgiving, I invited my company to lunch with six or seven friends. "At least," I thought, "they will be able to enjoy our incomparable view of the Ocean"—for we lived above a cliff overhanging the Atlantic—"if failing to participate in interesting conversation."

I had forgotten that everything interests travelers, and especially those of Bourget's stamp. I do not know if, on that first day, his myopic gaze reached so far as the sparkling sea sprawled at his feet; but I do know that our house and our guests interested him enormously. Our guests had been selected carefully, for it was not easy to find in Newport guests capable of any interest in intellectual life. But what Bourget wished was to see representative figures, chosen from social life, as it was then understood in our country; and from that point of view he certainly made at our home interesting acquaintances.

However, as he later told me, what especially surprised and interested him was to find in such a frivolous milieu a house so stocked with books. So unexpected was this to him that he returned, with his wife, as often as possible, delighted by the contrast between the pleasing library at *Land's End* with the grand bays opening upon the immensity of the Atlantic, and the life of the Casino and sports, yachting, bridge, sumptuous dinners, and the elegant dances, which constituted the "season" at Newport. At that time, when the villas lined along the cliffs were almost all inhabited by Old New York families—the Astors, the Van Allens, the Goelets, the Winthrops, the Chanlers, the Cushings, etc.—that season of the spa had still a sterling elegance; but the pleasant people who made up that small society were, with scarcely any exceptions, hermetically sealed against the intellectual and artistic movement which, in Paris and in London, had reached even the most shallow milieux. At Newport it was still unnecessary to seem interested in ideas.

I shall always recall that first meeting with the celebrated writer and his young wife. The beautiful head of Bourget, with its serious and tormented features, gay smile, and gaze perpetually on the alert, resembled one of those lifelike and vigorous busts of Roman senators that one sees in the Capitol Museum. . . . She [Mrs. Bourget] was very timid, or rather, I believe, little inclined to relate easily with others, with chance or fortuitous acquaintances, while Bourget, indefatigable scrutinizer of the human soul, could have taken as his motto the *Homo sum* of the poet.

Both, moreover, felt themselves at once in familiar country at *Land's End*, where the eighteenth-century Italian furniture, which my husband and I had brought back from our numerous voyages, recalled to Bourget his own sojourns in Tuscany and Umbria. It was perhaps due to my library and Venetian consoles that we were immediately at ease with one another and that I do not recall having had to pass through that first tiresome stage which often precedes a real understanding. It seems to me that from that first day we understood and liked each other.

The Bourgets, arriving at Newport for a few days, remained there a whole month. In leafing through the first pages of *Outre-mer* (which I had not reread since 1894), I note the interest which the author displayed in the most minute details of that life of elegant idleness. But I also am made aware that he did not escape the common error of nearly all sociologists coming from old Europe to study American manners. For Bourget, as for all other Europeans, North America was especially, before all else, the country of the dollar bill. Now this conception, which, since then, has become, alas, only all the more accurate, was not a true one, forty years ago, as regards the old Eastern cities in the United States. In New York, especially, the rich families were most often people of mediocre intelligence but of amiable manners, who had lived for several generations on their private incomes. The phenomenal increase in the value of real estate in New York had created a small society of wealth, idle and shut off, where only a few representatives, of more than modest means, of the new strata of the West, having earned through their mines and railroads millions which would soon eclipse the fortunes of old New Yorkers, just managed to enter. In the milieu in which I lived (and which formed, in my youth, the "society" of the little New York of that period), one never heard of Wall Street, and most men devoted their spare time to sports and hunting. . . .

After his departure from Newport Bourget undertook, with the family of John Gardner, of Boston, an extended tour of the Western states. It is probable that he already knew Mrs. Gardner, who possessed a palace in Venice and stopped each year for long stays in Paris and Italy. . . .

But to return to Bourget, and his voyage across the United States. He returned after several months, having seen much and noted much. But what strikes me particularly, in rereading his book, is to see him excessively fatigued and bewildered by the rapidity and din of a journey which would seem to us today a slow expedition across a peaceful and somnolent Arcadia!

It seems to me Bourget's mind was responsive to everything; his culture vast, his memory stocked with impressions from his literary and non-literary resources. In contrast with most of his French contemporaries, he had travelled much, not only to the United States, but to Italy, England, Ireland. . . . In the Bourget of that period there was nothing of that intense "nationalism" of spirit and culture which characterizes certain French men of letters, and which always recalls to mind the celebrated verse of Kipling: "How can they know England, that only England know?"

I wished, in these few notes, to speak not of the writer, but of the friend. I feel that the opinion of a foreigner on work as well known as Bourget's has only little interest for his compatriots; and yet I am aware that it is impossible for me to delay any longer the painful confession that I never very much liked his fiction. It is particularly painful because he did me the great honor of writing a very beautiful preface for the French translation of my first novel, *Chez les heureux du monde* [*The House of Mirth*, 1905]. It is even thanks to him that my friend Charles Du Bos (whom I did not know at that time) made his literary debut in translating my novel; and I shall always be grateful to Bourget for having rendered me this friendly assistance.

My admiration for his essays of literary criticism has always been great; but why did it have to be that the qualities which made his conversation so fascinating—the gaiety, irony, the light and lively way of recounting an anecdote or miming a dialogue—why was it that everything which rendered his conversation so brilliant and flavorsome, disappeared each time the novelist lifted his pen?

We spoke often of the art of fiction, because the technique of our métier engrossed us both; and soon I recognized that Bourget's ideas differed entirely from mine. As soon as he would begin a novel, Bourget would ascend a pulpit; it was necessary that each character be a pawn in a game cleverly arranged in advance and in which the disconnected contingencies of life were totally banished. Having discovered that our theories were never in accord, we took the wise resolution of no longer speaking of our respective works; but, on the other hand, we never tired of telling each other of the theories of our future books.

The irony and sadness of human fate, both of us envisaged in the same way; each incident provided him, as well as me, a new idea, and we would spend hours recounting them. Bourget always scolded me because in my books I did not sufficiently explain my characters; I responded that he underestimated the intelligence of his readers in supposing that it was necessary to dissect at length in advance the motive for each act, almost for each word, instead of letting the speech and behavior of the characters reveal themselves.

Needless to say, these discussions never left the least rancor in the minds of the discussants. Nothing altered the affectionate good will that Bourget exercised toward his friends. One could tease him, make fun of him, even scold him a bit, without his getting angry. During our long years of almost fraternal friendship, I never saw him display the least shade of impatience or resentment. . . .

Of his literary probity, I had one day a very moving proof. It was at the time of Tolstoi's death. For a long time this great Russian novelist had been the object of Bourget's scorn and odium. The latter, always very personal in his judgments, and strongly influenced, as he grew older, by the opinions of his entourage, had come to deny the literary genius of the writer because he disliked, with reason, his vague social theories. Often I had pointed out to him that the novelist's genius had remained intact despite the man's intellectural poverty. Bourget always answered:

—But, no, my dear, you are wrong; Tolstoi was never a great novelist. What do we find in *Anna Karenina, War and Peace, Resurrection?* A jumble of undigested theories, of disjointed scenes, without beginning or ending.—

The day of Tolstoi's death we took up the same discussion, and I never heard Bourget express himself with more injustice and violence. But on that very day a newspaper of importance requested of him an article on Tolstoi. To do so, he had to quickly peruse the novels which he certainly had not read for years; and having done so, Bourget wrote, for the Russian novelist whom he had never in reality dared to admire, one of the finest and most generous articles that an artist had ever devoted to the memory of a colleague.

All Bourget is in this story: his basically generous nature, his brusque changes of opinion, and especially his magnificent professional integrity.

PART VI

Poetic Cross-Currents

CHARLES BAUDELAIRE
(1821–1867)

New Notes on Edgar Poe

ONE OF THE STRANGEST PHENOMENA in modern literary history—a phenomenon that has been contemplated many times without a fully satisfactory explanation—is the comparative neglect of Edgar Allan Poe in his own country and the great influence and reputation he has enjoyed in France. From Walt Whitman to Henry James and T. S. Eliot, poets and critics in the United States have either disparaged him or extended a grudging approval. In France Poe has remained almost a religious cult. Charles Baudelaire, who began the adulation of Poe in France, followed by Stéphane Mallarmé and Paul Valéry—three significant modern French poets—have praised his genius and intellect. Poe, it should be recalled, was instrumental in the development of French Symbolism, and a host of literary figures, including Paul Verlaine, Arthur Rimbaud, Joris Karl Huysmans, Philippe-Auguste, Comte de Villiers de l'Isle Adam, Paul Claudel, and André Gide, have expressed intense interest in him.

Some show of interest in Poe in France, however, preceded Baudelaire. E. D. Forgues, who drew notice to several American authors, wrote in the *Revue des Deux Mondes* (October, 1846) a characteristically intelligent introduction to Poe's stories, and translations of several of Poe's stories also appeared in various journals. But the phenomenon of Poe in France began with Baudelaire's reading of some of Poe's tales in these French translations, probably in early 1847. Baudelaire, who saw in Poe an *alter ego*, a double of himself, conveyed his shock of recognition in correspondence: "The first time I opened one of his books I saw, to my amazement and delight, not simply certain subjects which I had dreamed of, but *sentences*, which I had thought out, written by him twenty years before" (quoted by Patrick F. Quinn, *The French Face of Edgar Poe* [Carbondale, Ill.: 1957], pp. 135–36). Poe's work filled him with a

193

"singular excitement" and "incredible sympathy." Subsequently, Baudelaire endeavored to make Poe better known in France. He translated and compiled five books of Poe's tales: *Histoires extraordinaires* (1856); *Nouvelles histoires extraordinaires* (1857)—published the same year as Baudelaire's masterpiece, *Fleurs du Mal*; translations of *Arthur Gordon Pym* (1858) and *Eureka* (1863); and *Histoires grotesques et serieuses* (1865). Baudelaire devoted more attention to Poe's stories than to his poems, and, in his comments, underscored their psychological content. He had written to Sainte-Beuve in 1856: "Edgar Poe, who isn't much in America, *must* become a great man in France—at least that is what I want" (quoted by Quinn, p. 9). Baudelaire's scrupulous translations helped him to accomplish this aim.

In addition to seven shorter notices, Baudelaire wrote three critical essays on Poe. The first, written in 1852, and published in two installments in the *Revue de Paris,* is largely biographical, borrowing heavily from American sources, two issues of the *Southern Literary Messenger* (November, 1849 and March, 1850). Here Baudelaire sees Poe as both outlaw and saint, an outcast and rebel in an America devoted to a materialism and a democratic mediocrity which Baudelaire hated. In Baudelaire we find the negation of the glowing sentiments about the young American democracy prevalent in France at the beginning of the century. He exaggerated, however, the extent to which Poe had rebelled against American society. In any event, Poe represented to Baudelaire the tragic fate of the poet in modern times. In 1856 Baudelaire recast and shortened his 1852 essay as an introduction to his translations of that year. This best known of his essays on Poe, "Edgar Allan Poe: sa vie et ses ouvrages," restates the theme of the poet as victim, justifies the poet's vices or weaknesses if they contribute to works of artistic merit, and sees as the proper subject-matter of poetry the original, the bizarre, or the abnormal.

The 1856 essay met with some strong opposition, notably an attack by Barbey d'Aurevilly, Baudelaire's friend and a prominent critic and man of letters. Barbey d'Aurevilly cited Poe's work as decadent and upheld, as against the image of Poe that Baudelaire had created, the values of religion, society, and family. Baudelaire's last essay, "New Notes on Egar Poe," which served as preface for his 1857 translations defends "decadent" literature in opposition to d'Aurevilly and, with much satire, delivers several other sociological and literary judgments on the contemporary scene. Again Baudelaire derides American cultural life, with its stress on utility and progress; he shares Poe's recognition of perverseness as a motive in human behavior, though he gives the notion a theological interpretation that Poe had not intended; and he praises Poe's emphasis on the poet's quest for supernal beauty. The essay also reflects the influence of Poe's critical essays on poetry, "The Philosophy of Composition" (1846) and "The Poetic Principle" (1850). Baudelaire cites Poe on the need for craftsmanship, brevity, and discipline in poetry. The French poet was to undertake a relentless attack against the undisciplined and the excessively rhetorical in verse, as is attested to by his criticism of Alfred de Musset, and to display his own mastery of the sonnet and the shorter poem.

Mallarmé's translation of Poe's poems, with a dedication to Baudelaire, was published in 1887. His famous sonnet, "Le Tombeau d'Edgar Poe," appeared in a memorial volume to Poe in Baltimore, 1876; and, in 1894, his poetic prose piece "Essay on Poe" appeared, in which Poe is called "an aerolith star—and lightning-born" and the "absolute model of the writer." The French poet (1842–1898) seemed particularly affected by Poe's "Poetic Principle," which drew an analogy between poetry and music and stressed musical suggestiveness in poetic language.

Paul Valéry (1871–1945), one of the most celebrated of twentieth-century French poets, also held Poe in reverence. He valued Poe as metaphysician and thinker, as is revealed in his essay on Poe's *Eureka*, which he wrote as a preface to a publication (1921) of Baudelaire's translation of *Eureka*. Valéry saw *Eureka* (which has never enjoyed much attention in the United States) as an original cosmological speculation, a rich "abstract poem." As such, Poe's essay seems to have exerted an influence on Valéry's development as a poet. When Valéry first read *Eureka* at the age of twenty, Poe seemed to mate poetry and science, spirit and matter, beyond the limits of impressionism, on the one hand, and of the materialism of classical physics, on the other.

Bibliography: The literature on Baudelaire and Poe is voluminous. A book to begin with is Patrick F. Quinn, *The French Face of Edgar Poe* (Carbondale, Ill.: 1957), with its useful bibliography. Valuable, too, are *Affidavits of Genius: Edgar Allan Poe and the French Critics*, ed. Jean Alexander (Port Washington, N.Y.: 1971), which contains French critical writings on Poe, translated into English, and W. T.

Bandy's brochure, "The Influence and Reputation of Edgar Allan Poe in Europe," (Baltimore: 1962). Baudelaire's overall criticism is discussed in Margaret Gilman, *Baudelaire the Critic* (New York: 1943).

A classic essay from the American point of view is T. S. Eliot, "From Poe to Valéry," *Hudson Review*, 2 (Autumn, 1949), 327–42, wherein Eliot proposes the idea that Poe might be worth reconsideration since the French have seen so much in him. A full-length study of Poe's influence on Mallarmé is Joseph Chiari, *Symbolism from Poe to Mallarmé* (New York: 2nd ed., 1970). In the most relevant chapters (III through VI), Chiari advances the thesis that Mallarmé translated Poe's imprecise formulas into more meaningful terms. Wallace Fowlie, *Mallarmé* (Chicago: 1952), has insightful paragraphs on Poe and Mallarmé.

This selection is excerpted from *Baudelaire as a Literary Critic*, ed. and trans. Lois B. Hyslop and Francis E. Hyslop, Jr. (College Park, Pa.: Pennsylvania State University Press, 1964). The selected pages are 117–23; 126–28; 129–32.

NEW NOTES ON EDGAR POE

(1857)

I

Decadent literature!—Empty words which we often hear fall, with the sonority of a deep yawn, from the mouths of those unenigmatic sphinxes who keep watch before the sacred doors of classical Aesthetics. Each time that the irrefutable oracle resounds, one can be sure that it is about a work more amusing than the *Iliad*. It is evidently a question of a poem or of a novel, all of whose parts are skillfully designed for surprise, whose style is magnificently embellished, where all the resources of language and prosody are utilized by an impeccable hand. When I hear the anathema boom out—which, I might say in passing, usually falls on some favorite poet—I am always seized with the desire to reply: Do you take me for a barbarian like you and do you believe me capable of amusing myself as dismally as you do? Then grotesque comparisons stir in my brain; it seems to me that two women appear before me: one, a rustic matron, repugnant in her health and virtue, plain and expressionless, in short, *owing everything to simple nature;* the other, one of those beauties who dominate and oppress one's memory, adding all the eloquence of dress to her profound and original charm, well poised, conscious and queen of herself—with a speaking voice like a well-tuned instrument, and eyes laden with thoughts but revealing only what they wish. I would not hesitate in my choice, and yet there are pedagogical sphinxes who would reproach me for my failure to respect classical honor.—But, putting aside parables, I think it is permissible to ask these wise men if they really understand all the vanity, all the futility of their wisdom. The phrase *decadent literature* implies that there is a scale of literatures, an infantile, a childish, an adolescent, etc. This term, in other words, supposes something fatal and providential, like an ineluctable decree; and it is altogether unfair to reproach us for fulfilling the mysterious law. All that I can understand in this academic phrase is that it is shameful to obey this law with pleasure and that we are guilty to rejoice in our destiny.—The sun, which a few hours ago overwhelmed everything with its direct white light, is soon going to flood the western horizon with variegated colors. In the play of light of the dying sun certain poetic spirits will find new delights; they will discover there dazzling colonnades, cascades of molten metal, paradises of fire, a sad splendor, the pleasure of regret, all the magic of dreams, all the memories of opium. And indeed the sunset will appear to them like the marvelous allegory of a soul filled with life which descends behind the horizon with a magnificent store of thoughts and dreams.

But what the narrow-minded professors have not realized is that, in the movement of life, there may occur some complication, some combination quite unforeseen by their schoolboy wisdom. And then their inadequate language fails, as in the case—a phenomenon which perhaps will increase with variants—of a nation which begins with decadence and thus starts where others end.

Let new literatures develop among the immense colonies of the present century and there will result most certainly spiritual accidents of a nature disturbing to the academic mind. Young and old at the same time, America babbles and rambles with an astonishing volubility. Who could count its poets? They are innumerable. Its *blue stockings?* They clutter the magazines. Its critics? You may be sure that they have pedants who are as good as ours at constantly recalling the artist to ancient beauty, at questioning a poet or a novelist on the morality of his purpose and the merit of his intentions. There can be found there as here, but even more than here, men of letters who do not know how to spell; a childish, useless activity; compilers in abundance, hack writers, plagiarists of plagiaries, and critics of critics. In this maelstrom of mediocrity, in this society enamored of material perfections—a new kind of scandal which makes intelligible the grandeur of inactive peoples—in this society eager for surprises, in love with life, but especially with a life full of excitements, a man has appeared who was great not only in his metaphysical subtlety, in the sinister or bewitching beauty of his conceptions, in the rigor of his analysis, but also great and not less great as a *caricature*.—I must explain myself with some care; for recently a rash critic, in order to disparage Edgar Poe and to invalidate the sincerity of my admiration, used the word jongleur which I myself had applied to the noble poet as a sort of praise.

From the midst of a greedy world, hungry for material things, Poe took flight in dreams. Stifled as he was by the American atmosphere, he wrote at the beginning of *Eureka:* "I offer this book to those who have put faith in dreams as in the only realities!" He was in himself an admirable protest, and he made his protest in his own particular way. The author who, in "The Colloquy of Monos and Una," pours out his scorn and disgust for democracy, progress and *civilization,* this author is the same one who, in order to encourage credulity, to delight the stupidity of his contemporaries, has stressed human sovereignty most emphatically and has very ingeniously fabricated hoaxes flattering to the pride of *modern man.* Considered in this light, Poe seems like a helot who wishes to make his master blush. Finally, to state my thought even more clearly, Poe was always great not only in his noble conceptions but also as a prankster.

II

For he was never a dupe! I do not think that the Virginian who calmly wrote in the midst of a rising tide of democracy: "People have nothing to do with laws except to obey them," has ever been a victim of modern wisdom; and: "The nose of a mob is its imagination. By this, at any time, it can be quickly led"—and a hundred other passages in which mockery falls thick and fast like a hail of bullets but still remains proud and indifferent.—The Swedenborgians congratulate him on his "Mesmeric Revelation," like those naïve

Illuminati who formerly hailed in the author of the *Diable amoureux* a discoverer of their mysteries; they thank him for the great truths which he has just proclaimed—for they have discovered (O verifiers of the unverifiable!) that all that which he has set forth is absolutely true;—although, at first, these good people confess, they had suspected that it might well have been merely fictitious. Poe answers that, so far as he is concerned, he has never doubted it.—Must I cite in addition this short passage which catches my eye while scanning for the hundredth time his amusing "Marginalia," which are the secret chambers, as it were, of his mind: "The enormous multiplication of books in all branches of knowledge is one of the greatest scourges of this age, for it is one of the most serious obstacles to the acquisition of all positive knowledge." Aristocrat by nature even more than by birth, the Virginian, the Southerner, the Byron gone astray in a bad world, has always kept his philosophic impassability and, whether he defines the nose of the mob, whether he mocks the fabricators of religions, whether he scoffs at libraries, he remains what the true poet was and always will be—a truth clothed in a strange manner, an apparent paradox, who does not wish to be elbowed by the crowd and who runs to the far east when the fireworks go off in the west.

But more important than anything else: we shall see that this author, product of a century infatuated with itself, child of a nation more infatuated with itself than any other, has clearly seen, has imperturbably affirmed the natural wickedness of man. There is in man, he says, a mysterious force which modern philosophy does not wish to take into consideration; nevertheless, without this nameless force, without this primordial bent, a host of human actions will remain unexplained, inexplicable. These actions are attractive only *because* they are bad or dangerous; they possess the fascination of the abyss. This primitive, irresistible force is natural Perversity, which makes man constantly and simultaneously a murderer and a suicide, an assassin and a hangman;—for he adds, with a remarkably satanic subtlety, the impossibility of finding an adequate rational motive for certain wicked and perilous actions could lead us to consider them as the result of the suggestions of the Devil, if experience and history did not teach us that God often draws from them the establishment of order and the punishment of scoundrels;—*after having used the same scoundrels as accomplices!* such is the thought which, I confess, slips into my mind, an implication as inevitable as it is perfidious. But for the present I wish to consider only the great forgotten truth—the primordial perversity of man—and it is not without a certain satisfaction that I see some vestiges of ancient wisdom return to us from a country from which we did not expect them. It is pleasant to know that some fragments of an old truth are exploded in the faces of all these obsequious flatterers of humanity, of all these humbugs and quacks who repeat in every possible tone of voice: "I am born good, and you too, and all of us are born good!" forgetting, no! pretending to forget, like misguided equalitarians, that we are all born marked for evil!

Of what lies could he be a dupe, he who sometimes—sad necessity of his environment—dealt with them so well? What scorn for pseudophilosophy on his good days, on the days when he was, so to speak, inspired! This poet, several of whose compositions seem deliberately made to confirm the alleged omnipotence of man, has sometimes wished to purge himself. The day that he wrote: "All certainty is in dreams," he thrust back his own Americanism into the region of inferior things; at other times, becoming again the true poet, doubtless obeying the ineluctable truth which haunts us like a demon, he uttered the ardent sighs of *the fallen angel who remembers heaven;* he lamented the golden age and the lost Eden; he wept over all the magnificence of nature *shrivelling up before the hot breath of fiery furnaces;* finally, he produced those admirable pages: "The Colloquy of Monos and Una" which would have charmed and troubled the impeccable de Maistre.

It is he who said about socialism at a time when the latter did not yet have a name, or when, at least, this name was not completely popularized: "The world is infested, just now, by a new sect of philosophers, who have not yet suspected themselves of forming a sect, and who, consequently, have adopted no name. They are the *Believers in everything Old.* Their High Priest in the East, is Charles Fourier—in the West, Horace Greeley; and they are well aware that they are high priests. The only common bond among the members is Credulity:—let us call it Insanity at once, and be done with it. Ask any one of them *why* he believes this or that, and, if he be conscientious (ignorant people usually are), he will make you very much such a reply as Talleyrand made when asked why he believed in the Bible. 'I believe in it first,' said he, 'because I am Bishop of Autun; and, secondly, because I don't know the least thing about it.' What these philosophers call 'argument' is a way they have 'de nier ce qui est et d'expliquer ce qui n'est pas.' "

Progress, that great heresy of decay, likewise could not escape Poe. The reader will see in different passages what terms he used to characterize it. One could truly say, considering the fervor that he expends, that he had to vent his spleen on it, as on a public nuisance or as on a pest in the street. How he would have laughed, with the poet's scornful laugh, which alienates simpletons, had he happened, as I did, upon this wonderful statement which reminds one of the ridiculous and deliberate absurdities of clowns. I discovered it treacherously blazoned in an eminently serious magazine:—*The unceasing progress of science has very recently made possible the rediscovery of the lost and long sought secret of* . . . (Greek fire, the tempering of copper, something or other which has vanished), *of which the most successful applications date back to a* barbarous *and very old period!!!* That is a sentence which can be called a real find, a brilliant discovery, even in a century of *unceasing progress;* but I believe that the mummy Allamistakeo would not have failed to ask with a gentle and discreet tone of superiority, if it were also thanks to *unceasing progress*—to the fatal, irresistible law of progress—that this famous secret had been lost.—Moreover, to become serious about a subject which is as sad as it is laughable, is it not a really stupefying thing to see a nation, several nations, and presently all humanity, say to its wise men, its magicians: I shall love you and I shall make you great if you convince me that we are progressing unconsciously, inevitably—while sleeping; rid us of responsibility, veil for us the humiliation of comparisons, turn history into sophistries and you will be able to call yourselves the wisest of the wise? Is it not a cause for astonishment that this simple idea does not flash into everyone's mind; that progress (in so far as there is progress) perfects sorrow to the same extent that it refines pleasure and that, if the epidermis of peoples is becoming delicate, they are evidently pursuing only an *Italian fugientem,* a conquest lost every minute, a progress always negating itself? . . .

III

Such a social environment necessarily engenders corresponding literary errors. Poe reacted against these errors as often as he could, and with all his might. We must not be surprised then that American writers, though recognizing his singular power as a poet and as a storyteller, have always tended to question his ability as a critic. In a country where the idea of utility, the most hostile in the world to the idea of beauty, dominates and takes precedence over everything, the perfect critic will be the most *respectable*, that is to say the one whose tendencies and desires will best approximate the tendencies and desires of his public—the one who, confusing the intellectual faculties of the writer and the categories of writing, will assign to all a single goal—the one who will seek in a book of poetry the means of perfecting conscience. Naturally he will become all the less concerned with the real, the positive beauties of poetry; he will be all the less shocked by imperfections and even by faults in execution. Edgar Poe, on the contrary, dividing the world of the mind into pure *Intellect, Taste,* and *Moral Sense,* applied criticism in accordance with the category to which the object of his analysis belonged. He was above all sensitive to perfection of plan and to correctness of execution; taking apart literary works like defective pieces of machinery (considering the goal that they wished to attain), noting carefully the flaws of workmanship; and when he passed to the details of the work, to its plastic expression, in a word, to style, examining meticulously and without omissions the faults of prosody, the grammatical errors and all the mass of dross which, among writers who are not artists, besmirch the best intentions and deform the most noble conceptions.

For him, Imagination is the queen of faculties; but by this word he understands something greater than that which is understood by the average reader. Imagination is not fantasy; nor is it sensibility, although it may be difficult to conceive of an imaginative man who would be lacking in sensibility. Imagination is an almost divine faculty which perceives immediately and without philosophical methods the inner and secret relations of things, the correspondences and the analogies. The honors and functions which he grants to this faculty give it such value (at least when the thought of the author has been well understood) that a scholar without imagination appears only as a pseudoscholar, or at least as an incomplete scholar.

Among the literary domains where imagination can obtain the most curious results, can harvest treasures, not the richest, the most precious (those belong to poetry), but the most numerous and the most varied, there is one of which Poe is especially fond; it is the *Short Story.* It has the immense advantage over the novel of vast proportions that its brevity adds to the intensity of effect. This type of reading, which can be accomplished in one sitting, leaves in the mind a more powerful impression than a broken reading, often interrupted by the worries of business and the cares of social life. The unity of impression, the *totality* of effect is an immense advantage which can give to this type of composition a very special superiority, to such an extent that an extremely short story (which is doubtless a fault) is even better than an extremely long story. The artist, if he is skillful, will not adapt his thoughts to the incidents but, having conceived deliberately and at leisure an effect to be produced, will invent the incidents, will combine the events most suitable to bring about the desired effect. If the first sentence is not written with the idea of preparing this final impression, the work has failed from the start. There must not creep into the entire composition a single word which is not intentional, which does not tend, directly or indirectly, to complete the premeditated design. . . .

IV

"*Genus irritabile vatum!* That poets (using the word comprehensively, as including artists in general) are a *genus irritabile*, is well understood; but the *why*, seems not to be commonly seen. An artist *is* an artist only by dint of his exquisite sense of Beauty—a sense affording him rapturous enjoyment but at the same time implying, or involving, an equally exquisite sense of Deformity or disproportion. Thus a wrong—an injustice—done a poet who is really a poet, excites him to a degree which, to ordinary apprehension, appears disproportionate with the wrong. Poets *see* injustice—*never* where it does not exist—but very often where the unpoetical see no injustice whatever. Thus the poetical irritability has no reference to 'temper' in the vulgar sense but merely to a more than usual clear-sightedness in respect to Wrong:—this clear-sightedness being nothing more than a corollary from the vivid perception of Right—of justice—of proportion—in a word, of the beautiful. But one thing is clear—that the man who is *not* 'irritable' (to the ordinary apprehension) is *no poet.*"

Thus the poet himself speaks, preparing an excellent and irrefutable apologia for all those of his race. Poe carried this sensibility into his literary affairs, and the extreme importance which he attached to things poetic often led him to use a tone in which, according to the judgment of the weak, a feeling of superiority became too evident. I have already mentioned, I believe, that several prejudices which he had to combat, false ideas, commonplace opinions which circulated around him, have for a long time infected the French press. It will not be useless then to give a brief account of some of his most important opinions relative to poetic composition. The parallelism of error will make their application quite easy.

But above all, I must point out that in addition to the share which Poe granted to a natural, innate poetic gift, he gave an importance to knowledge, work, and analysis that will seem excessive to arrogant and unlettered persons. Not only has he expended considerable efforts to subject to his will the fleeting spirit of happy moments, in order to recall at will those exquisite sensations, those spiritual longings, those states of poetic health, so rare and so precious that they could truly be considered as graces exterior to man and as visitations; but also he has subjected inspiration to method, to the most severe analysis. The choice of means! he returns to that constantly, he insists with a learned eloquence upon the adjustment of means to effect, on the use of rhyme, on the perfecting of the refrain, on the adaptation of rhythm to feeling. He maintained that he who cannot seize the intangible is not a poet; that he alone is a poet who is master of his memory, the sovereign of words, the record book of his own feelings always open for examination. Everything for the conclusion! he often repeats. Even a sonnet needs a plan, and the construction, the armature, so to speak, is the most important guarantee of the mysterious life of works of the mind.

I turn naturally to the article entitled "The Poetic Principle," and I find from the very beginning a vigorous protest against what could be called, in the field of poetry, the heresy of length or of dimension— the absurd importance attributed to bulky poems. "I hold that a long poem does not exist. I maintain that the phrase, 'a long poem,' is simply a flat contradiction in terms." In fact, a poem deserves its title only insomuch as it excites and uplifts the soul, and the real merit of a poem is due to this excitation, to this *uplifting* of the soul. But, from psychological necessity, all these excitations are fugitive and transitory. This strange mood into which the soul of the reader has been drawn by force, as it were, will certainly not last as long as the reading of a poem which exceeds human capacity for enthusiasm.

It is obvious then that the epic poem stands condemned. For a work of that length can be considered poetic only insofar as one sacrifices the vital condition of every work of art, Unity;—I do not mean unity in the conception but unity in the impression, the *totality* of effect, as I said when I had occasion to compare the novel with the short story. The epic poem then appears to us, aesthetically speaking, as a paradox. Bygone ages may have produced a series of lyric poems, later compiled into epic poems; but every *epic intention* obviously is the result of an imperfect sense of art. The time for these artistic anomalies has passed, and it is even very doubtful that a long poem has ever been truly popular in the full meaning of the word.

It must be added that a too short poem, one which does not furnish a *pabulum* that will sustain the excitation created, one which is not equal to the natural appetite of the reader, is also very defective. However brilliant and intense the effect may be, it is not lasting; memory does not retain it; it is like a seal which, placed too lightly and too hastily, has not had time to imprint its image on the wax.

But there is another heresy which, thanks to the hypocrisy, to the dullness, and to the baseness of human minds, is even more formidable and has a greater chance of survival—an error which has a hardier life—I wish to speak of the heresy of *teaching a lesson* which includes as inevitable corollaries the heresy of *passion,* of *truth,* and of *morality.* A great many people imagine that the aim of poetry is a lesson of some sort, that it must now fortify the conscience, now perfect morals, now in short *prove* something or other which is useful. Edgar Poe claims that Americans especially have supported this heterodox idea; alas! there is no need to go as far as Boston to encounter the heresy in question. Even here it attacks and breaches true poetry every day. Poetry, if only one is willing to seek within himself, to question his heart, to recall his memories of enthusiasm, has no other goal than itself; it cannot have any other, and no poem will be so great, so noble, so truly worthy of the name of poetry as that which will have been written solely for the pleasure of writing a poem.

I do not mean that poetry does not ennoble manners—let there be no mistake about it—that its final result is not to raise man above the level of vulgar interests; that would obviously be an absurdity. I say that, if the poet has pursued a moral aim, he has diminished his poetic force; and it is not rash to wager that his work will be bad. Poetry cannot, under penalty of death or failure, be assimilated to science or morality; it does not have Truth as its object, it has only Itself. The means for demonstrating truth are other and are elsewhere. Truth has nothing to do with songs. All that constitutes the grace, the charm, the irresistible attraction of a song, would take from Truth its authority and its power. Cold, calm, impassive, the demonstrative mood rejects the diamonds and the flowers of the Muse; it is then absolutely the inverse of the poetic mood. . . .

Victor Hugo
Note on Some French
Romantics
Baudelaire and Loti

BEST REMEMBERED TODAY as an interpreter to America of Japan, where he lived from 1890 until his death, earlier in his career Lafcadio Hearn had performed a similar function as interpreter and also translator of French literature. In the course of his restless and nomadic life, he had settled in New Orleans in 1877, and, for an audience that, in part, was French-speaking, he wrote frequently on contemporary French literature in New Orleans periodicals. Part of his checkered childhood had been spent in France.

His were the first English translations of François Coppée, Philippe-Auguste, Comte de Villiers de l'Isle-Adam, Guy de Maupassant, and Pierre Loti; and he also translated works by Théophile Gautier, Gustave Flaubert, Anatole France, and Emile Zola. Though he was distressed by Zola and the naturalistic school, he bitterly criticized poor translations of Zola, especially those by John Sterling, and insisted on high standards of accuracy and style in translating from the French. In his first book, a translation of six tales by Gautier (1882), he employed a poetic prose style derived from a study of Gautier, Baudelaire, and his personal favorite, Loti. His *Fantastics and Other Fancies* (1914), a collection of sketches, were modelled upon Baudelaire's prose poems.

Devoted more to the esthetics of beauty than of realism, Hearn is
206

classified among the Bohemians of his time. He promoted the French Romantics and their heirs while other Americans were championing the Realists and Naturalists. He reserved special praise for Nerval's originality, Baudelaire's melodies, Gautier's pictorialism, and Loti's exotic allure—qualities he tried to incorporate in his own writings. In his appreciation of French poetry (though drawn primarily to poetic prose), he stopped short of Mallarmé and the Symbolist movement, which remained beyond his scope. In the selections that follow, Hearn reveals the representative Bohemian outlook of his day in his adulation of Victor Hugo and his responsiveness to the French Romantics, and displays his personal preferences in his discussions of Baudelaire's and Loti's prose styles.

Bibliography: A collection of Hearn selections, mostly on French literature, is his *Literary Essays,* ed. Ichiro Nishizaki (Tokyo: 1939). Another helpful collection is his *Essays in European and Oriental Literature,* ed. Albert Modell (New York: 1923). A good study is Beongcheon Yu, *An Ape of Gods: The Art and Thought of Lafcadio Hearn* (Detroit: 1964).

"Victor Hugo" first appeared in the New Orleans *Item,* March 23, 1881. "Note on Some French Romantics" comes from Hearn's *Life and Literature,* ed. John Erskine (New York: Dodd Mead, 1917), pp. 247–65—originally a lecture delivered at the University of Tokyo between 1896 and 1902; "Baudelaire and Loti" derives from another lecture in Japan published as "Baudelaire" in *Interpretations of Literature,* vol. II, ed. John Erskine (New York: Dodd Mead, 1915), pp. 83–89. The last two selections appear here in excerpt.

VICTOR HUGO

(1881)

PROBABLY NO POET since the days of Pindar has received such honor during his lifetime as Victor Hugo, whose eightieth birthday has just been celebrated at Paris with the magnificence of a municipal holiday. Proscribed and banished by the last of the Napoleons, he has lived to be elevated to a height of glory rarely reached by mortals while his persecutor slumbers forever under an infamy weightier than the marble of his tomb. Victor Hugo is now the greatest and oldest monarch in the world of letters, and no sovereign's name is more familiar in all civilized lands. Like a victor in Panhellenic games statues have been wrought of him; and his verses have been graven on monuments like those odes of Pindar inscribed by Athenians and Rhodians in letters of gold. His great social romance, "Les Miserables," is read today in nine different languages,—his "Notre Dame de Paris" inspired some of the rarest masterpieces of modern sculpture and painting, and called out the skill of the finest living artist to illustrate. He remodeled the French stage, enriched the French language, and with some few daring disciples formed a school of literature whose productions are miracles of genius. The school itself was too beautiful and too perfect to endure; perhaps the white-haired author of "Les Orientales" is today the only survivor of the band of Romanticists who followed him in 1830 as the paladins followed Roland to Roncesvalles. But if the Romanticists have passed away, their works will live for generations; and their influence will be felt as long as the French language is spoken. Littré's great dictionary owes a considerable portion of its learned bulk to their strong alimentation. They coined new terms, they borrowed and adopted from other tongues, they resurrected words from the literary ruins of the fifteenth and sixteenth centuries, and rescued much of value from obsolescence. In architecture, sculpture, decoration, drama, music, painting, etching, in ceramics, in jewelry, in gold and silver work,—in everything into which the study of the beautiful enters,—the disciples of Victor Hugo have made their influence manifest as well as in the domain of letters. Theirs was the Renaissance greater and grander even than the Renaissance of a Medician age,—not a Renaissance of Greek or Latin antiquity alone, but of all that was beautiful or bizarre or grotesque in all the civilizations that have passed away. They resuscitated the Gothic fantasticality of the middle ages, and borrowed moresque grace and arabesque ingenuity from the Orient. They created a new worship of loveliness for its own sake and established forever the first foundation of that modern taste which compels the eyes of the world to look toward Paris as the Mecca of modern art. And Victor Hugo, the Prophet of the new and universal faith, the founder of the new religion of aesthetics which no Naturalism can ever kill, well deserves the honors paid him, as that man of the Nineteenth century whose work will make the deepest impression upon the literature of the Twentieth. Greater his glory, surely, than even that of the good old Greek father, who died of joy to know that all his sons had conquered in those Olympian games, at which all men of Hellenic blood in the ancient world contended together. The literary children of Victor Hugo have won mightier victories than any muscled-knotted wrestler of antiquity, any athletic of Magna Graecia.

NOTE ON SOME FRENCH ROMANTICS
(1917)

I DO NOT THINK the French romantic movement was so much superior to the English in poetry as in prose; indeed, the matter is very disputable, and if we grant the French superiority, it is rather because of the finer qualities of their language than because of higher qualities of thought or feeling. To the student in this country, moreover, the poetical part of the movement is the least likely to appeal. I do not know that it would do you any more good to read the French romantic poets than to read the great English romantic poets. The English poets will furnish you with quite as many ideas and sentiments. But the French poetry was of a totally different order—much more passionate, warm, musical and brightly colored than the average of English romantic poetry. And it was more perfect as to form; the English language is not capable of producing verses of such jewelled splendors as the "Émaux et Camées" of Théophile Gautier. For this reason, perhaps, it may be rather to your interest to give your first attention to French poetry. I shall, however, make this lecture deal chiefly with the story tellers among the French romantics, and their peculiarities as masters of style. . . .

The great names, of course, are Victor Hugo, Alfred de Musset, Sainte-Beuve, Théophile Gautier, Alexandre Dumas, Honoré de Balzac, Prosper Merimée and "George Sand" (Armandine Lucile Dudevant)—in the first group. Of Sainte-Beuve, the greatest critic who ever lived, I have already spoken, and of his influence upon English criticism; he need be mentioned here only as an infallible guide. Without reading him no one can hope to form a correct taste in French literature. . . .

Gautier I shall speak of first. He was a charming man and a very great scholar, and something of his character as well as of his scholarship accounts for the extraordinary beauty of his work. He was one of the few great journalists who never wrote an unkind word about any man, although he attacked parties and principles which he considered wrong. He proclaimed the doctrine of art for art's sake—the creation or reflection of beauty as the chief object of art. His knowledge of Greek thought and feeling particularly influenced his artistic doctrine; unless the subject were beauty, he would not touch it. In this he differed very much from Hugo, who delighted in the horrible and the grotesque. One of his eccentricities is worth mentioning; his chief pleasure was the reading of the dictionary, and it was his custom to ask any young aspirant for literary honors, "Do you like to read dictionaries?" If the young man said, "Yes," they were friends; if he said, "No," Gautier suspected that he would never become a sincere lover of art. Most certainly it was by the study of dictionaries that Gautier became a veritable magician of style, but it does not follow that the same method succeeds in all cases. It succeeded with him not only because he was a genius, but because he had had the very best classical training, and he put it to the most romantic use. We have nothing in English at all like his books—there is nobody to compare with him. You must try to remember just these two things about him—that he chose only subjects which he thought beautiful and heroic, and that he treated them in a most exquisite way. But his aesthetics were not narrow; beauty of any kind attracted him, no matter to what age or part of the world it might belong. . . .

Gautier must have taught a great deal about style to English writers; Merimée could only be admired. The Englishman who comes nearest to Merimée in style is Froude. Merimée is a much greater artist, writing in a much more perfect language, and I doubt whether any Englishman can ever succeed in producing exactly the same effects. In French, Merimée had no imitator before Maupassant; and even Maupassant could not surpass him. It is true that the charm of Merimée is partly due to the strange and exotic character of his subjects, but independently of the subject the method is always supreme. We may say that his was the most realistic of styles, although producing the most romantic effects.

Of the other writers, only a few need to be dealt with at some length. The prose of De Musset, the beautiful little stories of Italian and Parisian life, though romantic in feeling, are written also in a very plain style, approaching that of Mérimée but not equalling it. A better example of his style is in the famous "Confession d'un Enfant du Siècle" (The Confession of a child of the age), which is a passionate piece of autobiography. It tells us all the pain and despair and jealousy of a young man betrayed by the woman to whom he was attached, and the man was the author himself, though other names are of course used. . . .

De Nerval, romantic as he was, came by style closer to Mérimée than to Gautier; his method was very plain and very pure. A new kind of prose was, however, on the verge of appearing. This new kind of prose had been attempted in England and a little by Blake, and a little by Coleridge, but it was only perfected in France. I mean prose poetry in the full sense of the word.

Louis Bertrand is an important name, though his only famous book, "Gaspard de la Nuit," is now out of print, and difficult to obtain. He died very young and left nothing else of importance. But this little book had very great influence upon French letters. It was a book of prose poems, or, if you like, a volume of prose sketches of the most romantic kind, in which every sentence had the rhythm and quality of poetry, and all the text was divided into paragraphs like the verses of the Bible. Bertrand played very much the same part in French literature as Macpherson did, with his Ossian, in England in the latter part of the previous century. There is no evidence of exactly to what extent Bertrand was influenced by Ossian, of which a prose translation was then very popular in France, but it is probable that he was to some degree inspired by it. Bertrand's book did not attract much attention with the public, but men of letters saw its merit, and the poet Baudelaire seized upon the suggestion which it offered for the creation of a new kind of prose. The value of Bertrand was really the impulse which he gave to Baudelaire.

Charles Baudelaire, an eccentric and perhaps slightly mad man of letters, you have perhaps heard of as a poet. He wrote the most extraordinary volume of poetry called "Fleurs du Mal" (Flowers of Evil), and the book is not badly described by its title. As poetry, in regard to form, nothing better was produced by any romantic, but the subjects were most horrible, dealing with crimes and with remorse, despair and other unhealthy emotions. There was also a strange sensualism in the book, something quite exotic and new. But we are now dealing chiefly with Baudelaire chiefly as a prose writer, and you should know that he was quite as great in prose as in verse. He was also a great translator—translating into French the best of De

Quincey and of Edgar Poe. He himself had very much of the imagination of Poe, but it did not take the form of strange stories. Instead of writing stories, he wrote very short romantic sketches, each representing some particular mood, experience or sorrow. And these, which he collected into one volume, under the title of "Petits Poemes en Prose," represented the influence of Bertrand. But Baudelaire was much greater than Bertrand. He showed, as never has been shown before, the extraordinary resources of the French language in prose of poetical form. A year ago I translated for you one of these prose studies, a little composition about the moon, and you may remember what a strange thing it was. The new poetical prose was fairly established by the publication of this book. But such prose was not adapted to the writing of novels and long stories. It could only be used for very short studies of a highly emotional character. . . .

BAUDELAIRE AND LOTI
(1915)

BAUDELAIRE believed that prose could be made quite as poetical as verse or even more so, for a prose that could preserve the rhythm of poetry without its monotony, and the melody of poetry without rhythm, might become in the hands of the master even more effective than verse. I do not know whether this is really true. I am inclined to think that it is; but I do not feel sufficiently learned in certain matters related to the question to venture a definite opinion. Enough to say that Baudelaire thought it possible, and he tried to make a new kind of prose; and the book containing these attempts entitled "Little Poems in Prose" is a wonderful treasure. But Baudelaire did not say anything very extravagantly in its preface. He only expressed the conviction that a poetical prose might be used with good effects for certain particular subjects,—dreams, reveries, the thoughts that men think in solitude, when the life of the world is not about them to disturb their meditations; his prose essays are all reveries, dreams, fantasies. . . .

The greatest living prose writer among the French is Pierre Loti (Julien Viaud), a French naval officer, and you know a member of the Academy. I hope that you have not been prejudiced against him by the stupid criticisms of very shallow men; and that you do not make the mistake of blaming the writer for certain observations regarding Japan, which were made during a stay of only some weeks in this country. Although he was here only for some weeks, and could only describe exactly what he saw, knowing nothing about Japan except through his eyes, yet his sketches of Japan are incomparably finer and truer than anything which has been done by any other living writer. His comments, his inferences may be entirely wrong (they often are); but that has nothing really to do with the merit of his descriptions. When he describes exactly what he sees, then he is like a wonderful magician. There is nobody else living who could do the same thing. I suppose you know that his reputation does not depend upon his Japanese work, however, but upon some twenty volumes of travel containing the finest prose that has ever been written. . . .

Now after this little digression let me come back to the subject of variety in style. Loti knows the art of it; so does many another French writer; but very few Englishmen do. What I am going to say is this, that an author ought to be able to choose a different style for different kinds of work,—that is, a great author. But it is so much trouble to master even one style perfectly well, that very few authors attempt this. However, I think it can be laid down as a true axiom that the style ought to vary with the subject in certain cases; and I think that the great writers of the future will so vary it. The poetical prose, of which I gave you an example from Loti, is admirably suited for particular kinds of composition—short and dreamy things. . . .

Irony, Laforgue, and Some Satire

EZRA POUND, poet, critic, and literary gadfly, received the Bollingen Prize for Poetry in 1948 for the *Pisan Cantos*, written in an American prison at Pisa where Pound—born in Idaho and raised in Pennsylvania—was awaiting trial for treason. The prize set off a long and bitter controversy, centered on the question of the relationship between artist and society. The *Pisan Cantos* formed a section of the immensely long *Cantos*, designed as a kind of secular *Divine Comedy* (though Pound never created a Paradiso), in which the poet searches through past literature and history for the sources of our present political and cultural dilemmas. The *Cantos* increasingly displayed those attitudes that led Pound to fascism and radio broadcasts on behalf of Mussolini. Instead of later standing trial, Pound was hospitalized and eventually released.

A more attractive period of Pound's career was the decade from approximately 1912 to 1922, when he encouraged, advised, or publicized other writers, including Robert Frost, T. S. Eliot, W. B. Yeats, and James Joyce; at the same time he tried to find his own poetic voice, and to direct English poetry away from its Georgian, post-Romantic softness. He wrote that he aimed to "make new his own poetry" and "reform Anglo-American poetry completely." He sought help in past literature; indeed, much of his poetry, then and later, stems from a critical relationship to this literature. Trained as a teacher of Romance languages, he studied and translated Provençal and Italian Renaissance poetry, as well as Greek and Latin poetry, and sought models or "masks" in these works.

Like Henry James and T. S. Eliot, he remained an expatriate; like

214

them, too, he was devoted to French literature. Among nineteenth-century French poets he admired especially Théophile Gautier, whose 1852 collection *Emaux et Camées* (Enamels and Cameos) impressed him with its "hard, concise, lucidly outlined poetry," an antidote to the "soft" diction of much English poetry written at the time Pound was writing. Of more recent French poets he prized those who emphasized precise imagery (which Pound later termed "phanopoeia") and an intellectual and ironic play on words ("logopoeia"). Thus he valued Tristan Corbière, Arthur Rimbaud, and especially Jules Laforgue (1860–1887), three poets whom, in Pound's extended comment "A Study of French Poets" (printed in *The Little Review,* February, 1918), he was to call "permanent." Pound placed less value on Symbolist poets whose diction was evocative, associative, and indirect. And so, as T. S. Eliot commented on Pound, "he ignores Mallarmé; he is uninterested in Baudelaire." Pound sought to incorporate the devices of "phanopoeia" and "logopoeia" into his own verse and to avoid symbols.

Eliot probably introduced Pound to the poetry of Laforgue, a reversal of their usual roles. Pound, in many ways more attuned to the eighteenth century than to the Romantic tradition, praises Laforgue, in "Irony, Laforgue, and Some Satire," for his sophisticated detachment, his sense of irony, his allusiveness, and his use of the colloquial. Pound calls Laforgue a "purge and critic," a satirist of the sentimental and the banal in past literature. All these qualities find their due place in *Hugh Selwyn Mauberly* (1920), Pound's first group of poems of real distinction.

Bibliography: On Pound and French literature, see Hugh Kenner, "Ezra Pound and the Light of France," *Yale French Studies*, no. 10 (n.d.), 54–64. A necessary article is T. S. Eliot's Introduction to his edition of Pound's *Literary Essays* (London: 1954), pp. ix–xv. A revision of Pound's "Study of French Poets" appeared in *Make It New* (London: 1934), pp. 159–247.

On Pound and Laforgue, see N. Christopher de Nagy, "The Place of Laforgue in Ezra Pound's Literary Criticism," in the collection *Jules Laforgue: Essays in a Poet's Life and Work,* ed. Warren Ramsey (Carbondale, Ill.: 1969), pp. 111–29, an article which sheds valuable light on Pound's critical method. Also, see Warren Ramsey, *Jules Laforgue and the Ironic Inheritance,* (Toronto: 1953), which stresses the influence of Laforgue on Pound's poetry.

On Laforgue in America, see Malcolm Cowley, "Laforgue in America: A Testimony" (in the above-mentioned Ramsey collection, pp. 3–15), which cites Laforgue's influence on Hart Crane and himself. Another poet sometimes linked with Laforgue is Wallace Stevens; Michel Benamou, *Wallace Stevens and the Symbolist Imagination*, (Princeton: 1972), ch. 2, points to likenesses and differences between the two.

"Irony, Laforgue, and Some Satire," first published in *Poetry*, 11 (Nov. 1917), is reprinted in Ezra Pound's *Literary Essays* (New York: New Directions, 1954), pp. 280–84. The first page of the essay is omitted here.

IRONY, LAFORGUE, AND SOME SATIRE
(1917)

IT IS IMPOSSIBLE that Jules Laforgue should have written his poems in America in 'the eighties'. He was born in 1860, died in 1887 of *la misère,* of consumption and abject poverty in Paris. The vaunted sensitiveness of French perception, and the fact that he knew a reasonable number of wealthy and influential people, did nothing to prevent this. He had published two small volumes, one edition of each. The seventh edition of his collected poems is dated 1913, and doubtless they have been reprinted since then with increasing celerity.

He is perhaps the most sophisticated of all the French poets, so it is not to be supposed that any wide public has welcomed or will welcome him in England or America. The seven hundred people in both those countries, who have read him with exquisite pleasure, will arise to combat this estimate, but no matter. His name is as well known as Mallarmé's, his writings perhaps are as widely distributed. The anthology of Van Bever and Leautaud has gone into, I suppose, its fiftieth thousand.

> Un couchant des Cosmogonies!
> Ah! que la Vie est quotidienne . . .
> Et, du plus vrai qu'on se souvienne,
> Comme on fut piètre et sans génie. . . .

What in heaven's name is the man in the street to make of this, or of the *Complainte des Bons Ménages!*

> L'Art sans poitrine m'a trop longtemps bercé dupe.
> Si ses labours sont fiers, que ses blés décevants!
> Tiens, laisse-moi bêler tout aux plis de ta jupe
>   Qui fleure le couvent.

The red-blood has turned away, like the soldier in one of Plato's dialogues. Delicate irony, the citadel of the intelligent, has a curious effect on these people. They wish always to be exhorted, at all times no matter how incongruous and unsuitable, to do those things which almost anyone will and does do whenever suitable opportunity is presented. As Henry James has said, 'It was a period when writers besought the deep blue sea "to roll".'

The ironist is one who suggests that the reader should think, and this process being unnatural to the majority of mankind, the way of the ironical is beset with snares and with furze-bushes.

Laforgue was a purge and a critic. He laughed out the errors of Flaubert, i.e., the clogging and cumbrous historical detail. He left *Coeur Simple, L'Education, Madame Bovary, Bouvard.* His, Laforgue's, *Salome* makes game of the rest. The short story has become vapid because sixty thousand story writers have all set themselves to imitating De Maupassant, perhaps a thousand from the original.

I think Laforgue implies definitely that certain things in prose were at an end. I think also that he marks the next phase after Gautier in French poetry. It seems to me that without a familiarity with Laforgue one can not appreciate—i.e., determine the value of—certain positives and certain negatives in French poetry since 1890.

He is an incomparable artist. He is, nine-tenths of him, critic—dealing for the most part with literary poses and *clichés,* taking them as his subject matter; and—and this is the important thing when we think of him as a poet—he makes them a vehicle for the expression of his own very personal emotions, of his own unperturbed sincerity.

> Je ne suis pas 'ce gaillard-là!' ni Le Superbe!
> Mais mon âme, qu'un cri un peu cru exacerbe,
> Est au fond distinguée et franche comme une herbe.

This is not the strident and satiric voice of Corbière, calling Hugo *'Garde Nationale épique',* and Lamartine *'Lacrimatoire des abonnés'.* It is not Tailhade drawing with rough strokes the people he sees daily in Paris, and bursting with guffaws over the Japanese in their mackintoshes, the West Indian mulatto behind the bar in the Quartier. It is not Georges Fourest burlesquing in a café; Fourest's guffaw is magnificent, he is hardly satirical. Tailhade draws from life and indulges in occasional squabbles. Corbière is hard-bitten, perhaps the most poignant poet since Villon, in very much Villon's manner.

Laforgue was a better artist than any of these men save Corbière. He was not in the least of their sort. Corbière lived from 1842 to 1875. Tailhade was born in 1854, and is still living. During the eighties he seems to have been writing Swinburnian verse, and his satires *Au Pays du Mufle*, now part of *Poèmes Aristophanesques*, appeared in 1891. Corbière's poems, first printed in 1873, were hardly obtainable until the reprint of 1891. Thus, so far as the public is concerned, these poets are almost contemporary with each other.

They 'reached' England in the nineties. Beardsley's *Under the Hill* was until recently the only successful attempt to produce 'anything like Laforgue' in our tongue. *Under the Hill* was issued in a limited edition. Laforgue's *Moralités Légendaires* was issued in England by the Ricketts and Hacon press in a limited edition, and there the thing has remained. Laforgue can never become a popular cult because tyros can not imitate him. Recent translations of his prose are held up because of copyright laws.

I do not think one can too carefully discriminate between Laforgue's tone and that of his contemporary French satirists. He is the finest wrought; he is most 'verbalist'. Bad verbalism is rhetoric, or the use of *cliché* unconsciously, or a mere playing with phrases. But there is good verbalism, distinct from lyricism or imagism, and in this Laforgue is a master. He writes not the popular language of any country but an international tongue common to the excessively cultivated, and to those more or less familiar with French literature of the first three-fourths of the nineteenth century.

He has done, sketchily and brilliantly, for French literature a work not incomparable to what Flaubert was doing for 'France' in *Bouvard and Pécuchet*, if one may compare the flight of the butterfly with the progress of an ox, both proceeding toward the same point of the compass. He has dipped his wings in the dye of scientific terminology. Pierrot *imberbe* has

Un air d'hydrocephale asperge.

The tyro can not play about with such things, the game is too dangerous. Verbalism demands a set form used with irreproachable skill. Satire needs, usually, the form of cutting rhymes to drive it home.

Chautauquas, Mrs. Eddys, Dr. Dowies, Comstocks, societies for the prevention of all human activities are impossible in the wake of Laforgue. And he is therefore an exquisite poet, a deliverer of the nations, a Numa Pompilius, a father of light. And to the crowd this mystery, the mystery why such force should reside in so fragile a book, why such power should coincide with so great a nonchalance of manner, will remain forever a mystery.

> Que loin l'âme type
> Qui m'a dit adieu
> Parce que mes yeux
> Manquaient de principes!
>
> Elle, en ce moment,
> Elle, si pain tendre,
> Oh! peut-être engendre
> Quelque garnement.
>
> Car on l'a unie
> Avec un monsieur,
> Ce qu'il y a de mieux,
> Mais pauvre en génie.

Laforgue is perhaps incontrovertible. John B. Yeats has written of the relation of art and 'certitude' and we are perhaps too prone to connect 'certitude' only with the 'strong silent man' of the kinema. There are, however, various species.

T. S. ELIOT

(1888–1965)

Baudelaire

AMONG MAJOR AMERICAN AUTHORS, Henry Adams, Henry James, Ezra Pound, and T. S. Eliot have read most deeply in French literature and thought. Of these, T. S. Eliot, poet, critic, man of letters, and Nobel Prize winner (1948), has probably absorbed most directly into his moral point of view and into his poetic style the lessons of the French writers he studied.

After his graduation from Harvard, where his interest in French literature had been whetted by the teaching of Irving Babbitt, Eliot elected to spend an academic year (1910–11) at the Sorbonne. There he attended Henri Bergson's lectures. In Paris, also, he improved his conversation in French under the tutorship of Henri Alain-Fournier, a young French writer who left one significant novel, *Le Grand Meaulnes* (1912), before being reported missing in action in 1914. Fournier prescribed some of Paul Claudel's works for their lessons, and undoubtedly also introduced Eliot to the work of his friend and correspondent, Jacques Rivière, a neo-classicist, for whom Eliot was later to write an obituary notice (1925).

Eliot settled in London in 1915, the first step toward his eventual naturalization as a British subject in 1927 and his conversion to the Anglican Church the same year. During his years as assistant editor of the *Egoist* (until 1922), editor of the *Criterion* (1922–39), and contributor to *La Nouvelle Revue Française* (1922–27), he maintained his lively interest, indeed immersion, in French letters. In 1929 Eliot stated: "We feel some pride in the fact that the *Criterion* was the first literary review in England to print work by such writers as Marcel Proust, Paul Valéry, Jacques Rivière, Ramon Fernandez, Jacques Maritain, Charles Maurras, Henri Massis . . and others." Of his own prose, Donald Gallup's *T. S. Eliot: A Bibliography* (New York: 1969) lists more than forty-five prefaces, essays, translations,

220

and reviews dealing with French literature, mostly before 1935, extending in range from a preface (1931) to Pascal's *Pensées* to a preface for an English translation of Charles-Louis Philippe's *Bubu de Montparnasse* (1900), a novel about underground Parisian life. In 1930 Eliot made a notable translation of the poem *Anabase* (1924), by St. John Perse. Also, Eliot's body of poetry includes four poems written in French. His example lends weight to his statement that it is necessary to know at least two cultures in order to be really cultured. He himself in his writings has given evidence of his knowledge of Italian and Latin.

Eliot once declared himself a classicist in literature, a royalist in politics, and an Anglo-Catholic in religion. These attitudes had been bolstered by a reading of Charles Maurras, whose *L'Avenir de l'Intelligence* (1905) Eliot was to call in 1926 a specimen of the classical spirit in full play. The Anglo-American poet defended Maurras's political program, *L'Action Française*, until such time as Maurras displayed open fascist sympathies. Eliot also admired Julien Benda's *Belphégor* (1912), which espoused an antiromantic political and esthetic doctrine.

Eliot praised the "formal beauty" of Benda's criticism, and in his short essay "The French Intelligence" (included in *The Sacred Wood*, 1920), Eliot cites Benda's work as a demonstration of the French critical tradition, superior to the English. "The French Intelligence" follows the precedent set by earlier essays by Henry James ("The Reminiscences of Ernest Renan," 1883) and Matthew Arnold ("The Literary Influence of Academies," in *Essays in Criticism: First Series*, 1865) in commending the cogency and clarity of French critical analysis. Eliot was also influenced by the neo-Thomist work, *Réflexions sur l'Intelligence* (1924), of the Catholic philosopher, Jacques Maritain.

A second and different kind of French influence contributed to the development of his poetic style. A reading in 1908 of Arthur Symon's *The Symbolist Movement in Literature* (1899) led him to a reading of the French poets, particularly Baudelaire (1821–1867) and Laforgue, and he learned from them how to write poetry in a contemporary idiom. He wrote: "The kind of poetry that I needed to teach me the use of my own voice, did not exist in English at all; it was only to be found in French" ("Modern Education and the Classics," *Selected Essays*, 1951). From Corbière and, especially, Laforgue, he derived the witty, unexpectedly allusive, half-ironic, half-pathetic tone he was to use in "The Love Song of J. Alfred Prufrock" (1915). In addition to Baudelaire, Corbière, and Laforgue, he was to echo in his later verse lines and approaches from other French poets, chiefly Gautier, Mallarmé, Rimbaud, and Valéry.

Baudelaire taught him how poetry could reflect the horrors of city life; the French poet's imprint is evident in Eliot's "The Wasteland" (1922), a landmark in twentieth-century poetry, recording the sterility of modern society. After this poem Eliot turned toward religion, which would elevate him, he believed, above the ennui and disorder of our times. In the essay (1930) on Baudelaire that follows, Eliot explains Baudelaire's satanism as an antecedent to spiritual faith.

Bibliography: The following are pertinent to the subject of Eliot and France: René Taupin, *L'Influence du Symbolisme français sur la poésie américaine (1910–1920)* (Paris: 1929); E. J. H. Greene, *T. S. Eliot et la France* (Paris: 1951); Grover Smith, Jr., *T. S. Eliot's Poetry and Plays: A Study in Sources and Meanings,* (Chicago: 1956); Herbert Howarth, *Notes on Some Figures behind T. S. Eliot,* ch. 6 (Boston: 1964). A French appraisal by a fellow neo-classicist is Ramon Fernandez, "The Classicism of T. S. Eliot," in *Messages* (Port Washington, N. Y.: 1964).

"Baudelaire" is reprinted from *Selected Essays: 1917–1932* (New York: Harcourt, Brace and Company, 1932), pp. 335–45. The essay appears here in its entirety.

BAUDELAIRE

(1932)

I

ANYTHING like a just appreciation of Baudelaire has been slow to arrive in England, and still is defective or partial even in France. There are, I think, special reasons for the difficulty in estimating his worth and finding his place. For one thing, Baudelaire was in some ways far in advance of the point of view of his own time, and yet was very much of it, very largely partook of its limited merits, faults, and fashions. For one thing, he had a great part in forming a generation of poets after him; and in England he had what is in a way the misfortune to be first and extravagantly advertised by Swinburne, and taken up by the followers of Swinburne. He was universal, and at the same time confined by a fashion which he himself did most to create. To dissociate the permanent from the temporary, to distinguish the man from his influence, and finally to detach him from the associations of those English poets who first admired him, is no small task. His comprehensiveness itself makes difficulty, for it tempts the partisan critic, even now, to adopt Baudelaire as the patron of his own beliefs.

It is the purpose of this essay to affirm the importance of Baudelaire's prose works, a purpose justified by the translation of one of those works which is indispensable for any student of his poetry.[1] This is to see Baudelaire as something more than the author of the *Fleurs du Mal,* and consequently to revise somewhat our estimate of that book. Baudelaire came into vogue at a time when "Art for Art's sake" was a dogma. The care which he took over his poems, and the fact that contrary to the fluency of his time, both in France and England he restricted himself to this one volume, encouraged the opinion that Baudelaire was an artist exclusively for art's sake. The doctrine does not, of course, really apply to anybody; no one applied it less than Pater, who spent many years, not so much in illustrating it, as in expounding it as a *theory of life,* which is not the same thing at all. But it was a doctrine which did affect criticism and appreciation, and which did obstruct a proper judgment of Baudelaire. He is in fact a greater man than was imagined, though perhaps not such a perfect poet.

Baudelaire has, I believe, been called a fragmentary Dante, for what that description is worth. It is true that many people who enjoy Dante enjoy Baudelaire; but the differences are as important as the similarities. Baudelaire's inferno is very different in quality and significance from that of Dante. Truer, I think, would be the description of Baudelaire as a later and more limited Goethe. As we begin to see him now, he represents his own age in somewhat the same way as that in which Goethe represents an earlier age. As a critic of the present generation, Mr. Peter Quennell has recently said in his book, *Baudelaire and the Symbolists:*

He had enjoyed a *sense of his own age,* had recognized its pattern while the pattern was yet incomplete, and—because it is only our misapprehension of

[1] *Journaux Intimes,* translated by Christopher Isherwood, and published by the Blackamore Press and the Beacon Press.

the present which prevents our looking into the immediate future, our ignorance of today and of its real as apart from its spurious tendencies and requirements—had anticipated many problems, both on the aesthetic and on the moral plane, in which the fate of modern poetry is still concerned.

Now the man who has this sense of his age is hard to analyse. He is exposed to its follies as well as sensitive to its inventions; and in Baudelaire, as well as in Goethe, is some of the outmoded nonsense of his time. The parallel between the German poet who has always been the symbol of perfect "health" in every sense, as well as of universal curiosity, and the French poet who has been the symbol of morbidity in mind and concentrated interests in work, may seem paradoxical. But after this lapse of time the difference between "health" and "morbidity" in the two men becomes more negligible; there is something artificial and even priggish about Goethe's healthiness, as there is about Baudelaire's unhealthiness; we have passed beyond men with restless, critical, curious minds and the "sense of the age"; both men who understood and foresaw a great deal. Goethe, it is true, was interested in many subjects which Baudelaire left alone; but by Baudelaire's time it was no longer necessary for a man to embrace such varied interests in order to have the sense of the age; and in retrospect some of Goethe's studies seem to us (not altogether justly) to have been merely dilettante hobbies. The most of Baudelaire's prose writings (with the exception of the translations from Poe, which are of less interest to an English reader) are as important as the most of Goethe. They throw light on the *Fleurs du Mal* certainly, but they also expand immensely our appreciation of their author.

It was once the mode to take Baudelaire's Satanism seriously, as it is now the tendency to present Baudelaire as a serious and Catholic Christian. Especially as a prelude to the *Journaux Intimes* this diversity of opinion needs some discussion. I think that the latter view—that Baudelaire is essentially Christian—is nearer the truth than the former, but it needs considerable reservation. When Baudelaire's Satanism is dissociated from its less creditable paraphernalia, it amounts to a dim intuition of a part, but a very important part, of Christianity. Satanism itself, so far as not merely an affectation, was an attempt to get into Christianity by the back door. Genuine blasphemy, genuine in spirit and not purely verbal, is the product of partial belief, and is as impossible to the complete atheist as to the perfect Christian. It is a way of affirming belief. This state of partial belief is manifest throughout the *Journaux Intimes*. What is significant about Baudelaire is his theological innocence. He is discovering Christianity for himself; he is not assuming it as a fashion or weighing social or political reasons, or any other accidents. He is beginning, in a way, at the beginning; and being a discoverer, is not altogether certain what he is exploring and to what it leads; he might almost be said to be making again, as one man, the effort of scores of generations. His Christianity is rudimentary or embryonic; at best, he has the excesses of a Tertullian (and even Tertullian is not considered wholly orthodox and well balanced). His business was not to practise Christianity, but—what was much more important for his time—to assert its *necessity*.

Baudelaire's morbidity of temperament cannot, of course, be ignored: and no one who has looked at the work of Crépet or the recent small biographical study of François Porché can forget it. We should be misguided if we treated it as an unfortunate ailment which can be discounted or attempted to detach the sound from the unsound in his work. Without the morbidity none of his work would be possible or significant; his weaknesses can be composed into a larger whole of strength, and this is implied in my assertion that neither the health of Goethe nor the malady of Baudelaire matters in itself: it is what both men made of their endowments that matters. To the eye of the world, and quite properly for all questions of private life, Baudelaire was thoroughly perverse and insufferable: a man with a talent for ingratitude and unsociability, intolerably irritable, and with a mulish determination to make the worst of everything; if he had money, to squander it; if he had friends, to alienate them; if he had any good fortune, to disdain it. He had the pride of the man who feels in himself great weakness and great strength. Having great genius, he had neither the patience nor the inclination, had he had the power, to overcome his weakness; on the contrary, he exploited it for theoretical purposes. The morality of such a course may be a matter of endless dispute; for Baudelaire, it was the way to liberate his mind and give us the legacy and lesson that he has left.

He was one of those who have great strength, but strength merely to *suffer*. He could not escape suffering and could not transcend it, so he *attracted* pain to himself. But what he could do, with that immense passive strength and sensibilities which no pain could impair, was to study his suffering. And in this limitation he is wholly unlike Dante, not even like any character in Dante's Hell. But, on the other hand, such suffering as Baudelaire's implies the possibility of a positive state of beatitude. Indeed, in his way of suffering is already a kind of presence of the supernatural and the superhuman. He rejects always the purely natural and the purely human; in other words, he is neither "Naturalist" nor "humanist." Either because he cannot adjust himself to the actual world he has to reject it in favour of Heaven and Hell, or because he has the perception of Heaven and Hell he rejects the present world: both ways of putting it are tenable. There is in his statements a good deal of romantic detritus; *ses ailes de géant l'empêchent de marcher,* he says of the Poet and of the Albatross, but not convincingly; but there is also truth about himself and about the world. His *ennui* may of course be explained, as everything can be explained in psychological or pathological terms; but it is also, from the opposite point of view, a true form of *acedia,* arising from the unsuccessful struggle towards the spiritual life.

II

From the poems alone, I venture to think, we are not likely to grasp what seems to me the true sense and significance of Baudelaire's mind. Their excellence of form, their perfection of phrasing, and their superficial coherence, may give them the appearance of presenting a definite and final state of mind. In reality, they seem to me to have the external but not the internal form of classic art. One might even hazard the conjecture that the care for perfection of form, among some of the romantic poets of the nineteenth century, was an effort to support, or to conceal from view, an inner disorder. Now the true claim of Baudelaire as an artist is not that he found a superficial form, but that he was searching for a form of life. In minor form he never indeed equalled Théophile Gautier, to whom he significantly dedicated his poems: in the best of the slight verse of Gautier there is a satisfaction, a balance of inwards and form, which we do not find in Baudelaire. He had a greater technical ability than Gautier, and yet the content of feeling is constantly bursting the receptacle. His apparatus, by which I do not mean his command of words and rhythms, but his stock of imagery (and every poet's stock of imagery is circumscribed somewhere), is not wholly perdurable or adequate. His prostitutes, mulattoes, Jewesses, serpents, cats, corpses, form a machinery which has not worn very well; his Poet, or his Don Juan, has a romantic ancestry which is too clearly traceable. Compare with the costumery of Baudelaire the stock of imagery of the *Vita Nuova,* or of Cavalcanti, and you find Baudelaire's does not everywhere wear as well as that of several centuries earlier; compare him with Dante or Shakespeare, for what such a comparison is worth, and he is found not only a much smaller poet, but one in whose work much more that is perishable has entered.

To say this is only to say that Baudelaire belongs to a definite place in time. Inevitably the offspring of romanticism, and by his nature the first counter-romantic in poetry, he could, like any one else, only work with the materials which were there. It must not be forgotten that a poet in a romantic age cannot be a "classical" poet except in tendency. If he is sincere, he must express with individual differences the general state of mind—not as a *duty*, but simply because he cannot help participating in it. For such poets, we may expect often to get much help from reading their prose works and even notes and diaries; help in deciphering the discrepancies between head and heart, means and end, material and ideals.

What preserves Baudelaire's poetry from the fate of most French poetry of the nineteenth century up to his time, and has made him, as M. Valéry has said in a recent introduction to the *Fleurs du Mal,* the one modern French poet to be widely read abroad, is not quite easy to conclude. It is partly that technical mastery which can hardly be overpraised, and which has made his verse an inexhaustible study for later poets, not only in his own language. When we read

> Maint joyau dort enseveli
> Dans les ténèbres et l'oubli,
> Bien loin des pioches et des sondes;
> Mainte fleur épanche à regret
> Son parfum doux comme un secret
> Dans les solitudes profondes,

we might for a moment think it a more lucid bit of Mallarmé; and so original is the arrangement of words that we might easily overlook its borrowing from Gray's *Elegy*. When we read

> Valse mélancolique et langoureux vertige!

we are already in the Paris of Laforgue. Baudelaire gave to French poets as generously as he borrowed from English and American poets. The renovation of the versification of Racine has been mentioned often enough; quite genuine, but might be overemphasized, as it sometimes comes near to being a trick. But even without this, Baudelaire's variety and resourcefulness would still be immense.

Furthermore, besides the stock of images which he used that seems already second-hand, he gave new possibilities to poetry in a new stock of imagery of contemporary life.

> . . . Au cœur d'un vieux faubourge, labyrinthe fangeux
> Ou l'humanite grouille en ferments orageux,
>
> On voit un vieux chiffonier qui vient, hochant le tête
> Buttant, et se cognant aux murs comme un poéte.

This introduces something new, and something universal in modern life. (The last line quoted, which in ironic terseness anticipates Corbière, might be contrasted with the whole poem *Bénédiction* which begins the volume.) It is not merely in the use of imagery of common life, not merely in the use of imagery of the sordid life of a great metropolis, but in the elevation of such imagery to the *first intensity*—presenting it as it is, and yet making it represent something much more than itself—that Baudelaire has created a mode of release and expression for other men.

This invention of language, at a moment when French poetry in particular was famishing for such invention, is enough to make of Baudelaire a great poet, a great landmark in poetry. Baudelaire is indeed the greatest exemplar in *modern* poetry in any language, for his verse and language is the nearest thing to a complete renovation that we have experienced. But his renovation of an attitude towards life is no less radical and no less important. In his verse, he is now less a model to be imitated or a source to be drained than a reminder of the duty, the consecrated task, of sincerity. From a fundamental sincerity he could not deviate. The superficies of sincerity (as I think has not always been remarked) is not always there. As I have suggested, many of his poems are insufficiently removed from their romantic origins, from Byronic paternity and Satanic fraternity. The "satanism" of the Black Mass was very much in the air; in exhibiting it Baudelaire is the voice of his time; but I would observe that in Baudelaire as in no one else, it is redeemed by *meaning something else.* He uses the same paraphernalia, but cannot limit its symbolism even to all that of which he is conscious. Compare him with Huysmans in *A rebours, En route,* and *Là-bas.* Huysmans, who is a first-rate realist of his time, only succeeds in making his diabolism interesting when he treats it externally, when he is merely describing a manifestation of his period (if such it was). His own interest in such matters is, like his interest in Christianity, a petty affair. Huysmans merely provides a document. Baudelaire would not even provide that, if he had been really absorbed in that ridiculous hocus-pocus. But actually Baudelaire is concerned, not with demons, black masses, and romantic blasphemy, but with the real problem of good and evil. It is hardly more than an accident of time that he uses the current imagery and vocabulary of blasphemy. In the middle nineteenth century, the age which (at its best) Goethe had prefigured, an age of bustle, programmes, platforms, scientific progress, humanitar-ianism, and revolutions which improved nothing, an age of progres-sive degradation, Baudelaire perceived that what really matters is Sin and Redemption. It is proof of his honesty that he went as far as he could honestly go and no further. To a mind observant of the post-Voltaire France (*Voltaire . . . le prédicateur des concierges),* a mind which saw the world of *Napoléon le petit* more lucidly than did that of Victor Hugo, a mind which at the same time had no affinity for the *Saint-Sulpicerie* of the day, the recognition of the reality of Sin is a New Life; and the possibility of damnation is so immense a relief in a world of electoral reform, plebiscites, sex reform, and dress reform, that damnation itself is an immediate form of salvation—of salvation from the ennui of modern life, because it at last gives some significance to living. It is this, I believe, that Baudelaire is trying to express; and it is this which separates him from the modernist Protestantism of Byron and Shelley. It is apparently Sin in the Swinburnian sense, but really Sin in the permanent Christian sense, that occupies the mind of Baudelaire.

Yet, as I said, the sense of Evil implies the sense of good. Here too, as Baudelaire apparently confuses, and perhaps did confuse, Evil with its theatrical representations, Baudelaire is not always certain in his notion of the Good. The romantic idea of Love is never quite exorcised, but never quite surrendered to. In *Le Balcon,* which M. Valéry considers, and I think rightly, one of Baudelaire's most beautiful poems, there is all the romantic idea, but something more: the reaching out towards something which cannot be had *in,* but

which may be had partly *through,* personal relations. Indeed, in
much romantic poetry the sadness is due to the exploitation of the
fact that no human relations are adequate to human desires, but also
to the disbelief in any further object for human desires than that
which, being human, fails to satisfy them. One of the unhappy
necessities of human existence is that we have to "find things out for
ourselves." If it were not so, the statement of Dante would have, at
least for poets, done once for all. Baudelaire has all the romantic
sorrow, but invents a new kind of romantic nostalgia, a derivative of
his nostalgia being the *poésie des départs,* the *poésie des salles d'at-
tente.* In a beautiful paragraph of the volume in question, *Mon cœur
mis à nu,* he imagines the vessels lying in harbour as saying: *Quand
partons-nous vers le bonheur?* and his minor successor Laforgue
exclaims: *Comme ils sont beaux, les trins manqués.* The poetry of
flight—which, in contemporary France, owes a great debt to the
poems of the A. O. Barnabooth of Valery Larbaud—is, in its origin
in this paragraph of Baudelaire, a dim recognition of the direction of
beatitude.

But in the adjustment of the natural to the spiritual, of the bestial to
the human and the human to the supernatural, Baudelaire is a bungler
compared with Dante; the best that can be said, and that is a very
great deal, is that what he knew he found out for himself. In his book,
the *Journaux Intimes,* and especially in *Mon cœur mis à nu,* he has a
great deal to say of the love of man and woman. One aphorism which
has been especially noticed is the following: *la volupté unique et
suprême de l'amour gît dans la certitude de faire le mal.* This means, I
think, that Baudelaire has perceived that what distinguishes the
relations of man and woman from the copulation of beasts is the
knowledge of Good and Evil (of *moral* Good and Evil which are not
natural Good and Bad or puritan Right and Wrong). Having an
imperfect, vague romantic conception of Good, he was at least able to
understand that the sexual act as evil is more dignified, less boring,
than as the natural, "lifegiving," cheery automatism of the modern
world. For Baudelaire, sexual operation is at least something not
analogous to Kruschen Salts.

So far as we are human, what we do must be either evil or good;[2] so
far as we do evil or good, we are human; and it is better, in a

[2]"Know ye not, that to whom ye yield yourselves servants to obey, his servants ye
are to whom ye obey: whether of sin unto death, or of obedience unto
righteousness?"—Romans vi. 16.

paradoxical way, to do evil than to do nothing: at least, we exist. It is true to say that the glory of man is his capacity for salvation; it is also true to say that his glory is his capacity for damnation. The worst that can be said of most of our malefactors, from statesmen to thieves, is that they are not men enough to be damned. Baudelaire was man enough for damnation: whether he *is* damned is, of course, another question, and we are not prevented from praying for his repose. In all his humiliating traffic with other beings, he walked secure in this high vocation, that he was capable of a damnation denied to the politicians and the newspaper editors of Paris.

III

Baudelaire's notion of beatitude certainly tended to the wishy-washy; and even in one of the most beautiful of his poems, *L'Invitation au voyage,* he hardly exceeds the *poésie des départs.* And because his vision is here so restricted, there is for him a gap between human love and divine love. His human love is definite and positive, his divine love vague and uncertain: hence his insistence upon the evil of love, hence his constant vituperations of the female. In this there is no need to pry for psychopathological causes, which would be irrelevant at best; for his attitude towards women is consistent with the point of view which he had reached. Had he been a woman he would, no doubt, have held the same views about men. He has arrived at the perception that a woman must be to some extent a symbol; he did not arrive at the point of harmonising his experience with his ideal needs. The complement, and the correction to the *Journaux Intimes,* so far as they deal with the relations of man and woman, is the *Vita Nuova,* and the *Divine Comedy.* But—I cannot assert it too strongly—Baudelaire's view of life, such as it is, is objectively apprehensible, that is to say, his idiosyncrasies can partly explain his view of life, but they cannot explain it away. And this view of life is one which has grandeur and which exhibits heroism; it was an evangel to his time and to ours. *La vraie civilisation,* he wrote, *n'est pas dans le gaz, ni dans la vapeur, ni dans les tables tournantes. Elle est dans la diminution des traces du péché originel.* It is not quite clear exactly what *diminution* here implies, but the tendency of his thought is clear, and the message is still accepted by but few. More than half a century later T. E. Hulme left behind him a paragraph which Baudelaire would have approved:

In the light of these absolute values, man himself is judged to be essentially limited and imperfect. He is endowed with Original Sin. While he can occasionally accomplish acts which partake of perfection, he can never himself *be* perfect. Certain secondary results in regard to ordinary human action in society follow from this. A man is essentially bad, he can only accomplish anything of value by discipline—ethical and political. Order is thus not merely negative, but creative and liberating. Institutions are necessary.

PART VII

The Modern Novel:
French and American Perspectives

André Malraux: A Preface for Faulkner's *Sanctuary* (1933)
Jean-Paul Sartre: American Novelists in French Eyes (1946)
André Gidé: The New American Novelists (1949)
Henry Miller: Blaise Cendrars (1959)

ANDRE MALRAUX
(1901–1976)

A Preface for Faulkner's *Sanctuary*

AN ADVENTUROUS CAREER—encompassing an early archeological expedition to Indo-China (1923), possible participation in the Chinese
Civil War (1926–27), participation in the Spanish Civil War (1937–
38) and in the underground resistance during the Second World War,
and an escape from German imprisonment—made Malraux a legend
in his own time. His many political experiences served as the source
of inspiration for his novels, the best known of which is *La Condition
Humaine* (1933), set in Shanghai during the civil war of the 1920s.
Though Malraux's creative imagination is that of anguish and despair, he advocates that man transcend his tragic existence through a
philosophy of involvement, political and fraternal. After the Second
World War, Malraux devoted himself largely to the Gaullist program
and to art history, as attested to by his four-volume *Psychologie de
l'art* 1948–52).

When the Paris publishing House, Gallimard, decided to put out
French translations of the works of William Faulkner (1897–1962),
Malraux was selected to write the Preface to the first volume,
Sanctuary (trans. 1933). Of this Preface, W. M. Frohock, in *André
Malraux and The Tragic Imagination* (Stanford, Cal.: 1952), makes
this apt comment:

His frequently quoted Preface to the Gallimard edition of *Sanctuary* puts an
infallible finger upon the points where Faulkner's novels are most like his
own. With the modern detective story, Malraux asserts, Faulkner has
managed to combine much of the feeling of Greek tragedy, and, especially,
has captured the feeling that each of his characters is running headlong

235

toward his destiny. . . . Malraux is also intensely interested in the obsessions which shape the conduct of Faulkner's people, and is even more interested in the role of obsession in determining the relation of the author himself to his book. . . . The invitation to apply the insight to his own novels is Malraux's. What else had he done during the decade of his trips to Asia and of his first three novels than seek out what would obsess him and what at the same time would be his subject as well as his master? (p. 92.)

In a 1945 interview, reprinted in *Horizon* (Oct., 1945, 236–42), Malraux forsees the development of a new Atlantic culture, a blending of American and European attributes. He speaks of the impact of the American novelists—Hemingway, Caldwell, Steinbeck, Faulkner—on French writers, but suggests that Europe will help transform the American novel. American fiction suffers a lack: ". . . *to my mind, the essential characteristic of contemporary American writing is that it is the only literature whose creators are not intellectual.* . . . I am convinced that the great problem of this literature is to intellectualize itself without losing its direct approach." (Italics in the original text.) In the converging of national cultures, he continues, American literature will also be affected. Whatever the virtues of Malraux's predictions as prophecy, the interview reveals Malraux's search for cultural metamorphosis, a preoccupation manifesting itself in all his writings on art.

Bibliography: An examination of Malraux as literary critic can be found in Margaret Groves, "The Concept of Literary Creation in the Critical Writings of André Malraux: 1927 to 1935," *Romanic Review*, 61 (1970), 198–208.

The translation which follows was published in *Yale French Studies*, no. 10 (1952), 90–94. The translator is not named.

A PREFACE FOR FAULKNER'S *SANCTUARY*

(1933)

FAULKNER is well aware that detectives do not exist, that the police do not depend on psychology or perspicacity but rather on secret information, and that the escaping murderer is not caught by Mr. Gumshoe or Mr. Shadow, those modest thinkers of police headquarters, but by "plants" in suspicious neighborhoods. One has only to read the memoirs of police chiefs to discover that psychological penetration is not their great quality, and that a good police force is simply the one which has succeeded in organizing its army of informers most efficiently. Faulkner also knows that the gangster is first of all a dealer in alcohol. *Sanctuary* is therefore a novel with a detective-story atmosphere but without detectives, a novel of sordid gangsters who are sometimes cowardly and weak. In this way the author achieves a brutality justified by the setting, as well as the possibility, without abandoning a measure of verisimilitude, of getting credence for rape, lynching, and murder, the forms of violence which the plot imposes on the whole book.

It is probably erroneous to look for the essential part of a detective story in the plot or the hunt for the criminal. Taken by itself, the plot would be only a sort of chess game, an artistic failure. The plot is important in that it is the most efficient way of revealing an ethical or poetic fact in its greatest intensity. The worth of the plot is in what it engenders.

What does it engender in this case? An ill-assorted, powerful, and savagely personal world, sometimes one not without crudity. In Faulkner, there is no particular presentation of man, there are no values, nor, in spite of the stream-of-consciousness monologues in his early books, is there even any psychology. But there is the figure of Destiny, standing alone behind all these similar and diverse beings like Death in a hospital ward of incurables. An intense obsession crushes each of his characters, and in no case do the characters succeed in exorcizing it. The obsession still hovers behind them, unchanging, summoning them instead of awaiting their summons.

Such a realm was for a long time the subject for gossip; even if American rumors did not kindly inform us that alcohol was an integral part of Faulkner's personal legend, the relationship between his universe and those of Poe and Hoffmann would be clear. The same psychological material, the same hatreds, horses, coffins, and obsessions. What differentiates Faulkner and Poe is their individual notions of the work of art. To be more exact, the work of art existed for Poe and dominated the will to express; and this is probably what most separates him from us. When the story was finished, it took on in his mind the limited and independent existence of a picture on the easel.

In the weakening of importance accorded to things, I see the principal element of transformation of our art. In painting, it is clear that a Picasso picture is ever less a canvas, and more and more the indication of a discovery, a landmark left for the passage of tormented genius; in literature, the supremacy of the novel is significant, since, of all the arts (and I am not forgetting music), the novel is the least tractable, the one in which the realm of will is most limited. One can best appreciate how much *The Brothers Karamazoff* and *Illusions perdues* dominate Dostoevsky and Balzac by reading these works after the splendid passive novels of Flaubert. The important thing is not that the author is dominated, but that for the last fifty years he has been increasingly selecting what will dominate him, that he has been arranging the resources of his art with that end in view. Certain great novels have been for their authors primarily the creation of the one thing that could engulf them. And, just as Lawrence wraps himself up in sexuality, so does Faulkner dig down into the irreparable.

A secret force, sometimes an epic one, is released in him every time he succeeds in placing one of his characters face to face with the irreparable. Perhaps his one true subject is the irreparable; perhaps for him there is no question other than that of successfully crushing man. I should not be surprised if he often thought out his scenes before imagining his characters, if the work were in his eyes, not a story whose unfolding determined tragic situations, but contrarily that the plot was created from the dramatic opposition or crushing of unknown characters, and imagination merely served to bring forth characters for this preconceived situation. The impassioned tension, which is Faulkner's strength, stems either from enslaved powerlessness fully comprehended (the girl in the gangster's house), or from irreparable absurdity (the corn-cob rape, the burning of the innocent victim, Popeye the fugitive stupidly condemned for a crime he did not commit; in *While I Lay Dying* the farmer who treats his injured knee by encasing it in cement, the extraordinary monologue of hatred). It is, moreover, absurdity which gives to his almost comical secondary characters (the keeper of the brothel with her dogs) an intensity comparable to that of Shchedrin. I shall not suggest the name of Dickens, for even the secondary characters of Faulkner move in the aura of feeling which gives the work its worth—hatred. Here it is not a matter of the struggle against one's own set of values, of that fatalistic passion by which all the great artists, from Baudelaire to half-blind Nietzsche singing of light, express the essential part of their being; it is a question of a psychological state on which almost all tragic art depends and which has not ever been studied because esthetics do not reveal it: fascination. Just as the opium eater does not discover his universe until he has used the drug, so does the tragic poet express his world only when he is in a particular state, so persistent that it becomes a need. The tragic poet expresses what obsesses him, not to exorcize the obsession (the obsessive object will reappear in his next work), but to change its nature: for, by expressing it with other elements, he makes the obsession enter the relative universe of things he has conceived and dominated. He does not defend himself against anguish by expressing it, but by expressing something else with it, by bringing it back into the universe. The deepest form of fascination, that of the artist, derives its strength from being both horror and the possibility of conceiving horror.

Sanctuary is the intrusion of Greek tragedy into the detective story.

JEAN-PAUL SARTRE

(1905–   )

American Novelists in French Eyes

DURING THE NINETEENTH CENTURY American authors often looked to French fiction—especially the novels of Balzac, Flaubert, Maupassant, and Zola—as setting standards for realism and vigor. In the twentieth century the current of influence has usually run the other way. Beginning in about 1930 and reaching a crescendo in the decade following the Second World War, French writers found in American fiction an originality and force, both in technique and subject matter, lacking in the European novel, and sought to emulate their American counterparts.

Les Cinq Grands ("The Big Five") whom the French admired most—William Faulkner, Ernest Hemingway, John Dos Passos, John Steinbeck, and Erskine Caldwell—employed unconventional prose styles that seemed to probe radically into characters and events. They impressed French writers also with their vitality, their virile pessimism, and above all, their "violence"—an unabashed examination of life's brutalities and a projection of the displaced and disoriented in modern existence. This trait of "violence" so struck the French that Caldwell and Dashiell Hammett, who also cultivated "violence" but did not enjoy critical fame in the United States, won the same approval in France as did Hemingway and Faulkner. (In *Transatlantic Migration,* Thelma Smith and Ward L. Miner note that such American writers as Thomas Wolfe, Willa Cather, and Ellen Glasgow, whose styles were more conventionally realistic or whose approaches to life were more quiet, did not attract French writers.) Defeat in the Second World War and the period of German occupation seemed to validate for the French the postulates of American fiction.

240

The dismembered world of experience, the cruelty and disorienta-
tion, in the works of Richard Wright (1908–1960) also moved French
writers. Wright, in turn, read the Existentialists and emigrated to
Paris in 1946. His novella "The Man Who Lived Underground"
(1944) couples a picture of the terrors of Negro life in America and
some tenets of French Existentialist philosophy.

While some American novelists were possibly overrated by the
French, it is also true that Faulkner, for one, achieved a respect he
deserved earlier in France than in his own country. Among trans-
lators and scholars, Maurice-Edgar Coindreau contributed notably,
over a period of thirty-odd years, to an understanding of Faulkner, as
well as other novelists, in France. Among novelists, André Malraux
was similarly prominent in establishing Faulkner's claims.

Sartre's essay exemplifies the vital involvement of a post-war
generation of French writers with the American novel. In his comprehensive survey, Sartre details the specific indebtedness of certain
French novelists.

Sartre elsewhere has written more specifically of individual American novelists. Among his significant early reviews were: "John Dos
Passos and 1919" (1938), "William Faulkner's *Sartoris*" (1938), and
"On *The Sound and The Fury*: Time in The Work of Faulkner"
(1939). In his essay on Dos Passos, Sartre praises Dos Passos's
narrative technique, which, with its journalistic devices, blends
individual character and social event together, to achieve a total
interpenetration of these qualities. Thus Dos Passos maintains a
consistently phenomenological point of view—a point of view Sartre
seeks to incorporate in his own fiction. In his essays on Faulkner,
Sartre stresses Faulkner's brilliant use of *time* in narrative. In *Sartoris*,
Faulkner mingles past and present with the future nowhere in
evidence; in *The Sound and the Fury*, Faulkner is completely obsessed with the past, with no progression into the future possible.
Intrigued as Sartre is by Faulkner's use of time, the French writer is
unwilling to accede to the notion of a completely closed future. All
three essays illustrate Sartre's discovery in American fiction of new
insights into time and reality.

Bibliography: Some useful references, in an extensive critical literature, are: Claude-Edmond Magny, *L'Age du Roman Américain*
(Paris: 1948); Henri Peyre, *French Novelists of Today*, (New York:
1967), pp. 339–45; Thelma M. Smith and Ward L. Miner, *Transatlantic Migration: The Contemporary American Novel in France*

(Durham, N.C.: 1953); *The Literary Reputation of Hemingway in Europe,* ed. Roger Asselineau, (Paris: 1965), pp. 39–72.

"American Novelsts in French Eyes" was published in the *Atlantic Monthly,* 178 (Aug., 1946), 114–18, as translated by Evelyn de Solis.

AMERICAN NOVELISTS IN FRENCH EYES
(1946)

I

THERE IS ONE American literature for Americans and another for the French. In France the general reader knows *Babbitt* and *Gone With the Wind,* but these books have had no influence on French literature. The greatest literary development in France between 1929 and 1939 was the discovery of Faulkner, Dos Passos, Hemingway, Caldwell, Steinbeck. The choice of these authors, many people have told me, was due to Professor Maurice Coindreau of Princeton, who sent us their works in translation with excellent prefaces.

But a selection by any one man is effective only if he foresees the demands of the collective group to which he addresses himself. With Coindreau as intermediary, the French public selected the works it needed. It is true that these authors have not had in France a popular success comparable to that of Sinclair Lewis. Their influence was far more restricted, but infinitely more profound. We needed them and not your famous Dreiser. To writers of my generation, the publication of *The 42nd Parallel, Light in August, A Farewell to Arms,* evoked a revolution similar to the one produced fifteen years earlier in Europe by the *Ulysses* of James Joyce. Their reception was prepared for by the excellent *Bridge of San Luis Rey* of Thornton Wilder.

It seemed to us suddenly that we had just learned something and that our literature was about to pull itself out of its old ruts. At once, for thousands of young intellectuals, the American novel took its place, together with jazz and the movies, among the best of the importations from the United States. America became for us the country of Faulkner and Dos Passos, just as it had already been the home of Louis Armstrong, King Vidor, the Blues. The large frescoes of Vidor joined with the passion and violence of *The Sound and the Fury* and *Sanctuary* to compose for us the face of the United States—a face tragic, cruel, and sublime. Malraux wrote in a famous preface, "The novels of Faulkner are eruptions of Greek tragedy in the detective story."

What fascinated us all really—petty bourgeois that we were, sons of peasants securely attached to the earth of our farms, intellectuals entrenched in Paris for life—was the constant flow of men across a whole continent, the exodus of an entire village to the orchards of California, the hopeless wanderings of the hero in *Light in August*, and of the uprooted people who drifted along at the mercy of the storms in *The 42nd Parallel*, the dark murderous fury which sometimes swept through an entire city, the blind and criminal love in the novels of James Cain.

It takes some time for an influence to produce its effect, and it was during the German occupation, when the Germans forbade all printing and reprinting of American books, that we began to see in France the greatest number of works inspired by this new manner of writing. It seemed as if, cut off from their habitual dose of American novels, the French began to write some themselves in order to have something to read.

The French novel which caused the greatest furor between 1940 and 1945, *The Stranger*, by Albert Camus, a young writer who was then director of the clandestine newspaper, *Combat*, deliberately borrowed the technique of *The Sun Also Rises*. In *Un Homme Marche dans la Ville*, the only and posthumous book of Jean Jansion, a very young man who was killed by the Germans in 1944, you might be reading Hemingway—the same short, brutal sentences, the same lack of psychological analysis, the same heroes. *Les Mendicants,* by Desforêts, and *Gerbebaude,* by Magnane, used the technique of Faulkner's *As I Lay Dying* without changing anything. They took from Faulkner the method of reflecting different aspects of the same event, through the monologues of different sensitivities.

The technique of Simone de Beauvoir, also, was inspired by Faulkner. Without him she never would have conceived the idea, used in *Le Sang des Autres,* of cutting the chronological order of the story and substituting instead a more subtle order, half logical, half intuitive. And as for me, it was after reading a book by Dos Passos that I thought for the first time of weaving a novel out of various, simultaneous lives, with characters who pass each other by without ever knowing one another and who all contribute to the atmosphere of a moment or of a historical period.

These attempts provoked others. Moulouji, the young son of an Arabian workman, found himself suddenly, at thirteen, adopted by French writers and actors who made him read Faulkner and Steinbeck long before he ever heard of Racine or Voltaire. His culture is entirely surrealist and American. Not very long ago, when he was nearly twenty, he spoke to me enthusiastically about a book he had just read, which related events "in such a new and such an original manner." It was *The Three Musketeers* of Alexandre Dumas *Père!* Moulouji writes "American" as naturally as one breathes, and with the same innocence. His first book, *Enrico,* which won the Prix de la Pléiade—is not inferior in its violence, its naïve perversity, realism, and poetry, to *Tobacco Road* or *Tragic Ground.*

Today two thirds of the manuscripts which young writers submit to the review which I direct are written à la Caldwell, à la Hemingway, à la Dos Passos. A student named Guicharnaud even showed me short stories so profoundly inspired by Saroyan that, not content with using "the American technique" (we speak today in France of "the American technique" in literature as if it referred to dental surgery or a taste for champagne, as we said a while back about a pianist that he had "the American touch"), he locates all his stories in the United States—a United States filled with speak-easies, gangsters, motorcycle cops, all of which derive from novels and films at least twenty years old.

These stories bring to mind that other America of fantasy which Kafka described in *Amerika.* Guicharnaud, like Kafka, had never set foot in the United States. He achieved his ideal the day he attempted to retell, in the Saroyan manner, while listening to Duke Ellington's music, an American pre-war film, *Only Angels Have Wings,* which he had seen the day before. You can imagine that, in spite of these new works, we missed American books during the occupation.

A black market for American books was established. The headquarters was the Café de Flore, where poor students resold at a profit books which they found in the bookstalls along the Seine. Snobbishness played its part during the period when the underground was unorganized and not yet hazardous and when amateurs thought they could save France by scratching V signs on the walls. The reading of novels by Faulkner and Hemingway became for some a symbol of resistance. Stenographers believed they could demonstrate against the Germans by reading *Gone With the Wind* in the Métro. In 1944,

Marc Barbizat, director of the luxurious review *L'Arbalète,* which he published himself with a hand press at Lyons, prepared secretly one number consisting of extracts from American books which had not yet been translated. He intended to publish them without submitting them to the censor, right in the midst of the occupation. The work took longer than he anticipated, however. This number of the review appeared shortly after the liberation. It was eagerly read.

II

It is easy to understand my eagerness to see the country of these great writers when I was flying to America in January, 1945. I must confess that in one respect I was disappointed. First, it was impossible to meet any of these men. They were in France, in England, in the Orient—everywhere, indeed, except in the United States. Also, the majority of the cultivated Americans whom I met did not share my enthusiasm for them. An American lady who knew Europe very well asked me one day what American writers I preferred. When I mentioned Faulkner, the other people present started to laugh. The lady, gently amused, said, "Good heavens—that *old* Faulkner!"

Later I met a young liberal writer—the author of some very good historical novels. I told him I had been asked by my publishers to get in touch with literary agents of several writers who were particularly admired in France. He asked me the names of these writers. When I mentioned Caldwell, his friendly smile vanished suddenly; at the name of Steinbeck he raised his eyebrows; and at the mention of Faulkner he cried indignantly, "You French! Can't you ever like anything but filth?" At this same time a New York editor refused to allow the *Nouvelle Révue Française* to publish a particular novel— very amusing, and hardly malicious at all—about the American publishing world, because, he said, "the book is anti-American." I discussed Faulkner with students in the universities of the East. These young people, who often knew the works of obscure eighteenth-century writers, had, in some cases, never heard his name.

Because of these experiences I concluded that the American public does not react to its writers in the same way as the French public. This discovery dulled my enthusiasm. Everywhere people told me, "You like Faulkner because you have never read any other novel about the South. We have hundreds of them. Read Dreiser, read Henry James. These are our great writers."

I have also concluded that at the moment there is a very strong reaction against the "pessimistic" literature of the period between the two wars. I must admit that we have the same reaction in France against writers of that period. And finally I observed among many American intellectuals a lively concern about the success in France of certain writers who could not fit into American life. "Between France and us," they told me, "there are today misunderstandings which are inevitable but momentary. We do not attach much importance to them, of course. But is this the time—when all countries must combine their efforts to understand one another better—to present the French with an unjust and black picture of our civilization?"

This is why I feel it necessary to explain to the American readers of this article two essential points. I should like to show them that these unflattering books do not make bad propaganda for the United States. I should also like to make them understand why the French have chosen precisely these books from so many excellent works.

It is true that the Germans tried to use the "pessimistic" works of your authors for propaganda purposes—particularly Steinbeck, because Steinbeck was the most severe critic of the capitalistic form of production in the United States. They permitted the publication of *In Dubious Battle*, although they had previously forbidden all translation of American authors. I recall the care with which the proprietor of the collaborationist bookshop "Rive Gauche" in the heart of the Boulevard Saint-Michel had arranged his anti-American window. He exhibited side by side *The Disunited States* of Vladimir Pozner and the works of Steinbeck and, above and below, photographs of Negro lynchings and of policemen battling with strikers. The result was quite different from what he expected. Few people stopped in front of the shop. Then a week later all the windows of the bookshop were smashed with rocks. From that day on, it was necessary for two French policemen to stand on melancholy guard before the display.

Later these same German propagandists tried again by offering Gallimard permission to publish *The Grapes of Wrath*. Gallimard suspected something and refused. This work was later translated and published by a Belgian collaborationist editor, and the offices of the Franco-Germanic Institute were preparing to flood the French market with *The Grapes of Wrath* when the Americans broke through the Nazi line in Normandy. But at the same time, the clandestine Éditions de Minuit which had published *Le Silence de la Mer*, began to circulate *The Moon Is Down* by the same Steinbeck—which seemed to us all like a message from fighting America to the European underground. Thus the most rebellious, perhaps, of your writers held the ambiguous position of being acclaimed at the same time by the collaborationists and by the underground.

In another instance the friends of the Germans miscalculated. When the Vichy newspapers published an extract from the American or English press severely criticizing some Allied military operation, or loyally recognizing some Allied defeat, they thought they would discourage us. They provoked on the contrary among most of us a profound respect for Anglo-Saxon democracy and bitter regret for our own. "Such people," we told ourselves, "have confidence in their rights. They must be both disciplined and stout-hearted to withstand without flinching the announcement of a defeat."

The harsh criticism that your writers made against your social regime we took in the same way. It never disgusted us with America—on the contrary, we saw in it a manifestation of your liberty. We knew that in Germany such a book as *The Grapes of Wrath* could never have been published. Then, need I add, no matter what evils your writers denounced, we have the same faults in our own country. Yes, the Negroes of Chicago are housed in hovels. That is neither just nor democratic. But many of our white work-men live in hovels that are even more miserable.

These injustices have never seemed to us a defect of American society but rather a sign of the imperfections of our time. In December, 1944, at the same time that the Aubert Palace movie theater in Paris was showing an old movie by Fritz Lang, *Fury*, which depicted a Chicago lynching, Frenchmen in the Midi were hanging and shooting without much discrimination, such members of the "militia" and collaborationists as they were able to capture. They were shaving the heads of women in our provinces. Thus, when we saw on the screen the adventures of Spencer Tracy, we did not think about your lynchings, but of ours—we took the lesson to ourselves. Your authors, like your producers, always appeared to us as critics of your society, moralists who report on humanity. What we looked for above all else in the American novel was something quite different from its crudities and its violence.

III

This brings me to the other point which I want to make. I was asked, "What do you see in Faulkner? Why don't you admire rather our Henry James, our Dreiser?" I answered that we do admire them both, but coldly.

It is entirely natural that the American public, weary of direct and brutal novels which attempt to paint groups or sociological developments, should return to novels of analysis. But analytical novels flood our country. We created the genre, and the best of the analysts, Benjamin Constant and Marcel Proust, are French. Henry James can please us, charm us, but he teaches us nothing—nor does Dreiser. The techniques Dreiser uses to depict his Americans he borrowed directly or indirectly from French realists—from Flaubert, from Maupassant, from Zola. How can we get excited over methods which originated with us, which we learned in school, and which, when we are already weary of them, are shipped back to us from America?

What has aroused our enthusiasm among the recent novelists whom I have mentioned is a veritable revolution in the art of telling a story. The intellectual analysis which, for more than a century, had been the accepted method of developing character in fiction was no longer anything but an old mechanism badly adapted to the needs of the time. It was opposed to a psychology of synthesis which taught us that a psychological fact is an indivisible whole. It could not be used to depict a group of facts which present themselves as the ephemeral or permanent unity of a great number of perceptions.

All around us clouds were gathering. There was war in Spain: the concentration camps were multiplying in Germany, in Austria, in Czechoslovakia. War was menacing everywhere. Nevertheless analysis—analysis à la Proust, à la James—remained our only literary method, our favorite procedure. But could it take into account the brutal death of a Jew in Auschwitz, the bombardment of Madrid by the planes of Franco? Here a new literature presented its characters to us synthetically. It made them perform before our eyes acts which were complete in themselves, impossible to analyze, acts which it was necessary to grasp completely with all the obscure power of our souls.

The heroes of Hemingway and Caldwell never explain themselves—do not allow themselves to be dissected. They act only. Some have said they were blind and deaf, that they allowed themselves to be buffeted about by destiny. This is false and unjust. On the contrary, each of their spontaneous reactions is completely what it would be in real life—something that lives and that does not contemplate itself. We learned from Hemingway to depict, without commentaries, without explanations, without moral judgments, the actions of our characters. The reader understands them because he sees them born and formed in a situation which has been made understandable to him. They live because they spurt suddenly as from a deep well. To analyze them would be to kill them.

When Camus shows us his hero, Meursault, emptying his revolver at an Arab, he takes care not to explain. But he describes the pitiless heat of the day, the merciless horror of the sun. He encircles his hero with a criminal aura. After this, the act is born of itself; it is obvious to us without any analysis.

For a long time we have been using certain techniques to make our readers understand what was going on in the souls of our characters. We wrote bravely: "He told himself, 'It is warm. How shall I ever climb the hill?' " Or else we used the "indirect" style which Flaubert, according to Thibaudet,—La Fontaine according to others—introduced into our literature: "Paul walked with difficulty. It was warm. Good Lord, how would he have the strength to climb the hill?' " Or still another technique recently taken from England and imitating Joyce: "One, two, one two, atrocious heat and I—the hill—how shall I ever . . . ?" These different artifices, equally true or equally false, allowed us to reveal only what the character said consciously to himself. They omitted necessarily the whole obscure zone where feelings and intentions seethe, those feelings and intentions which are not expressed in words.

The American writers freed us from these obsolete techniques. Hemingway never enters inside his characters (except in *For Whom the Bell Tolls,* the least impressive of his books, and one which has not yet appeared in France). He describes them always from the outside. He is only the witness of their conduct. It is from their conduct that we must, as in life, reconstruct their thought. He does not admit that the writer has the power to lift the tops of their skulls as the Club-footed Devil raised the roofs of houses to see what went on inside. We have to wait with him—page after page—to understand the actors in the drama. We are, as he pretends to be, reduced to conjectures.

Faulkner also elects to present his heroes from the outside, when their consciousness is complete, and then to show us, suddenly, the depths of their souls—when there is no longer anything there. Thus he gives the illusion that everything which impels them to act lies somewhere below the level of clear consciousness. Dos Passos, in order to make us feel more keenly the intrusion of the group thinking in the most secret thoughts of his characters, invented a social voice, commonplace and sententious, which chatters incessantly round about them, without our ever knowing whether it is a chorus of conformist mediocrity or a monologue which the characters themselves keep locked in their hearts.

All these procedures were new to us in 1930, and they were what first attracted us. There is something more: just as Riemann and Lobachevsky showed the way which permitted Russell and others to reveal the postulates which are the bases of Euclidian geometry, so these American authors have taught us that what we thought were immutable laws in the art of the novel were only a group of postulates which one might shift about without danger. Faulkner has taught us that the necessity of relating a story in chronological order was only a postulate and that one may use any order in telling the story as long as that order allows an author to evaluate the situations, the atmosphere, and the characters.

Dos Passos has revealed the falsity of the unity of action. He has shown that one might describe a collective event by juxtaposing twenty individual and unrelated stories. These revelations permitted us to conceive and to write novels which are to the classic works of Flaubert and Zola what the non-Euclidian geometry is to the old geometry of Euclid. In other words, the influence of American novels has produced a *technical* revolution among us. They have placed in our hands new and supple instruments, which allow us to approach subjects which heretofore we had no means of treating: the unconscious; sociological events; the true relation of the individual to society, present or past.

We have not sought with morose delight stories of murder and rape, but lessons in a renewal of the art of writing. We were weighted down, without being aware of it, by our traditions and our culture. These American novelists, without such traditions, without help, have forged, with barbaric brutality, tools of inestimable value. We collected these tools but we lack the naïveté of their creators. We thought about them, we took them apart and put them together again, we theorized about them, and we attempted to absorb them into our great traditions of the novel. We have treated consciously and intellectually what was the fruit of a talented and unconscious spontaneity.

When Hemingway writes his short, disjointed sentences, he is only obeying his temperament. He writes what he sees. But when Camus uses Hemingway's technique, he is conscious and deliberate, because it seems to him upon reflection the best way to express his philosophical experience of the absurdity of the world. If Faulkner breaks the chronological order of his story, it is because he cannot do otherwise. He sees time jumping about in disordered leaps. But when Simone de Beauvoir borrows his methods of mixing periods of time, she does so deliberately, and because she sees a possibility of placing her characters and action in better relief. In this way your American novelists have enriched French writers with new techniques, and French writers have absorbed these and have used them in a different manner.

Soon the first French novels written during the occupation will appear in the United States. We shall give back to you these techniques which you have lent us. We shall return them digested, intellectualized, less effective, and less brutal—consciously adapted to French taste. Because of this incessant exchange which makes nations rediscover in other nations what they have invented first and then rejected, perhaps you will rediscover in these foreign books the eternal youth of that "old" Faulkner.

ANDRE GIDE

(1869–1951)

The New American Novelists

In a distinguished literary career of more than fifty years, André Gide, novelist, essayist, dramatist, and critic, explored particularly the complexities arising from the issue of personal freedom, the dialectical pulls of convention and resistance to convention. A perspicacious critic as well as artist, he expressed an interest in many foreign writers; among Americans he felt the influence of Emerson and especially Whitman, whose homosexuality, individuality, and optimism attracted him and whose poetry he helped to translate and propagate in France in the 1910s.

In the imaginary dialogue that follows, written toward the end of his life, Gide showed an alert awareness of the new American fiction but confessed that he approached these new American writers as an amateur. These novelists did not help mold his psyche or develop his art; they did not have the shaping influence on him as they did on Sartre's generation. The essay's interest is that it reveals drifts of French opinion on American literature. Also, like Malraux, Gide sees in the new American fiction a freedom from the moral burden of "our too rich past." In his Journal dated 1921, he quoted with approval Walter Rathenau's statement that America had not yet "deigned to *plunge into the abyss of suffering and sin.*"

Bibliography: An adverse comment on Gide's essay appears in F. W. Dupee, "An International Episode," *Partisan Review*, 13 (1946), 259–65.

"The New American Novelists" appears in Gide's *Imaginary Interviews*, trans. Malcolm Cowley (New York: Alfred A. Knopf, 1949), 140–46.

252

THE NEW AMERICAN NOVELISTS
(1949)

I HADN'T seen my interviewer for more than a year, but at last he ran me to earth again; he wanted to talk about the issue of *Fontaine* that would be devoted to American literature. In what I thought was a rather disrespectful manner, he expressed surprise at my interest in the subject, hinting that nothing in the world seemed farther from my proper field.

"I have met two sorts of people in my long career," was what I began by saying. "The first sort consists of those who fall in love with everything that resembles themselves, in literature and art as well as in nature, and who feel cheated by any work that doesn't offer their image in a mirror. The second consists of those who travel through countries or books in search of an admonitory strangeness, and who enjoy a landscape all the more for its being different from themselves. I belong to the second class. There is no contemporary literature that arouses my curiosity more than that of the United States; not even that of the new Russia."

I added that there was nothing recent about my eagerness to hear what America was saying, and that I was probably one of the first in France to admire Melville, having urged my friends to read him long before Giono undertook his translation of *Moby Dick*. It was the same with Thoreau's *Walden;* I remember the day when Fabulet met me in the Place de la Madeleine and told me about his discovery. "An extraordinary book," he said, "and one that nobody in France has heard about." It happened that I had a copy of *Walden* in my pocket.

"As regards more recent books," I continued, "other Frenchmen were ahead of me; it was Malraux who had me read Hemingway and Faulkner. I have to admit that it took me some time to become acclimated to the latter, although I now regard him as one of the most important, perhaps *the* most important, of the stars in this new constellation. It was Steinbeck, however, who gave me the keenest satisfaction. When it comes to Dos Passos, I admire him more than he captivates me. He gives the impression of having a formula; his pointillism wears me out, even though it is highly effective; and his intrepid modernism is the sort that seems old before its time. I have trouble following him through a series of snapshots that dazzle me one after the other; they remain so unrelated in my mind that, after patiently reading the 500-odd pages of *Manhattan Transfer* or *The*

42nd Parallel, I should have been completely incapable of grouping my successive impressions around a center, and even of deciding what the author had said, about whom. Nevertheless I had been held and dominated from page to page; I was forced to admit that here was 'something big.' "

HE.—Might I ask whether you have read these new authors in the original?

I.—The truth is that I usually have to depend on translations, but several of these impress me as being first-class; those by Maurice Coindreau and Michel Tyr in particular. I have no trouble understanding English, but it seems to me that American has been tending more and more to become a separate language. Very often I find myself halted by phrases or idioms that make me wish for a new dictionary, since they aren't to be found in those we now possess.

HE.—That must be quite troublesome.

I.—Much less so than one might suppose. It might even be that the author sometimes gains by these fleeting misapprehensions, since his meaning perhaps falls short of what I imagine it to be. The difficulty of the language also keeps me from making hasty judgments. Thus I can't be sure about the accuracy of certain dialogues; in *The Grapes of Wrath,* for example—

HE.—That is supposed to be Steinbeck's best book.

I.—I should prefer *In Dubious Battle,* a novel in which the most urgent and bitterly argued of social questions is presented (I almost said "played") in a wholly impartial light, with a profound feeling for psychology and a very sure artistic sense that leads to compelling simplifications and formalizations, thus transforming this picture of a strike and all its complicated issues into something bold and legendary. But Steinbeck, in my opinion, has written nothing more skillful and nearly faultless than some of the stories in a volume called *The Long Valley;* they equal or surpass the best tales of Chekhov.

HE.—I hear that *Fontaine* has asked you to write an essay on the present status of literature in the United States.

I.—I feel that I am not at all qualified for the task. Although I have read more than a score of books by their new novelists, I know scarcely anything about their poets. It is good to hear that our friend Jean Wahl is presenting their work in translation.

HE.—Mightn't you at least make some general statement about the work of their novelists?

I.—Not even that. It would require more perspective, in spite of the fact that distance in space is often equivalent to distance in time, as Racine maintained in the preface to *Bajazet*. Some of these novels seem very far from us, and yet—don't you agree?—they touch us closely. Above all this is true of Hemingway, and particularly of *A Farewell to Arms,* which is so palpitating with life and rich in a sensibility that is interfused with intelligence. I have none of his love for bull-fighting, and yet there is no American author I would rather meet.

HE.—I grant you Hemingway, since he is the most European of them all. As for the others, I have to confess that their strangeness appals me. I thought I would go mad with pain and horror when I read Faulkner's *Sanctuary* and his *Light in August.* Dos Passos makes me suffocate. I laugh, it is true, when reading Caldwell's *Journeyman* or *God's Little Acre,* but I laugh on the wrong side of my mouth. There is no doubt that each of these great novelists impresses me as having a powerful individuality; and yet, after the simple but resolute and instinctive optimism of Whitman and Emerson and Melville, how do you explain that these more recent writers have chosen to portray an equal depth of abject suffering and blindness? If one believes what they are saying, the American cities and countrysides must offer a foretaste of hell.

I.—Don't believe a word of it. Each of these authors is a realist, it is true, but in his own fashion. When he paints the American world for us, he isn't so much reflecting as opposing it. One might say that each of them is achieving a consciousness of his own nature by reacting. Faulkner in particular, with his Southern background, is and remains essentially, powerfully, and in the full sense of the word a *Protestant.*

HE.—I remember a remark of Rathenau's that you set down in your *Journal.* "America," he told you in 1921, "has no soul and will not deserve to have one until it consents to plunge into the abyss of human sin and suffering." I quote these words from memory because they impressed me.

I.—Ever since the last war, American literature has done its best to draw people out of the soulless contentment that Rathenau was talking about, not to mention the state of quivering lethargy and mechanized innocence that was depicted in Sinclair Lewis's *Babbitt.* Dreiser already, the first of their somber authors—unless we go back to Edgar Allan Poe . . .

HE.—Yes, these new writers have taken the great plunge into the abyss, Faulkner especially; and yet there is not one of his characters who, properly speaking, has a soul. For them and for him the moral question simply doesn't exist.

I.—It doesn't exist in the new Russia either. Perhaps it doesn't exist anywhere except as a human invention. I wonder whether it hasn't tormented us long enough. Might it be that a new humanity is preparing to abolish it? . . . But that discussion would carry us too far.

HE.—Something else surprises me: the stubbornly and violently æsthetic, literary, and at times even artificial aspect of some of these recent productions. I was thinking, for instance, of Faulkner's extraordinary *As I Lay Dying.* Does that represent still another reaction?

I.—Against reporting; there isn't much doubt of it. America is the country of reporters. Now, just as photography absolved painting from reproducing nature and imitating the real world, might we not say that in America, more than anywhere else on earth, reporting carried to a state of perfection—as in Dana's masterpiece, *Two Years before the Mast*—had the effect of purging literature of everything that did not properly belong to it? I don't know, I am asking a question. We are speaking of random impressions.

And speaking at random, there is one recent author, Dashiell Hammett, who is doubtless not in the same class as the four great figures we began by discussing. Again it was Malraux who drew my attention to him; but for the last two years I have been vainly trying to find a copy of *The Glass Key,* which Malraux specially recommended; it couldn't be procured either in the original or in translation, whether on the Riviera or in North Africa. Hammett, it is true, squanders his great talent on detective stories; they are unusually good ones, no doubt, like *The Thin Man* and *The Maltese Falcon,* but a little cheap—and one could say the same of Simenon. For all of that, I regard his *Red Harvest* as a remarkable achievement, the last word in atrocity, cynicism, and horror. Dashiell Hammett's dialogues, in which every character is trying to deceive all the others and in which the truth slowly becomes visible through the haze of deception, can be compared only with the best in Hemingway. If I speak of Hammett, it is because I seldom hear his name mentioned.

HE.—You haven't said anything about Caldwell. Is that because you think he is less important?

I.—Not at all. But I haven't been drawing up a list of prize-winners for commencement day. If I haven't spoken about Erskine

Caldwell, it is because he puzzles me. He evades the categories and theories that I am trying to elaborate; what I was saying about the others does not wholly apply to him, and that is all to his credit. But the quality in which he resembles them is the interest he takes in life. All these new American novelists are seized and held like children by the present moment, by the here and now; they are far from books and free from the ratiocinations, the preoccupations, the feelings of remorse that darken and complicate our old world. That is why a closer acquaintance with them can be very profitable to those of us who are burdened with the weight of our too rich past. Good-by. Leave me quickly before I start thinking of objections.

HENRY MILLER
(1891–   )

Blaise Cendrars

In 1931 *Panama,* consisting of poems by Blaise Cendrars (1887–1961), was translated into English by John Dos Passos. The cinematic, documentary techniques of these poems manifest themselves in the Camera Eye sections of Dos Passos' *U. S. A.* (1930–1936). In his foreword to the 1931 translations, Dos Passos reveals the creative excitement of Paris before and after the First World War. Numerous Americans left for Paris in the 1920s to participate in a renaissance of the arts and to share the exhilarating freedom the city promised. Gertrude Stein, Ernest Hemingway, F. Scott Fitzgerald, E. E. Cummings, as well as Dos Passos, found in France an ambiance conducive to literary production. Something, too, of the gaiety of the time was captured in Hemingway's introduction to *Kiki's Memoirs* (1930), an autobiography of a French prostitute.

The Paris depicted by Henry Miller, who left for France in 1930 and lived there until the outbreak of war in 1939, is harsher and less carefree than Hemingway's Paris a decade earlier. Miller's Bohemian, idiosyncratic, and Depression-ridden existence in Paris is described in *Tropic of Cancer* (1934), an autobiographical novel, and in other novels and essays that followed. Miller's value as a writer has not yet been firmly established; controversy swirls around him—assessing whether he is a genius or an eccentric, nihilistic or optimistic in point of view, realistic or nonrealistic, tedious and long-winded or energetically prolific.

In any event, he has often written on French literature, including essays on Balzac, Lautréamont, Rimbaud—in a long, discursive piece called "The Time of the Assassins," Giono, Ionesco, and the poet and novelist Blaise Cendrars.

Cendrars appealed to Miller because of his concern with all phases of life, not to the neglect of adventure and escape, and to quote
258

Miller, because "he restores to contemporary life the elements of the heroic, the imaginative and the fabulous." Indeed, as Miller wrote, if in the early stages of his career it was Knut Hamsun whom Miller idolized, it was Cendrars whom, in the latter stages, he most desired to imitate.

Bibliography: Stephen Longstreet, in *We All Went to Paris: Americans in the City of Light, 1776–1971* (New York: 1971), presents an historical survey more popular than scholarly in intent. Nevertheless, he assembles much interesting information. Chapters 52 and 53 are devoted to Miller. George Wickes, in *Americans in Paris* (New York: 1969), traces some literary affinities between Americans in Paris in the 1920s and French predecessors.

The following selections are taken from pp. 328–52 of *The Henry Miller Reader,* ed. by Lawrence Durrell (New York: New Directions, 1959).

BLAISE CENDRARS

(1959)

CENDRARS was the first French writer to look me up, during my stay in Paris, and the last man I saw on leaving Paris. I had just a few minutes before catching the train for Rocamadour and I was having a last drink on the *terrasse* of my hotel near the Porte d'Orléans when Cendrars hove in sight. Nothing could have given me greater joy than this unexpected last-minute encounter. In a few words I told him of my intention to visit Greece. Then I sat back and drank in the music of his sonorous voice which to me always seemed to come from a sea organ. In those last few minutes Cendrars managed to convey a world of information, and with the same warmth and tenderness which he exudes in his books. Like the very ground under our feet, his thoughts were honeycombed with all manner of subterranean passages. I left him sitting there in shirt sleeves, never dreaming that years would elapse before hearing from him again, never dreaming that I was perhaps taking my last look at Paris.

I had read whatever was translated of Cendrars before arriving in France. That is to say, almost nothing. My first taste of him in his own language came at a time when my French was none too proficient. I began with *Moravagine,* a book by no means easy to read for one who knows little French. I read it slowly, with a dictionary by my side, shifting from one café to another. It was in the Café de la Liberté, corner of the Rue de la Gaieté and the Boulevard Edgar Quintet, that I began it. I remember well the day. Should Cendrars ever read these lines he may be pleased, touched perhaps, to know that it was in that dingy hole I first opened his book.

. . . I think of two . . . passages . . . deeply engraved in my mind, from *Une Nuit dans la Forêt,** which I read about three years later. I cite them not to brag of my powers of memory but to reveal an aspect of Cendrars which his English and American readers probably do not suspect the existence of.

1. I, the freest man that exists, recognize that there is always something that binds one: that liberty, independence do not exist, and I am full of contempt for, and at the same time take pleasure in, my helplessness.

2. More and more I realize that I have always led the contemplative life. I am a sort of Brahmin in reverse, meditating on himself amid the hurly-burly, who, with all his strength, disciplines himself and scorns existence. Or the boxer with his shadow, who, furiously, calmly, punching at emptiness, watches his form. What virtuosity, what science, what balance, the ease with which he accelerates! *Later, one must learn how to take punishment with equal imperturbability.* I, I know how to take punishment and with serenity I fructify and with serenity destroy myself: in short, work in the world not so much to enjoy as to make others enjoy (it's others' reflexes that give me pleasure, not my own). Only a soul full of despair can ever attain serenity and, to be in despair, you must have loved a good deal and *still love the world.*†

These last two passages have probably been cited many times already and will no doubt be cited many times more as the years go by. They are memorable ones and thoroughly the author's own. Those who know only *Sutter's Gold, Panama* and *On the Trans-siberian,* which are about all the American reader gets to know, may indeed wonder on reading the foregoing passages why this man has not been translated more fully. Long before I attempted to make Cendrars better known to the American public (and to the world at large, I may well add), John Dos Passos had translated and illustrated with water colors *Panama, or the adventures of my seven uncles.**

*Editions du Verseau, Lausanne, 1929.
†Italics mine.
*See chapter 12, "Homer of the Trans-siberian," *Orient Express;* Jonathan Cape & Harrison Smith, New York, 1922.

However, the primary thing to know about Blaise Cendrars is that he is a man of many parts. He is also a man of many books, many kinds of books, and by that I do not mean "good" and "bad" but books so different one from another that he gives the impression of evolving in all directions at once. An evolved man, truly. Certainly an evolved writer.

His life itself reads like the *Arabian Nights' Entertainment*. And this individual who has led a super-dimensional life is also a book-worm. The most gregarious of men and yet a solitary. ("*O mes solitudes!*") A man of deep intuition and invincible logic. The logic of life. Life first and foremost. Life always with a capital L. That's Cendrar's.

To follow his career from the time he slips out of his parents' home in Neufchâtel, a boy fifteen or sixteen, to the days of the Occupation when he secretes himself in Aix-en-Provence and imposes on himself a long period of silence, is something to make one's head spin. The itinerary of his wanderings is more difficult to follow than Marco Polo's, whose trajectory, incidentally, he seems to have crossed and recrossed a number of times. One of the reasons for the great fascination he exerts over me is the resemblance between his voyages and adventures and those which I associate in memory with Sinbad the Sailor or Aladdin of the Wonderful Lamp. The amazing experiences which he attributes to the characters in his books, and which often as not he has shared, have all the qualities of legend as well as the authenticity of legend. Worshiping life and the truth of life, he comes closer than any author of our time to revealing the common source of word and deed. He restores to contemporary life the elements of the heroic, the imaginative and the fabulous. His adventures have led him to nearly every region of the globe, particularly those regarded as dangerous or inaccessible. (One must read his early life especially to appreciate the truth of this statement.) He has consorted with all types, including bandits, murderers, revolutionaries and other var-ieties of fanatic. He has tried at no less than thirty-six métiers, according to his own words, but, like Balzac, gives the impression of knowing every métier. He was once a juggler, for example—on the English music-hall stage—at the same time that Chaplin was making his debut there; he was a pearl merchant and a smuggler; he was a plantation owner in South America, where he made a fortune three times in succession and lost it even more rapidly than he had made it. But read his life! There is more in it than meets the eye.

Yes, he is an explorer and investigator of the ways and doings of men. And he has made himself such by planting himself in the midst of life, by taking up his lot with his fellow creatures. What a superb, painstaking reporter he is, this man who would scorn the thought of being called "a student of life." He has the faculty of getting "his story" by a process of osmosis; he seems to seek nothing deliberately. Which is why, no doubt, his own story is always interwoven with the other man's. To be sure, he possesses the art of distillation, but what he is vitally interested in is the alchemical nature of all relationships. This eternal quest of the transmutative enables him to reveal men to themselves and to the world; it causes him to extol men's virtues, to reconcile us to their faults and weaknesses, to increase our knowledge and respect for what is essentially human, to deepen our love and understanding of the world. He is the "reporter" par excellence because he combines the faculties of poet, seer and prophet. An innovator and initiator, ever the first to give testimony, he has made known to us the real pioneers, the real adventurers, the real discoverers among our contemporaries. More than any writer I can think of he has made dear to us *"le bel aujourd'hui."*

Whilst performing on all levels he always found time to read. On long voyages, in the depths of the Amazon, in the deserts (I imagine he knows them all, those of the earth, those of the spirit), in the jungle, on the broad pampas, on trains, tramps and ocean liners, in the great museums and libraries of Europe, Asia and Africa, he has buried himself in books, has ransacked whole archives, has photographed rare documents, and, for all I know, may have stolen invaluable books, scripts, documents of all kinds—why not, considering the enormity of his appetite for the rare, the curious, the forbidden?

He has told us in one of his recent books how the Germans *(les Boches!)* destroyed or carried off, I forget which, his precious library, precious to a man like Cendrars who loves to give the most precise data when referring to a passage from one of his favorite books. Thank God, his memory is alive and functions like a faithful machine. An incredible memory, as will testify those who have read his more recent books—*La Main Coupée, l'Homme Foudroyé, Bourlinguer, Le Lotissement du Ciel, La Banlieue de Paris.*

On the side—with Cendrars it seems as though almost everything of account has been done "one the side"—he has translated the works of other writers, notably the Portuguese author, Ferreira de Castro

(*Forêt Vierge*) and our own Al Jennings, the great outlaw and bosom friend of O. Henry.* What a wonderful translation is *Hors-la-loi* which in English is called *Through the Shadows with O. Henry*. It is a sort of secret collaboration between Cendrars and the innermost being of Al Jennings. At the time of writing it, Cendrars had not yet met Jennings nor even corresponded with him. (This is another book, I must say in passing, which our pocket-book editors have overlooked. There is a fortune in it, unless I am all wet, and it would be comforting to think that part of this fortune should find its way into Al Jennings' pocket.)

One of the most fascinating aspects of Cendrars' temperament is his ability and readiness to collaborate with a fellow artist. Picture him, shortly after the First World War, editing the publications of La Sirène! What an opportunity! To him we owe an edition of *Les Chants de Maldoror,* the first to appear since the original private publication by the author in 1868. In everything an innovator, always meticulous, scrupulous and exacting in his demands, whatever issued from the hands of Cendrars at La Sirène is now a valuable collector's item. Hand in hand with this capability for collaboration goes another quality—the ability, or grace, to make the first overtures. Whether it be a criminal, a saint, a man of genius, a tyro with promise, Cendrars is the first to look him up, the first to herald him, the first to aid him in the way the person most desires. I speak with justifiable warmth here. No writer ever paid me a more signal honor than dear Blaise Cendrars who, shortly after the publication of *Tropic of Cancer,* knocked at my door one day to extend the hand of friendship. Nor can I forget that first tender, eloquent review of the book which appeared under his signature in *Orbes* shortly thereafter. (Or perhaps it was *before* he appeared at the studio in the Villa Seurat.)

There were times when reading Cendrars—and this is something which happens to me rarely—that I put the book down in order to wring my hands with joy or despair, with anguish or with desperation. Cendrars has stopped me in my tracks again and again, just as implacably as a gunman pressing a rod against one's spine. Oh, yes, I am often carried away by exaltation in reading a man's work. But I am alluding now to something other than exaltation. I am talking of a sensation in which all one's emotions are blended and confused. I am

---

*Cendrars has also translated Al Capone's autobiography.

talking of knockout blows. Cendrars has knocked me cold. Not once, but a number of times. And I am not exactly a ham, when it comes to taking it on the chin! Yes, *mon cher* Cendrars, you not only stopped *me,* you stopped the clock. It has taken me days, weeks, sometimes months, to recover from these bouts with you. Even years later, I can put my hand to the spot where I caught the blow and feel the old smart. You battered and bruised me; you left me scarred, dazed, punch-drunk. The curious thing is that the better I know you—through your books—the more susceptible I become. It is as if you had put the Indian sign on me. I come forward with chin outstretched—"to take it." *I am your meat,* as I have so often said. And it is because I believe I am not unique in this, because I wish others to enjoy this uncommon experience, that I continue to put in my little word for you whenever, wherever, I can.

I incautiously said: "the better I know you." My dear Cendrars, I will never know you, not as I do other men, of that I am certain. No matter how thoroughly you reveal yourself I shall never get to the bottom of you. I doubt that anyone ever will, and it is not vanity which prompts me to put it this way. You are as inscrutable as a Buddha. You inspire, you reveal, but you never give yourself wholly away. Not that you withhold yourself! No, encountering you, whether in person or through the written word, you leave the impression of having given all there is to give. Indeed, you are one of the few men I know who, in their books as well as in person, give that "extra measure" which means everything to us. You give all that *can* be given. It is not your fault that the very core of you forbids scrutiny. It is the law of your being. No doubt there are men less inquisitive, less grasping, less clutching, for whom these remarks are meaningless. But you have so refined our sensitivity, so heightened our awareness, so deepened or love for men and women, for books, for nature, for a thousand and one things of life which only one of your own unending paragraphs could catalogue, that you awaken in us the desire to turn you inside out. When I read you or talk to you I am always aware of your inexhaustible awareness: you are not just sitting in a chair in a room in a city in a country, telling us what is on your mind or in your mind, you make the chair talk and the room vibrate with the tumult of the city whose life is sustained by the invisible outer throng of a whole nation whose history has become your history, whose life is your life and yours theirs, and as you talk or write all these elements, images, facts, creations enter into your thoughts and feeling, forming a web which the spider in you ceaselessly spins and which spreads in us, your listeners, until the whole of creation is involved, and we, you, them, it, everything, have lost identity and found new meaning, new life. . . .

[*Editors' Note:* After addressing Cendrars personally, Miller returns here to the third person.]

Many are the things which have been said against this writer . . . that his books are cinematic in style, that they are sensational, that he exaggerates and deforms *à outrance*, that he is prolix and verbose, that he lacks all sense of form, that he is too much the realist or else that his narratives are too incredible, and so on ad infinitum. Taken altogether there is, to be sure, a grain of truth in these accusations, but let us remember—*only a grain!* They reflect the views of the paid critic, the academician, the frustrated novelist. But supposing, for a moment, we accepted them at face value. Will they hold water? Take his cinematic technique, for example. Well, are we not living in the age of the cinema? Is not this period of history more fantastic, more "incredible," than the simulacrum of it which we see unrolled on the silver screen? As for his sensationalism—have we forgotten Gilles de Rais, the Marquis de Sade, the *Memoirs* of Casanova? As for hyperbole, what of Pindar? As for prolixity and verbosity, what about Jules Romains or Marcel Proust? As for exaggeration and deformation, what of Rabelais, Swift, Céline, to mention an anomalous trinity? As for lack of form, that perennial jackass which is always kicking up its heels in the pages of literary reviews, have I not heard cultured Europeans rant about the "vegetal" aspect of Hindu temples, the façades of which are studded with a riot of human, animal and other forms? Have I not seen them twisting their lips in distaste when examining the efflorescences embodied in Tibetan scrolls? No taste, eh? No sense of proportion? No control? *C'est ça. De la mesure avant tout!* These cultured nobodies forget that their beloved exemplars, the Greeks, worked with Cyclopean blocks, created monstrosities as well as apotheoses of harmony, grace, form and spirit; they forget perhaps that the Cycladic sculpture of Greece surpassed in abstraction and simplification anything which Brancusi or his followers ever attempted. The very mythology of these worshipers of beauty, whose motto was "Nothing to the extreme," is a revelation of the "monstrous" aspect of their being.

Oui, Cendrars is full of excrescences. There are passages which swell up out of the body of his text like rank tumors. There are detours, parentheses, asides, which are the embryonic pith and substance of books yet to come. There is a grand efflorescence and exfoliation, and there is also a grand wastage of material in his books. Cendrars neither cribs and cabins, nor does he drain himself completely. When the moment comes to let go, he lets go. When it is expedient or efficacious to be brief, he is brief and to the point—like a dagger. To me his books reflect his lack of fixed habits, or better yet, his ability to break a habit. (A sign of real emancipation!) In those swollen paragraphs, which are like *une mer houleuse* and which some readers, apparently, are unable to cope with, Cendrars reveals his oceanic spirit. We who vaunt dear Shakespear's madness, his elemental outbursts, are we to fear these cosmic gusts? We who swallowed the *Pantagruel* and *Gargantua*, via Urquhart, are we to be daunted by catalogues of names, places, dates, events? We who produced the oddest writer in any tongue—Lewis Carroll—are we to shy away from the play of words, from the ridiculous, the grotesque, the unspeakable or the "utterly impossible"? It takes a *man* to hold his breath as Cendrars does when he is about to unleash one of his triple-page paragraphs without stop. *A man*? A deep-sea diver. A whale. A whale of a man, precisely.

It has been my lot to prowl the streets, by night as well as day, of these God-forsaken precincts of woe and misery, not only here in my own country but in Europe too. In their spirit of desolation they are all alike. Those which ring the proudest cities of the earth are the worst. They stink like chancres. When I look back on my past I can scarcely see anything else, smell anything else but these festering empty lots, these filthy, shrouded streets, these rubbish heaps of jerries indiscriminately mixed with the garbage and refuse, the forlorn, utterly senseless household objects, toys, broken gadgets, vases and pisspots abandoned by the poverty-stricken, hopeless, helpless creatures who make up the population of these districts. In moments of high fettle I have threaded my way amidst the bric-a-brac and shambles of these quarters and thought to myself: What a poem! What a documentary film! Often I recovered my sober senses only by cursing and gnashing my teeth, by flying into wild, futile rages, by picturing myself a benevolent dictator who would eventually "restore order, peace and justice." I have been obsessed for weeks and months on end by such experiences. But I have never succeeded in making music of it. (And to think that Erik Satie, whose domicile Robert Doisneau gives us in one of the photos, to think that his man also "made music" in that crazy building is something which makes my scalp itch.) No, I have never succeeded in making music of this insensate material. I have tried a number of times, but my spirit is still too young, too filled with repulsion. I lack that ability to recede, to assimilate, to pound the mortar with a chemist's skill. But Cendrars *has* succeeded, and that is why I take my hat off to him. *Salut, cher* Blaise Cendrars! You are a musician. Salute! And glory be! We have need of the poets of night and desolation as well as the other sort. We have need of comforting words—and you give them—as well as vitriolic diatribes. When I say "we" I mean all of us. Ours is a thirst unquenchable for an eye such as yours, an eye which condemns without passing judgment, an eye which wounds by its naked glance and heals at the same time. Especially in America do "we" need your historic touch, your velvety backward sweep of the plume. Yes, we need it perhaps more than anything you have to offer us. History has passed over our scarred *terrains vagues* at a gallop. It has left us a few names, a few absurd monuments—and a veritable chaos of bric-a-brac. The one race which inhabited these shores and which did not mar the work of God was the redskins. Today they occupy the wastelands. For their "protection" we have organized a pious sort of concentration camp. It has no barbed wires, no instruments of torture, no armed guards. We simply leave them there to die out . . .

But I cannot end on this dolorous note, which is only the backfire of those secret rumblings which begin anew whenever the past crops up. There is always a rear view to be had from these crazy edifices which our minds inhabit so tenaciously. The view from Satie's back window is the kind I mean. Wherever in the "zone" there is a cluster of shabby buildings, there dwell the little people, the salt of the earth, as we say, for without them we would be left to starve, without them that crust which is thrown to the dogs and which we pounce on like wolves would have only the savor of death and revenge. Through those oblong windows from which the bedding hangs I can see my pallet in the corner where I have flopped for the night, to be rescued again in miraculous fashion the next sundown, always by a "nobody," which means, when we get to understand human speech, by an angel in disguise. What matter if with the coffee one swallows a mislaid emmenagogue? What matter if a stray roach clings to one's tattered garments? Looking at life from the rear window one can look down at one's past as into a still mirror in which the days of desperation merge with the days of joy, the days of peace, and the days of deepest friendship. Especially do I feel this way, think this way, when I look into my *French* backyard. There all the meaningless pieces of my life fall into a pattern. I see no waste motion. It is all as clear as "The Cracow Poem" to a chess fiend. The music it gives off is as simple as were the strains of "Sweet Alice Ben Bolt" to my childish ears. More, it is beautiful, for as Sir H. Rider Haggard says in his autobiography: "The naked truth is always beautiful, even when it tells of evil."

My dear Cendrars, you must at times have sensed a kind of envy in me for all that you have lived through, digested, and vomited forth transformed, transmogrified, transubstantiated. As a child you played by Vergil's tomb; as a mere lad you tramped across Europe, Russia, Asia, to stoke the furnace in some forgotten hotel in Pekin; as a young man, in the bloody days of the Legion, you elected to remain a corporal, no more; as a war victim you begged for alms in your own dear Paris, and a little later you were on the bum in New York, Boston, New Orleans, Frisco . . . You have roamed far, you have idled the days away, you have burned the candle at both ends, you have made friends and enemies, you have dared to write the truth, you have known how to be silent, you have pursued every path to the end, and you are still in your prime, still building castles in the air, still breaking plans, habits, resolutions, because *to live* is your primary aim, and you *are* living and will continue to live both in the flesh and in the roster of the illustrious ones. How foolish, how absurd of me to think that I might be of help to *you*, that by putting in my little word for you here and there, as I said before, I would be advancing your cause. You have no need of *my* help or of anyone's. Just living your life as you do you automatically aid us, all of us, everywhere life is lived. Once again I doff my hat to you. I bow in reverence. I have not the right to salute you because I am not your peer. I prefer to remain your devotee, your loving disciple, your spiritual brother in *der Ewigkeit*.

You always close your greetings with "*ma main amie.*" I grasp that warm left hand you proffer and I wring it with joy, with gratitude, and with an everlasting benediction on my lips.

A Selected Bibliography of Secondary Sources

(This list does not include items recorded elsewhere in this volume)

Baym, Max I. "Franco-American Literary Relations" in Sidney D. Braun, ed., *Dictionary of French Literature*. New York: Philosophical Library, 1958.
———. *The French Education of Henry Adams*. New York: Columbia University Press, 1956.
Block, Haskell. "The Impact of French Symbolism on Modern American Poetry" in Melvin J. Friedman and John B. Vickery, eds., *The Shaken Realist: Essays in Modern Literature in Honor of Frederick J. Hoffman*. Baton Rouge: Louisiana State University Press, 1970. A comprehensive survey.
Brodin, Pierre. *Les Maîtres de la littérature américaine*. Paris, 1948. Based on a series of lectures.
———. *Les Ecrivains américains de l'entre-deux-guerres*. Montreal, 1945. Based on a series of lectures.
Brown, Ruth Elizabeth. "A French Interpreter of New England's Literature, 1846–1865," *New England Quarterly*, 13 (June, 1940), 305–21. On Émile Montégut's pioneering articles in the *Revue des Deux Mondes* and *Le Moniteur Universel*.
Cabeen, D. C., ed. *Critical Bibliography of French Literature*. See "Foreign Influences and Relations," ch. XI, in vol. IV, George R. Havens and Donald F. Bond, eds. Syracuse, N. Y.: Syracuse University Press, 1951. Basic bibliographical source for the impact of foreign literature on the French.
Chinard, Gilbert. *L'Amérique et le rêve exotique dans la littérature française au 17ᵉ et au 18ᵉ siecle*. Paris, 1913. Definitive.
Coindreau, Edgar. *The Time of William Faulkner: A French View of Modern American Fiction*. George M. Reeves, ed. and trans.

Columbia: University of South Carolina Press, 1971. The collected essays of the translator of Faulkner and Hemingway; an unsympathetic view of recent American fiction.

De Mille, George E. *Literary Criticism in America: A Preliminary Survey*. New York: Lincoln MacVeagh, 1931; reprint, New York: Russell and Russell, 1967.

Earnest, Ernest. *Expatriates and Patriots: American Artists, Scholars, and Writers in Europe*. Durham, N.C.: Duke University Press, 1968.

Foerster, Norman. *American Criticism: A study in Literary Theory from Poe to the Present*. Boston and New York: Houghton Mifflin Company, 1928.

Frohock, W. M. *The Novel of Violence in America*. Dallas: Southern Methodist University Press, 1957.

Jeune, Simon. *De F. T. Graindorge à A. O. Barnabooth: les types américains dans le roman et le théâtre français, 1867–1917*. Paris, 1963. American types and stereotypes in French literature from Taine to Larbaud.

Jones, Howard Mumford. *America and French Culture, 1750–1848*. Chapel Hill: University of North Carolina Press, 1927. An historical and cultural survey, not directly concerned with literature.

Jourda, Pierre. *L'Exotisme dans la littérature française*. 2 vols. Paris, 1938. Chapter VIII, "L'Amérique," in vol. II, discusses the American scene as described by French writers since 1880.

Levin, Harry. "France-Amérique: The Transatlantic Refraction" in *Refractions: Essays in Comparative Literature*. New York: Oxford University Press, 1966. Witty, knowledgeable.

Lowell, Amy. *Six French Poets: Studies in Contemporary Literature*. New York: Macmillan, 1915; reprint, Freeport, N. Y.: Books for Libraries, 1969. On Émile Verhaeren, Albert Samain, Rémy de Gourmont, Henri de Regnier, Francis Jammes, and Paul Fort, with translations. Displays a special affection for Jammes, who seemed more interested in the "exteriority" than in the "interiority" of his subjects.

Lynes, Carlos, Jr. "The 'Nouvelle Revue Française' and American Literature, 1909–1940," *French Review*, 19 (January, 1946), 159–67. The *Nouvelle Revue Française* was instrumental in promoting American literature in France between the two World Wars.

McGee, Sidney Lamont. *La Littérature américaine dans la Revue des Deux Mondes, 1831–1900*. Montpellier, 1927. A good survey of the critical comments on American writing in the journal.

Michaud, Régis. *The American Novel Today: A Social and Psychological Study*. Boston: Little, Brown and Company, 1928. A French perspective influenced by Freud and the anti-Puritanical stance of the 1920s.

Morissette, Bruce. "Early English and American Critics of French Symbolism" in *Studies in Honor of Frederick W. Shipley*. (Washington University Studies, new series, Language and Literature no. 3.) St. Louis, 1942. Pp. 159–80.

———. "Vance Thompson's Plagiarism of Teodor de Wyzewa's Article on Mallarmé," *Modern Language Notes*, 67 (1952), 175–78.

O'Brien, Justin. "American Books and French Reviewers," *College English*, 1 (March, 1940), 480–87. Bibliographical information on contemporary French responses to American literature.

Peyre, Henri. *Observations on Life, Literature, and Learning in America*. Carbondale, Ill.: Southern Illinois University Press, 1961.

Poulet, George. "Time and American Writers" in *Studies in Human Time*, Elliott Coleman, trans. New York: Harper and Brothers, 1959.

Spiller, Robert E. et al. *Literary History of the United States*. 4th ed., revised. 2 vols. New York: Macmillan, 1974.

Stovall, Floyd, ed. *Eight American Authors: A Review of Research and Criticism*. New York: W. W. Norton & Company, 1963. Bibliographical information.

Taupin, René. *L'Influence du Symbolisme français sur la poésie américaine (de 1910 à 1920)*. Paris, 1929. A pioneering study.

Wilson, Edmund. *Axel's Castle: A Study in the Imaginative Literature of 1870–1930*. New York: Charles Scribner's Sons, 1931. Influential comparative study of one Symbolist inheritance.

Yale French Studies, no. 10 [1952]: *French-American Literary Relationships*. Miscellaneous articles of value.